March of the Lemmings

Stewart Lee began stand-up in 1988 at the age of twenty and won the Hackney Empire New Act of the Year Award in 1990. In 2001 he co-wrote the libretto for Richard Thomas's *Jerry Springer: The Opera*, which went on to win four Olivier awards. His most recent live shows have been *Carpet Remnant World* (2011), *Much A-Stew About Nothing* (2013), *Room with a Stew* (2015), *Content Provider* (2017) and *Snowflake/Tornado* (2019). In December 2011 he won Best Male TV Comic and Best Comedy Entertainment Performance at the British Comedy Awards and his BBC show *Stewart Lee's Comedy Vehicle* won a BAFTA in 2012. In 2018, he was described by *The Times* as the world's greatest living stand-up comedian.

Praise for Stewart Lee:

'The most exciting comedian in the country bar none.' *The Times*

'The worst comedian in Britain, as funny as bubonic plague.' *Sun*

'Stewart Lee is a true original.' *Observer*

'I've always thought of Stewart Lee's comedy as doing the opposite of what really good comedy should do.' Toby Young, BBC Radio 4

'[A] brave and doomed comedian . . . Innovative.' *New York Times*

Stewart
LEE

MARCH OF THE LEMMINGS

BREXIT IN PRINT
AND PERFORMANCE
2016–2019

faber

First published in the UK and the USA in 2019
by Faber & Faber Limited
Bloomsbury House
74–77 Great Russell Street
London WC1B 3DA

This paperback edition published in 2020

Typeset by Ian Bahrami
Printed and bound in the UK by CPI Group (UK) Ltd, Croydon, CR0 4YY

A CIP record for this book
is available from the British Library

ISBN 978–0–571–35703–1

2 4 6 8 10 9 7 5 3 1

Contents

PART II: BREXIT IN PERFORMANCE 2016–2018

PART III: WHAT NOW?

Preface

'May you live in interesting times.'
ANCIENT CHINESE CURSE, 2000 BC

'You were only supposed to blow the bloody doors off!'
SARAH VINE ON THE EU REFERENDUM, 24 JUNE 2016

'Twat!'
DANNY DYER ON DAVID CAMERON, 27 JUNE 2018

My first book of collected columns, *Content Provider*, written in the five years between April 2011 and April 2016, compiled supposedly humorous prose and charted my attempts to discover a 'columnist voice'. This period seems so long ago now, a time before Brexit and Trump, and the daily concerns of the era suddenly appear to be largely trivial, the luxurious petty anxieties of the concerned citizen of a relatively stable liberal democracy, and one who had access to as much insulin as he could drink.

Conveniently, from April 2016 onwards, I found the focus of my semi-regular newspaper columns became almost monomaniacally fixated upon Brexit; and my stand-up comedy live work – principally the 2016–18 touring show, also called *Content Provider* – couldn't escape the referendum's toilet-flush pull either, however far I stuffed my hand down the news bowl.

Whatever our position on the referendum, I am sure we have all lost friends over Brexit. I hope so anyway. Today, I see these losses not as some terrible tragedy, but as a necessary cull, a chopping away of dead wood, a winnowing of chaff. In the three years since the EU referendum, I find myself increasingly furious, cynical and depressed. I am politically homeless. I wish I spoke another language or had some transferable skills – tanning hide perhaps, or contemporary dance – so I could gather up my family and start again, somewhere far away.

I don't recognise my country or many of the people I thought I knew. And I am not sure I recognise myself any more, and the angry, disillusioned person I have become in reality, rather than just on stage. I also seem to have put on a lot of weight, developed high blood pressure and erectile dysfunction, become partially blind and gone completely grey, all of which I also blame on Brexit in general, and Jacob Rees-Mogg specifically.

I aimed to hand the edited and completed manuscript of this book in to my high-class literary publishers, Faber & Fucking Faber, of Bloomsbury, on the day we were due to leave the EU, Friday 29 March 2019. And I aimed to do this irrespective of whether that bold leap into the void had finally been made, deal or no deal, Brexit or no Brexit. I didn't want there to be time to further reassess the book's contents in the light of whatever happened next. And that is what I have done.

It is for others who come after me – perhaps alien historians alighting on our burned and lifeless planet millions of years in the future – to decide if the work collected herein represents a valuable and enlightening study of this tumultuous time in the rich pageant of our island nation's spangled history, or if it is just a load of old stuff all mashed up. And maybe this book will become the basis of an alien religion, a death cult no less. And I will be its prophet, the Lawgiver.

With a view towards shaping the inevitable book-length collection into a coherent whole, I tried, throughout the last three years of writing the columns, to concentrate on certain themes and recurring characters. And in assembling this collection I have tried, dishonestly, but to the best of my ability, to remove any columns that didn't shadow the story of Brexit. In Part II of the book, which deals with the live work I generated since the referendum, footnotes indicate how it was both sabotaged and shaped by the wet hand of Brexit. Rarely has a minor celebrity's cash-in book creaked so loudly under such a lofty weight of intent.

Now, together, let us start to heal this divided land.

Stewart Lee, writer/clown
Stoke Newington, March 2019

PART I:
BREXIT IN PRINT
2016–2019

Introduction

I always maintain that I take on a persona when writing columns for the *Observer*: that of an adopted man, from a relatively normal social background, who is an obvious victim of imposter syndrome. I don't so much write the columns as transcribe them. The adopted man stands at my shoulder, just out of sight, biting his nails and chewing the inside of his face, mumbling things into my ear, some of which I mishear. He simply can't believe he is being employed by a posh left-leaning newspaper that his own parents wouldn't have read, and knows there has been some mistake.*

* I was initially brought in to the *Observer*'s Sunday funnies slot to fill in for David Mitchell's absences, not, as online commenters suggest, as a replacement for Frankie Boyle and his writing team, who produced weekly columns for the *Sun* until September 2013, and occasional ones for the *Guardian* since. With so many comedians producing newspaper column content, their minor-celebrity status driving traffic through a dead medium, it does get confusing. Mark Steel in the *Independent* is the best of the comedian columnists, and Marina Hyde is the best of the legitimate journalist-humourists. Even though I have gradually been promoted to a fifty–fifty share of the *Observer* column, like a divorced dad given greater access to the kids having conquered his drinking, in my mind I will always think of it as David Mitchell's column and of myself as a kind of cat that does a smell in David Mitchell's lovely garden and then goes back over the fence where it belongs. I couldn't cope with the responsibility of being a newspaper columnist otherwise. My whole professional life, it seems to me as I enter my sixth decade on this planet, has been an act of cowardly retreat from commitments and opportunities, deludedly disguised as legitimate moral objections, which accidentally coalesced into a successful career. I find myself with a beautiful spouse, with a beautiful life, and I ask myself, 'How did I get here?' And I say to myself, 'Great Scott! What have I done?'

Thus, he tries to compensate by employing over-finessed language and attempting to give a good account of himself, politically and intellectually, aware that he is being scrutinised by his betters.

Obviously, as this persona is the same as me, it is not a massive stretch to channel it, although I am surprised this other me hasn't been sacked. What is true of both the columnist and the stand-up characters of me is that over the period of producing work in the interregnum between the EU referendum, in June 2016, and the supposed activation of Article 50, in March 2019, both became increasingly angry, bitter and incoherent.

Similarly, the comments on the newspaper columns included here, from members of the public who uploaded their views to social media or the paper's website,* while often astute in identifying weaknesses in the work, also become more frenzied as the months pass, as if we are witnessing a collective national unravelling of sense. Many of them, it is increasingly clear, are also the work of anonymous agents, perhaps hired for the purpose, intent on advancing very specific disruptive processes on behalf of unnamed paymasters.

The only voice you can trust in this entire book is the one the footnotes are written in, which seems to be pursuing its own agenda: an autobiographical unburdening intent on setting various stories straight, as if the author, now suddenly finding himself in his fifties and watching the world he knows fall apart and decay as he himself in turn falls apart and decays, can sense death on the horizon and wants to leave his personal effects in order, to minimise the inconvenience caused to his family.

And this? This is this.

* Unless otherwise attributed, all the readers' comments are from the online editions of the publication the pieces appeared in.

8

The EU debate is a cynical battle of big beasts, not belief

1 May 2016

Last weekend I found myself trapped on an isolated, monster-infested Pacific atoll with a pair of twin psychic Japanese school-girls. A skyscraper-sized lizard, with three fire-breathing heads, the result of careless radioactive experiments in the '50s, and now a huge and clumsy metaphor for both the dangers of human scientific meddling with Mother Nature and post-war Japanese identity anxiety, had cornered us in a cave on the beach.*

---

* From 1977 onwards, the Midlands television region had a slot called 'The ATV Thursday Picture Show', broadcasting innocuous movies from 4.30 p.m. to 6 p.m., after school. In my favourites, the giant monster epics of Japan's Toho studios, skilled kabuki theatre practitioners in rubber lizard suits battled giant canvas moths and massive stucco lobsters in the beautiful ruins of miniature hand-crafted cityscapes. I was lucky enough to be able to recreate my childhood enthusiasm for the genre in a film item for series two of *Stewart Lee's Comedy Vehicle*, in which I, dressed in a half-Godzilla costume, attacked the physical theatre performer Rob Thirtle (*Space Precinct*, *Brum*, Philip Glass's *Satyagraha*), who appeared as some kind of crustacean, with a shopping bag. These Japanese monster performances still move me more than any computer-generated artifice because I can see the human hand at work. I would rush home from Widney Junior School every Thursday, let myself in with the flowerpot latchkey and make toast, my mum still at work, ready for the highlight of the week. My favourite Japanese monster movie was Jun Fukuda's 1967 effort *Son of Godzilla*, in which Godzilla fights giant web-shooting spiders to save his ugly turnip-faced crying son, Minilla. My own father wasn't around much when I was young, and Godzilla taught me everything I know about parenting. You basically roar and stomp and

9

My new friends Lora and Moll hoped to summon to our aid a gigantic moth, with roughly the dimensions of an airship, over which they exercised a strange interspecies erotic sway. Anticipating this titanic struggle of equally matched opponents, each driven by blind instinct and insensible to reason, my thoughts naturally turned to June's forthcoming Brexit vote.

Arguments about Brexit are tearing my family apart. In March, drunk in the late dark, and loose on the Internet, I had ordered a European flag from Amazon, intending to fly it from the roof come the week of the Eurovote, so as to annoy any divs living locally.

But I forgot about the flag and left it on the sofa, and now the cat has taken to sleeping under it.* Which is odd, as previously he

---

everything works out in the end, as long as you love your kids and make sure that they know that. For God's sake, make sure that they know that. And kill any lobster that threatens them. Burn it! Burn its face off!!

* This cat died in mysterious circumstances in 2017. We were all inconsolably distraught, to the point where friends and relatives must have worried that we had lost all sense of perspective. But for the first ten years of our marriage, my wife and I toured our stand-up acts relentlessly, trying to consolidate our appeal before it was too late, one of us away performing, the other at home parenting tiny children, in lonely rotation. And that cat was a constant, the family member you saw when you got in at 4 a.m. from Telford, waiting to greet you and welcome you home. He was a conduit that closed all four of us into a circle. How many substandard spaghetti westerns did I watch in the small hours, with the cat my only companion? How many late nights would I have spent drinking alone to kill the post-show adrenaline, like some sad alcoholic, unless that cat had been sitting up with me, making a legitimate social event of what would otherwise have been evidence of a gradual slide into a terrible addiction? 'Have you caught any mice today?' I would ask him. That cat saved our marriage, I suspect, and when he knew we would be OK, he sensed his work was done and took himself away. Anyone who doesn't like cats must be dead inside.

was an avowed Eurosceptic, and would hiss aggressively whenever I put any European free jazz on the stereo. Indeed, we have on occasion used Günter 'Baby' Sommer's *Hörmusik* solo percussion album to drive him from the room when he made a smell.*

In a heated late-night argument with my pro-Brexit stepbrother two weeks ago, I used the contented cat's obvious happiness underneath the European flag to show him how Europe could shelter and comfort us, like cats under a flag. My stepbrother, brilliantly, snatched the European flag off the cat's back to show how the creature, and by association the nation, was quite capable of functioning without the embrace of Europe. I think this is an example of the kind of easy-to-understand argument the British public claim has been denied them in favour of tedious figures and facts about trade, environmental legislation, human rights and immigration.

The cat looked annoyed and eyed both of us with resentment. Already, the Brexit debate is tearing families apart, stepbrother against stepbrother, stepbrother against stepbrother-in-law, stepbrother-in-law against stepcat. 'Shouldn't you be in Japan by now, anyway?' he said, throwing my flag on the fire.

---

* A few years ago I was with a group of improvised-music practitioners on a train to Bexhill-on-Sea, where we were due to interpret the works of John Cage, when the subject of the East German free-jazz drummer Günter 'Baby' Sommer came up. Don't you wish you lived my life? Some of the group were convinced that because he seemed able to travel regularly from the Eastern Bloc to collaborate with free-jazz musicians in the West before the Wall came down, Baby must have been a Stasi agent, reporting back on the political persuasions of his co-workers. The conversation was speculative, free-flowing and fun, until the spouse of one of the younger musicians used his mobile phone to discover that yes, there was a suspicion that Günter was an undercover jazz drummer, and so the fun ended, another flight of fancy killed by modern technology. It is vagueness that makes the magic happen.

A few days later I arrived in the so-called Land of the Rising Sun for a meeting with the famous Studio Haino, who had begun work on an anime version of my multiple BAFTA- and British Comedy Award-winning BBC2 series, *Stewart Lee's Comedy Vehicle*, which they believed would play well with young Asian hipsters, jaded geisha and disillusioned samurai.*

Because *Fuck! Stewart Lee Pee-Pee Charabanc* (the literal Japanese translation of Studio Haino's new title for the show) was already expected to be a big hit, various merchandise spin-offs were almost up and running. A string of love beads, each sporting a different picture of my face, is already available in Japanese adult stores.

And since January I have been wearing four or five new pairs of pants a day, all of which will eventually take pride of place, when suitably soiled, in vending machines on the streets of Tokyo's most fashionable districts.

My wife, of course, finds this turn of events ridiculous, but she will be laughing on the other side of her stupid face when the flyblown briefs she currently uses as dishcloths become priceless collector's items.

And in the increasingly likely event of a British Brexit, the sale of these fetishised items will then fund our family's relocation to the newly independent free Scotland, from where I will harry the airwaves of England and Wales with liberally biased left-wing satire, the Lord Haw-Haw of sparkling-wine socialism.

In retrospect, the scrum of the Scottish independence

* There is no Japanese version of *Stewart Lee's Comedy Vehicle*, though much of my stand-up appears on YouTube with handmade Russian subtitles, and a Russian comedy fan has had a tattoo of one of my jokes, about the '70s Liverpudlian comedian Tom O'Connor, done on his arm, despite none of my work, or that of Tom O'Connor, being available commercially in Russia. How did I get here?

referendum looks dignified compared to the dirty war of Brexit. In Scotland, politicians on both sides of the divide at least seemed sincere in their beliefs, rather than selfishly using the nation's concerns about its future to try and secure theirs.

Indeed, the day when Boris Johnson cynically accused the pro-Europe and 'part-Kenyan' President Obama of being ancestrally ill-disposed towards Britain marks the moment at which the mayor of London changed from being merely a twat into a full-blown cunt.

It is appropriate to describe Boris Johnson with pure witless swearing, for that is all he deserves. He is of a political class where any insult, no matter how vicious, is acceptable, if it is delivered with the rhetorical flourishes and classical allusions of the public-school debating society. Hence, Cameron can scornfully sneer at Jeremy Corbyn and describe Dennis Skinner as a dinosaur, yet the venerable beast himself is dismissed from the house when he calls Cameron merely 'dodgy'.

The problem for the pro-Europe voter currently is that while obviously despising Cameron as both a person and a politician, one nonetheless wants him to prevail over Johnson, Gove, Iain Duncan Smith and the Brexit camp.

And as the giant moth arrived above the beach, momentarily blocking out the Japanese sun itself, and set about the three-headed lizard with electric rays from its head, I continued to ponder the Brexit campaign.

'Did he who made the lamb make thee?' asks William Blake of the Tyger. It was instinct that drove the moth and the lizard to fight, not ethics. They were as they were. Likewise, Johnson's Brexit position represents only a fight for personal betterment, not a considered view on Europe.*

---

* Last year, I organised a benefit to raise money for a memorial stone

There is an African fly that lays its eggs in the jelly of children's eyes, the hatching larvae blinding them by feeding on the eye itself. But the fly has no quarrel with the child. It is merely following its nature.

Likewise, Boris Johnson, a vile grub laying his horrible eggs in the soft jelly of the EU debate, has no agenda beyond his own advancement. He believes in nothing, and neither does his spiritual soulmate, the eye-scoffing African fly.

We cowered in our cave, the twins and I, and watched the combat of the monsters. The honest open war of the giant moth and three-headed lizard made Prime Minister's Questions seem contrived and banal. The earth shook beneath their feet, triggering tidal waves and rivers of lava from the atoll's smouldering volcano; vast explosions of startled birds scarred the sky; the landscape cracked. There was no 'Mr Speaker', no 'order, order', no classical allusion and no drawing-room wit. There was only war, terrible war.

Can we please keep this sort of hysteria out of the EU debate? We need sober analysis and reflection, not this. Richard Whittington

Stewart Lee: a propagandist masquerading as a comedian, who is promoted as sophisticated and as a confidence trick to make people buy into the narrative. Williebaldtschmidt

---

for William Blake, my favourite autodidact poet-artist, even though I suspect he would have been a Leave voter. I couldn't attend the unveiling, which was lucky, as I was frightened of a lot of the people who were going to be there, but the William Blake Society gave me an impressive chunk of the leftover marble, inscribed with a gilded 'B' by the engraver, which I was able to pretend was a birthday present I had had specially made for my wife.

I suppose everyone has a right to write as much unfunny, impenetrable gobbledygook mas they judge will make them rich and famous. Freespeechoneeach

Painfully unfunny as per usual. Markb35

It's worth saying that Japan had a vending machine selling used schoolgirl's panties for only about three weeks 20 years ago. But if you do allow that even for a number of days, don't be surprised if people never let you live it down. Saintexmin

If your country had been razed by the elective, arguably unnecessary, use of multiple nuclear weapons from a country that thinks of itself as a God, perhaps you would see the fictional radioactive God-named creature destroying your country as representing something more tangible than a clumsy 'mother nature' thing. As Japanese Admiral Isoroku Yamamoto said of Godzilla in *Mothra II – Bora! Bora! Bora!*, 'I fear we have awoken a sleeping giant and filled him with a great and terrible resolve.' Plantphotonics420

Poppycock. Ferdinand8

Typical public school socialist. Kontrol

'Want stories like this in your inbox?', it reads at the bottom of the article. What? Do I want more stories about giant three headed lizards fighting to the death with giant moths with X Ray eyes that also manage to describe Boris Johnson as an eye eating grub laying vile eggs in the EU membership debate? Are you kidding? Of course I do! Have you actually got any though? Tybo

Stuart, you are a total arse using 'pro-Europe' for 'pro-EU.' It occurred to us last night that calling the EU 'Europe' is like calling NATO 'the Atlantic ocean,' or FIFA 'Earth.' Jean Noir

That was three minutes I will never get back. Mustapha Mondeo

To become an 'edgy, funny comedian' in Guardianista terms you have to say 'Thatch was evil' every couple of minutes in the *Guardian* or on Radio 4. This, apparently, is biting satire at its finest and is, hilariously, deemed to be 'courageous' and 'anti-establishment'. The *Guardian* seems determined to identify and boost the careers of people striving to achieve the title of 'the left's Bernard Manning'. Campbellgoebells

Stewart Lee – another smug, millionaire Marxist from the well heeled comedy establishment. Henry Clift

This probably the most ridiculous article I have seen! Can't the remainers come up with any sensible arguments about the issues? Jemima15

You too? Underwear turned into dishcloth (by being cut in half)? Trouble is the dishcloth ones often end up back in my underwear drawer, so on a dark winters morning I frequently find myself trying to struggle into tatty half-sized briefs with no leg holes. Cloud9cuckoo

I'm not saying Michael Gove is a bit of an animal but . . .

19 June 2016

The so-called EU referendum debate on so-called ITV (let us not dignify either by naming them) filled me and all my ABC1 liberal friends with despair. Oh! The humanity!! Drunk on Belgian wine, I watched the Barrier Reef of the Britain I know bleach to nothing in the twin glare of Brexit's burning certainties and Julie Etchingham's gleaming teeth.

Leave had no arguments or facts, just pornographically arousing soundbites and lies they knew were lies, but which they calculated might stick to a wall in a depressed town somewhere, if flung with enough force, like compacted pellets of Priti Patel's shit.

Even Remain's Amber Rudd, the Countess Bathory of Energy and Climate, seemed clever by comparison to Boris Johnson, who managed to make the word 'expert' a pejorative term. Nonetheless, it was bleakly obvious that the audience's disillusion led them to favour the Leavers' lies.

I wondered how Leave could rationalise their blind stab in the dark and live with the untruths they had told. And my mind turned again to Michael Gove, who, to put their relationship in terms of Gove's beloved Dennis Wheatley, is the supplicant Simon Aaron to Johnson's satanic Mocata, their joint prize the mummified phallus of Conservative Party power. 'Only they who love without desire shall have power granted them in their darkest hour!'

As I have confessed before, in 1992 I was a gag writer on a doomed Channel 4 show, *A Pig in a Poke*. The experimental

satire programme broke new ground by positioning its performers on balsa ladders in a smoke-filled Bat Cave, while they delivered belligerent journalistic monologues to camera, the stylistic
integrity of which I and the comedian Richard Herring were
encouraged to compromise with jokes.*

Lucky Richard was assigned to *Poke*'s most affable hosts, the
restaurant critic Tracey MacLeod and her colleague, the rap-
per LL Cool J,† who plied him with fudge and polystyrene‡
all day, while I was understandably ignored by my master, a

* In 1992 I was a gag writer on a short-lived Channel 4 show called *Stab
in the Dark*. The football comedian David Baddiel, the critic Tracey
MacLeod and the columnist, and soon-to-be Conservative politician,
Michael Gove walked around a dimly lit industrial unit reciting
televisually unfriendly monologues about the week's news to a shifty
crowd. Future podcast king Richard Herring and I, hot from Radio 4's
weekly shit satire show *Weekending*, were pimped to MacLeod, to insert
our own leftover topical jokes into her prose. MacLeod showed us
undreamed-of kindnesses, letting us write in her Battersea flat, making
us lovely lunches, telling us funny showbiz anecdotes about Loudon
Wainwright III and The Brinsley Schwarz, and bequeathing me her
unwanted promo CDs, including my future favourite, *Girlfriend* by
Matthew Sweet, the first of the then newfangled silver discs I ever owned.
And she got Sid Griffin of the LA country-rock band The Long Ryders
to sign their *State of Our Union* sleeve for me, albeit with such gusto and
violence that he rather spoiled it. I was twenty-four years old and living
the provincial-boy-loose-in-London dream. Could life get any better?
† I can only assume my subconscious plucked LL Cool J out of the air
here to replace David Baddiel in the *Stab* team because in the early '90s
David Baddiel had a funny routine about LL Cool J.
‡ Richard Herring hated the sound of polystyrene, which both terrified
and enraged him, so Tracey MacLeod used to hide behind parked cars in
her street at the time he said he would arrive, squeaking polystyrene as
he approached to scare him.

capable young comic newspaper columnist called Michael Andrew Fizzwigg Gove.

Gove attended one writers' roundtable meeting a week, where all he did was badger the producers to book the former BBC newsreader Jan Leeming, upon whom he was oddly fixated, before leaving with all the office washroom's toilet rolls secreted in his satchel.

Instead of asking me for jokes, Gove would make me wait on the fire escape outside his Notting Hill flat, occasionally emerging to assign me mundane tasks, such as taking his weekly washing – usually just seven white pants, seven white vests, fourteen grey socks and one yellowing sock – to the dry-cleaners.

One week, the old Greek couple in Dryee-Fast seemed unduly amused by Gove's unusually bulky package. 'Tell Michael we try and try but can't get the stains outta the crotch this time!' they laughed, unravelling a full-size fur suit, the reasonably realistic costume of an unidentified Gove-size rodent. I rolled up the outfit and returned it to Gove without comment. I needed this job. I couldn't afford to rock the boat. Scruples were a luxury I didn't have.

Later that day, Gove suddenly appeared beside me on the fire escape, high above the Notting Hill street. He had a habit of sneaking up on you. 'Ah, Lee,' he said, 'contemplating the incalculable, I see?' 'Mr Gove?' I asked, as I felt his hand upon the small of my back, applying gentle pressure.

'The leap, Lee. If you were to leap now, Leapy Lee, from this fire escape, what would happen?' 'I'd die, I think, Mr Gove,' I answered, unsure where this line of questioning was going. 'Perhaps,' Gove countered, 'and experts would agree with you, I am sure. But would it not be thrilling to find out if one could profit from such a bold leap?' 'There's nothing to find out, Mr Gove,' I replied. 'No one could survive that leap. This is the seventh floor.' 'Was it not our lord Christ', Gove hissed, return-ing inside, 'who urged us to consider the lemming?' I don't think Christ did say that, did he? Wasn't it 'consider the lily'? What did Gove mean?

The next day, Gove suddenly emerged from his room, carry-ing a brown parcel, and told me he was going for a walk on Wormwood Scrubs common. 'Carry on, Lee,' he called, 'with whatever it is *A Pig in a Poke* pay you for.' I availed myself of my absent master's sofa and tried in vain to think of a funny intro-duction for Jan Leeming, should Gove's ambition of grilling her ever find favour with the producers.

Gove had a crackpot idea that he and Leeming should appear together, both dressed as some kind of rat, and jump off a high diving board into a swimming pool, and he had offered me a bonus, out of his own pocket, if I could contrive a scenario – somehow related to the week's news – that would convince the producers this would be a good idea.

In Gove's office, his phone rang persistently, and in the end I thought it best to enter, against his strict orders, and answer it. The producer of *Pig in a Poke* was saying something about how Gove was needed immediately for an urgent overdub of haughty snorting, but my eyes were adjusting to the dark. Gove's previ-ously unseen office slowly revealed itself to me in the full depth of its demented insanity.

Tiny, tiny . . . rodents – some soft and grey, some brown with black stripes, in paintings, posters, wallcharts, thumb-tacked magazine clippings and poorly executed crayon drawings, hurl-ing themselves fatally in their thousands over the cliff of their island home; or crudely taxidermied and mounted, eyes glazed and little paws frozen stiff – on every available surface.

Lemmings. Hundreds and hundreds of lemmings. Michael Gove was obsessed with lemmings. And I wasn't about to let him hurl himself to his death on my watch, although had I known what he would become, to do so would have been the most moral course of action. I ran to Wormwood Scrubs common.

On a patch of waste ground, upon a filthy mattress, prostrate beneath the abandoned silo from which he had jumped, lay Michael Gove, winded but alive, and dressed in the lemming costume – for that is what it was – that the dry-cleaners had laughed at, the crotch dark once more.

Gove's eyes flashed open inside the circle of fake fur that surrounded his excited face. 'Am I dead?' he bellowed. 'Am I dead, Lee?' 'No, Michael,' I said, 'you're not dead.' 'Experts,' he said, 'what do they know? Help me up, boy! Help me up!!'

The acceptable face of bigotry. Finnrkn

A dreadful piece of writing, absolute rubbish. John Gibbons

I can't think of a single thing likeable about Michael Gove – from his obnoxious face to his obnoxious wife. Except that he's funnier than Stewart Lee. Even his wife's funnier than Stewart Lee. Offshoretomorrow

What a pathetic article. It's obviously deeply unfunny but more than that – is this part of the new culture of respect we are all supposed to be adopting at the behest of the *Guardian*? Linking one of our foremost Asian female polticians to sh*t seems less than tolerant to me. Joking about the death of a leading Leave politician seems a little of keeping with the national mood as well, following recent events. Pretty sick all round. Does Stewart Lee consider, on reflection, whether he made a mistake in describing Priti Patel in relation to pieces of faeces? Is that really a tolerant approach in relation

to the foremost Asian woman in the Leave campaign? And how come did this article get published? Did no one read it beforehand? Progresstoleave

Did anyone read this from start to finish? If you did you'll never get that time back you know. Garyhoo1

Latest in the line of 'big in the nineties' has-beens trying to make their points. Nataliebeni0

Where was Putin when
Corbyn needed him?

28 August 2016

In Edinburgh, where I write this, there is concern that the city's newly opened branch of the Kremlin-backed news agency Sputnik is intended specifically to destabilise post-Brexit English–Scottish relations. Message to Putin: 'Don't worry, Vladimir baby! We can handle this one ourselves!!'

Nonetheless, let us compare the contrasting media-manipulation strategies of Putin's Russia and, for example, the Labour Party, both of them organisations that have, at times, abandoned their left-wing core beliefs in an attempt to adapt to a shifting geopolitical landscape.

In the autumn of 2015, it was suggested that Putin's deliberately penis-shaped submarines, designed specifically to subconsciously exaggerate our perceptions of Russian genitalia, are poking around the transatlantic data cables to ensure the maverick anarcho-superpower's ability to cut continental Europe off from America. Two campaigns working in opposition might then mean American media were full of phallic Russian propaganda that we in Europe weren't actually able to view.

On the other hand, this kind of strategy would be typical of Putin's confusion guru Vladislav Surkov, a surrealist artist who, despite dressing like a disgraced *Top Gear* presenter, uses creatively chaotic double-think to sculpt our perceptions of Russia as determinedly as Richard Dreyfuss mushes mashed potato into mountains in *Close Encounters of the Third Kind*.

On the one hand, dope-fiend Russian athletes' disqualification from the Rio feelgood festival was embarrassing; on the other, it creates the impression of a country of unpredictable law-defying crazies so convincingly Surkov himself may have masterminded it. There's no way of knowing any more. Surkov may even have written this. I may actually be him without my even knowing it.*

In March 2015, I wrote, for this paper, a silly fantasy about a giant statue of a naked Putin landing in my garden. Reading the below-the-line Internet comments later, I realised how thorough Russia's determination to muddy the waters of opinion was: many of them were clearly generated by almost-literate Kremlin cyber-slaves, rather than by the usual alt-right trolls taking time off from masturbating over old videos of Toby Young on a rowing reality TV show.†

Briefly, I adopted a strategy of writing borderline meaningless gibberish about Russia to try and provoke weird responses from the full-time Kremlin-backed commenters. Indeed, in a column about the Eurovision Song Contest three months later I discreetly included the following irrelevant paragraph:

> One may as well give the kosovorotka-marinading wazzocks
> something incomprehensible to feed to their bewildered

* By February 2019, the terrifying conclusions of the Digital, Culture, Media and Sport Select Committee's eighteen-month investigation into Facebook's dissemination of 'fake news', and the way Russia weaponised it, made me nostalgic for comic exaggerations like this, which now just seem like statements of fact. We know without a doubt that our referendum was rigged, and yet we roll forward with its result.

† I thought it was just me that was being systematically trolled by Russians. It now turns out they were doing it to Western democracy in general. It's possible some of the readers' comments included at the end of this piece were from fake Russian accounts.

brainstems. To me, then, Vladimir Putin is a giant, prolapsed female worker bee that sucks hot ridicule out of langoustines' cephalothoraxes. Let's see what crunchy, expansionist lavatory honey this notion causes the parthenogenetic Russian keyboard wendigos to inflate for us this week, in the shadow of Paul McGann and his art gnome.

The problem here was twofold. Firstly, many *Observer* readers found this nonsense indistinguishable from my usual writing. (As has been pointed out by contributors many times, I am no A. A. Gill. Now that man can write! Bring back Frankie!!) And, secondly, many of the pro-Putin below-the-line comments the incoherence provoked were, I suspect, actually placed by sassy readers attempting to parody the usual Kremlin posts.

Consider, for example, this convincingly odd submission from General Dreedle: 'Russia is very well doing without your Opra Winfrey western pornography and youre decadent music. More lies about Ukraine which was only the size of a biscuit before transsexual won.'

Whether the supposed *Observer* contributor General Dreedle is real or not, the fact is Putin's Russia has taken political propaganda to the next level, motherfuckers! Meanwhile, here at home, Jeremy Corbyn is filmed sitting on the floor of a train.

There is a long tradition of essentially dishonest photo opportunities being used by politicians to cement policy in the public mind. Consider Margaret Thatcher in that tank in 1986; or Michael Dukakis in that tank in 1988; or John Major on that tank in 1991.

But politicians' photo opportunities don't only use tanks. In 2006, David Cameron, who went on to ruin Britain for ever, was photographed in Norway hugging a husky, as he launched the barefaced lie that he was unleashing the 'greenest government ever'. But within a few years, Theresa May would close the Department of Energy and Climate Change and, post-Piggate, Conservative propagandists would have gone to any lengths to avoid David Cameron being photographed embracing an animal.

But instead of being photographed in a tank like a normal politician, Jeremy Corbyn last week chose to be filmed sitting on the floor of a train. While clearly intended to highlight the scandal of private rail company ownership, the Labour Party's release of the footage gives the same two blokes that secretly write all the jokes for the comedians on all those shitty TV comedy panel shows the opportunity to observe, 'Corbyn should have sat in his own back benches. There's plenty of room there!'

Our Left needs to raise its game. If you ever got to see film of Putin sprawled on public transport, every single possible interpretation of the footage would already have been minutely mapped.

This is very poor journalism, seemingly more interested in amusing the reader than informing them. I suggest that this 'Stewart Lee' – if that is his real name – should consider a career in a different field where such flights of fancy might be more welcome. Stand-up comedy, perhaps? Grover Rancid

What a ridiculous article. More propagandist scaremongering and association with conflated ad hominem arguments with pure partisan, non-objective reporting as usual without balance. On Corbyn, Putin and by contrast our establishment. Geopolitical and national politics rhetoric combined. MSM is not only source, adapt, tell the truth or risk going under, buried by the same failing neoliberalism that gave power. Notice the same trolls are out with their Latin usernames too.

Soros basement etc must be getting crowded. Equitable Effigy

This attempt to somehow associating Corbyn with Putin is despicable. Freeblood*

Corbyn the evil leftie – oh, how many ways can we smear him and associate him with . . . my god . . . the diabolical PUTIN!! EEEk. Laffcadio1944

This sort of stuff is not going to play in the crucible of Brexit post-intellectualism. Howard Beale

Sad that many Corbynistas who were previously hanging on every word of these 'alternative comedians' like Brand, will now find out the hard way that you don't get a nice gig on the telly without basically conforming to the neo liberal consensus. Hugodegauche

Does anyone still pretend to understand Lee's stuff, or is liking it it just part of being in the Corbyn cult? John Winwin

It's as funny as a burning orphanage. Mr Badger1966

Bring back Frankie. This is shit. Alan Tyndall

Incisive writing, for once exposing the link between Putin and Corbyn. The *Guardian* should keep up the Russia and Putin bashing, rather than wasting time delving into meaningless social, environmental and evonomic issues that affect ordinary working people. Icelandicmaiden

---

* The hysteria of the comments by some Corbyn loyalists here, blind to nuance and overreacting to trigger words without looking at the wider context, is tiresome and dispiriting. If indeed they are genuine Corbyn extremists, not people pretending to be Corbyn extremists to discredit the Labour Party. Who knows any more?

Odd piece of propaganda. Randomly tying in a hated reformer with Putin – pure Democrat playbook. Shtove

The usual *Guardian* anti-Corbyn verbiage. Silvertown

Another pathetically veiled article to bash Corbyn . . . Really low stuff. Forageforfood

No more schmoozing with the enemy on TV shows

20 November 2016

The danger in meeting politicians is that they seem all right and then, even as a multiple award-winning comedian, it is much harder to summon up the manufactured anger required to despise them for personal commercial gain. I have a mortgage. I can't afford to find myself thinking things like, 'You know, Ken Clarke isn't so bad once you get to know him.'* Hate is money! And, like a Danish sperm donor, I have to pump it out to a deadline by the bucketful!!

In the '00s I had a twenty-five-minute routine about Michael Portillo looking like the Cuprinol wood stain goblin, which was gradually becoming the spine of a new three-hour show. But after I met Portillo on BBC1's *This Week*, he seemed belatedly reasonable in that way that ex-Tories often do, and I found I could no longer suggest he was a wood stain goblin with any conviction. Another revenue stream ran dry.

I don't like going on TV, but I will make an exception for *This Week*, of which I am a huge fan. People always ask me what Andrew Neil's dogs are like in real life. To answer that question once and for all, Scrubber is nice, but Molly stinks and the BBC had to hush it up when she bit Jacob Rees-Mogg in his North East Somerset constituency. Though to be fair, Rees-Mogg had subjected the dog to cruel and sustained floccinaucinihilipilification.†

---

* Ken Clarke once presented a very sympathetic radio documentary on the heroin addict jazz trumpeter Lee Morgan.

† I gave up appearing on *This Week* in 2018, about the same time as they stopped asking me to appear, like someone trying to seem victorious by

quitting a job before they are sacked. Andrew Neil started firing off weird 2 a.m. tweets about left-wing bias in BBC TV comedy, while simultaneously being chairman of the *Spectator*. The last few times I did the show, a researcher would keep me on the phone for three hours, telling me what Andrew Neil was going to ask me, and asking me how I would respond, and then on the actual show at midnight, Neil would just ask me something mildly, and yet also impossibly, different to what was agreed, which threw the whole thing off. (I think this also annoyed Bobby Gillespie of Primal Scream, whose silent protest during the show's closing dance number went viral.) And by the end, Michael Portillo used to just sit there with his arms folded, making a condescending face and waiting for an opportunity to interrupt, as if everything you said was beneath his consideration. Big nose! Watching the show during the Brexit era, its once invigorating levity seemed inappropriate, and most of its apparently unaccountable co-presenters were part of the problem that brought us to disaster. Its cancellation appeared to be announced on 14 February 2019, but perhaps wasn't, and Neil began that night's programme with a heavily editorialised speech about Churchill, clearly designed to discredit the Labour Party for perceived unpatriotic attitudes towards the war hero, before he, Portillo and The Mod Postman all ganged up on Stella Creasy, the Talulah Gosh of British politics, like rats. Both incidents revealed how the once mighty show had run its course anyway, and it had become difficult for anyone to defend it. I did used to enjoy *This Week*, though, and once appeared on it with the delightfully surly Scottish nationalist Pat Kane, formerly of '80s band The Kane Gang. But I was disappointed to read on Twitter subsequently that he thought I was smelly, as he wrote, 'Jolly end-of-term feel backstage. Got to meet (somewhat odiferous) hero Stewart Lee.' Paddy Ashdown's former press secretary Miranda Green was on the show too, and kept vomiting into a bin, which I now worry was something to do with me. Come to think of it, when I went with the actor Paul Putner to see the German progressive-rock band Faust at the Southbank Centre sometime in the late '90s, he said I smelt so bad people were moving away from me. And in 1983, my mum told me I smelt of stale urine when I sat next to her once in the front seat of her Mini Metro on Whitefields Road, and that I had to go home and wash. Have I been stinking the place out my whole life? Does that explain everything?

Last Sunday morning, I further compromised my embargo and appeared on Peston's ITV politics niche, *Peston's Weekly Thought Nook*™. Peston introduced himself to me while reclining in a make-up chair: 'Hello, I'm Peston. And today I'll be talking to ballroom-dancing politico Ed Balls and UKIP's Suzanne Evans. Stay with me.'

I thought Peston's greeting oddly formal and impersonal, and then realised he was being filmed for a trailer and was addressing the British public en masse, not me individually. I felt stupid for not understanding how TV worked, like when I was little and I thought Harold Wilson could see me through the television.[*]

Next, I went to the green room, which is showbiz language for the place where the stars wait their turn to go on TV with Peston, or Andrew Neil, or whoever's show it is. In the old days it could have been Russell Harty, for example. Or Gus Honeybun.[†]

---

[*] Our cat used to run round the back of the television searching for the tiny men during the widescreen gunfight sections of Sergio Leone westerns. He was twenty-eight years old. Which is fucking old for a cat. (Without the word 'fucking' here, this joke wouldn't be good enough to work. It's just a rhythmical thing, really. Nonetheless, I apologise.)

[†] Today's digitally connected children, with all media at their fingertips, will never understand the dimension-shattering thrill of travelling to a different television region and realising they had an entirely bespoke pantheon of local television presenters and magazine programmes. It was like visiting a parallel reality, where, instead of Birmingham's Chris Phipps talking about punk rock on *Look! Hear!*, there was Manchester's Tony Wilson talking about punk rock on *So It Goes*. The pod-lord Richard Herring has spoken at length of the trauma of moving, as a child, from Yorkshire, where *Tiswas* was broadcast, to Somerset, where it wasn't. Gus Honeybun was a birthday-announcing rabbit who once ruled the south-western television region, and who could only be seen by other children when they were on holiday there, lending him a magical air. Rumoured to be obsessed with his co-star Fern Britton, Honeybun

The green room doesn't have to be green, or even a room. There isn't a green room on *This Week* on BBC1 in case the *Daily Mail* says it's too luxurious. On *This Week* there's just some chairs in a corridor and a table with old fishing magazines on it, like at the proctologist's. 'Andrew Neil will see you now.' Peston is much better.

I'm aware that writing about what happens in the green room is a betrayal of an unspoken showbiz-politics rule. Like Vegas, what happens in the green room stays in the green room. It's supposed to be a safe space, in a theatre or at a TV studio, where performers and contributors shouldn't feel they are being watched. Journalists went into my dressing room at the Leicester Square Theatre and reported that I used Lynx deodorant. I felt violated.

Nowadays, I find it very difficult being in the green room with younger, newer comedians, as I feel my age and supposed status mean I am permanently required to be in presidential mode. And I mean this in the old sense of 'presidential', meaning magnanimous, patient and generous, rather than in the modern sense, meaning being a corrupt, pussy-grabbing racist. How quickly words change their meanings.

In the Peston green room I sat next to Suzanne Evans from the Ukips. I tried to make small talk. She agreed that when Nigel

---

died from auto-asphyxiation in a Honiton hotel room on New Year's Eve 1992 after she rejected his advances, though children were told he had returned to live in the countryside like a wild rabbit. I first became aware of his work while I was in a caravan near Tenby, circa 1978, where my grandparents would take me in the school holidays, when my mum was working. Now, my middle-class son has middle-class friends who go on skiing trips at half-term. They will never know the pleasure of chips at sunset on a windswept rainy beach, with the promise of a pocket of 2ps to try and tip over an amusement arcade waterfall. But my kids will. I deny them luxurious holidays and take them to Prestatyn out of season so they will understand.

Farage, earlier that week, had threatened to unleash a pussy-grabbing Trump sex-attack robot on Theresa May, it had been a bit much.*

Suzanne Evans from the Ukips was wearing a giant Remembrance Day poppy made of cloth. Jeremy Corbyn came on TV wearing a tiny badge of a poppy. I said, 'Your poppy's massive, isn't it, Suzanne? Jeremy Corbyn's is tiny. He's a traitor, isn't he?'

Suzanne Evans from the Ukips didn't say much, and I worried that she had my card marked for being one of the liberal comedians that dominate all comedy now, to little or no effect in real terms. Perhaps she thought I was trying to generate material for a funny column. Which I wasn't. At the time.

Later on, when Marine Le Pen came on the BBC news being really, really racist, Suzanne Evans from the Ukips shook her head disapprovingly, as if Le Pen had crossed a racist line in the racist sand. I started wondering about gradations of tolerance, about how our relationship with someone, however minimal, affects our attitude towards them.

On Christmas morning 1995, I came down to our kitchen, hungover, and the first sentence that was said to me, on Christmas morning, apropos of nothing, was: 'You can say what you like about Hitler, but he had some good ideas. He just went about them the wrong way.' It was Auntie Hattie, on seasonal secondment from the old people's home, praising Hitler, on Christmas Day! On Christmas Day!! On Christmas Day in the morning!!! *Sieg Heil!!!!*†

---

* Farage had intimated that Trump might not be trusted to negotiate with Theresa May safely, and there was a sexual undertone to his perceived threat.

† I've referenced this odd exchange in various media, and people always say it couldn't have happened. It did, but I have changed the

But we make allowances for the madness of our relatives, because they are little old ladies, and little old men, and are a bit confused probably; but we must not allow ourselves to make allowances for far-right politicians and their followers. Because the American woman with mixed-race kids I talk to at swimming lessons every Tuesday is afraid to go home; and the day after Brexit, in our cosy comedy community, an Asian comedian was told to go back where he came from by an emboldened heckler at the Comedy Store, historic home of politically correct alternative comedy, the sort of incident I haven't seen since the '80s.*

And that's why, after next week's *This Week*, I'm not meeting any more TV politicians. These aren't the times for self-loathing liberals to seek to understand the leaders of the global far right, or their supporters. That ship sailed when Trump put Breitbart into the White House.† We should be in crisis-management mode.

It's time to reassert a fundamental principle, namely that there's no excuse for bigotry, whichever alt-right buzzword you get Boris or Steve Bannon to rebrand it with. And if that means

---

names, and I have changed them to different names on different occasions.

* Every Remain voter has observed evidence of the sudden shift in gear regarding what racists feel they can say in public since the referendum. Someone needs to compile some kind of archive of all this anecdotal material, so we can remember what we were like after Vote Leave uncorked the rage flask. It could be the Domesday Book of low-level anecdotal race hate.

† In January 2018, just over twelve months later, Trump had Breitbart's Steve Bannon removed from the White House for criticising him in the book *Fire and Fury*. As a result, Bannon was free to pursue his avowed intent of creating a global infrastructure for right-wing populism, which appeared to be based on his reading of Richard Allen's 1970s *Skinhead* novels.

no more free green-room bacon sandwiches on Sunday morning for me, then so be it. We are all going to have to make sacrifices.

The role of a comedian is to entertain with humour, not to preach his politics in the misguided belief that they are anything other than a professional entertainer. ID44390070

This Week is a horror show of how far to the right any politics on the beeb has gone. In the run up to the 2015 election. Anyone, Lee included, happy to go on any be best chums with Neill & Portillo should be openly ridiculed and shamed for hob-nobbing with the enemy. Alfiehisself

UKIP isn't spelt with an 's', who is this guy? Lukefisher

Stewart, it's 'Ukip' no 's'. Simples. DefendantK

I want to hear what frankie Boyle thinks about our current predicament. Tdlx

Give up and go home, you lost, you're on the wrong side of history and your 'comedy' is not sufficiently mitigating. Notguilt

Does anyone actually have a clue what this article is about? I know there are a lot of Lee groupies on here who will clam they enjoyed it enormously, and laughed their heads off, and saw a coruscating critique of the debased times in which we live. But did they actually have a clue what this article is about? JohnWinWin

I have just realised that it is only Lee's physical persona & delivery I dislike, as I quite enjoyed reading that piece. Mysteron

Needless to say Mr Lee attended public school followed by Oxford. I am shocked I tell you, shocked. Observer1951

Steward said he's had enough of meeting politicians, now he has to make money a different way. Stewart needs more money so he can pay his bank-rent. Stewart used to do stand-up like a proper comedian, now he demands Viner lets him write lefty click-bait. Stewart sits at home in the dark, underwhelmed and drifting through the abyss. Stewart wakes up at 3am to gorge on disgusting, delicious food. Stewart hopes he can fill this void one way or another. Shame those green room bacon sarnies are over. HPCMini

A middle-class lad, out of touch with anything contrary to his own experience, seeking to characterise people who don't agree with him as troglodytes. Reminiscent of early 19th century Tory attitudes in the face of the clamour for democracy. The aristocracy and land owners used to know what was best for the rest of us, now it's the well-educated, middle-class liberal. Mouthymike

Unfortunately for Stewart Lee's mortgage it may also be time to stop allowing self-loathing liberal comedians sate our sense of horror with clever, circular rhetoric. Alexlydiate

Do people believe the 'aunt Hattie' Hitler story actually happened?! Quingurzula

Firstly, are these luvvies allowed to mention bacon butties in case it upsets the peaceful religion? Secondly, it is advisable for a comedian to actually be funny . . . rather than the bland 'right on' wallahs these days. Kloppite

My Paul Nuttalls routine has floated back up the U-bend

4 December 2016

I believe it was a frog who wrote, 'Explaining a joke is like dissecting the American writer Elwyn Brooks White. You understand it better but Elwyn Brooks White dies in the process, ideally before completing *Stuart Little*.' I may have got this the wrong way round.

I am a multiple British Comedy and Bafta Award-winning 'comedian'. Once, my 'comedy' routines were written, performed and then largely forgotten. Now, they hang around the street corners of YouTube like homeless drunks, shouting and shorn of context, detached from the peculiarities of the times that shaped them, their relative merits debated enthusiastically by furious and illiterate racists from all over the globe. 'Who is this faggot?' Isn't technology amazing!

Whenever Paul Nuttalls of the Ukips hits the news, a routine I wrote about him on 25 April 2013 lurches back into involuntary digital circulation. Indeed, 'Stewart Lee' is now the third most popular Google appendage to Paul Nuttalls, below 'MEP' and above 'wife'. (The 'wife' search is presumably the result of patriotic women all over England, keen to be the broodmares for a better tomorrow, checking to see if Mr Nuttalls of the Ukips is available.)

Every time I think my Paul Nuttalls of the Ukips bit has been forgotten it returns to the public consciousness, more powerful and frightening than before, like a horrible Frankingstein, a persistent faecal clod that keeps floating back up the U-bend, or Paul Nuttalls of the Ukips himself.

In 2008 I wrote a forty-five-minute routine on *Top Gear*, imagining the presenters' Christmas drinks ending with Clarkson kicking a tramp to death, while Hammond and May fail to intervene, laughing and filming the attack on cameraphones.*

Predictably, every time Clarkson was nasty, the *Top Gear* bit accumulated more hits, the routine oddly foreshadowing the assault which was to end his BBC career. Sometimes I wonder if I am some kind of god. Does my work reflect reality, or am I actually shaping it? Was my 2008 routine a sort of sigil that ultimately drove Clarkson's steak-crazed fists into the face of his cheese-proffering servant?

And, in turn, was it the traffic my Paul Nuttalls routine generated over the past few years that actually raised his profile to the point where he was able to become leader of the Ukips? I wonder, typically as one of today's self-lacerating liberals, was it I who baked this golem and sent it out to rampage around the ghetto?†

Some routines take years to write. But the Paul Nuttalls of the Ukips routine shot out hot and fast, in one unbroken coil, like a good shit. I was running late on the morning of 25 April 2013 and so I drove my son to school, with the *Today* programme on the radio. Paul Nuttalls of the Ukips came on and said something odd

* Because I have no dramatic training, I acted out Clarkson kicking a tramp by kicking the floor of the stage hard and repeatedly. I did this probably over two hundred times. As a result of this (and being fat and old), my knees don't really work now. My health has been damaged by pretending to be Jeremy Clarkson. And so has Jeremy Clarkson's, if you think about it.

† The golem, again. I keep mentioning it. I have no imagination. Why can't Czech folk tales stay in the Czech Republic, where they belong, and enrich the Czech collective subconscious, instead of coming over here and clogging up my English imagination?

about Bulgarians, which seemed to me an attempt to portray his hostility to immigration as a genuine concern for the Bulgarians' own welfare. I went home and transcribed the interview from the iPlayer, and by midday the ten-minute bit, imagining the escalating absurd rhetoric of the Ukips' opposition to Britain's historic waves of immigration, was done.

In performance, I played up self-consciously to a stereotype of myself as a metropolitan liberal, angry that the lack of east European immigration would affect my ability to get cheap cups of coffee in central London, which was funny because it was true.* And I extended my hostility to Huguenots and Anglo-Saxons† and Neanderthal man into a general hatred of matter

---

* Many an eastern European, serving me across a counter in a hotel or railway station, has since told me how much they love this bit, before telling me they have a degree in astrophysics or something.

† When I performed this routine in *Comedy Vehicle* I quoted accurately lines in Anglo-Saxon from the ninth-century poem 'The Wanderer', the fatalistic outlook of which permanently informed my worldview when I studied it at university: '*Swa cwæð eardstapa, earfeþa gemyndig, wraþra wælsleahta, winemæga hryre.*' (So spoke the Wanderer, mindful of hardships, of fierce slaughters, and the downfall of kinsmen.) Billy Childish's literary garage-folk Medway combo The Spartan Dreggs have a deceptively beautiful setting of 'The Wanderer', entitled 'So Spake the Wanderer', on their 2012 album *Coastal Command*. I specifically wanted to get into Oxford University as a teenager for two reasons: firstly, because I knew the student drama society took comedy shows to the Edinburgh Fringe, and a doctor called Mark Payne, whom I did filing for on Saturday mornings, told me he had done that and it was brilliant; and secondly, to study Anglo-Saxon literature, which I turned out to be terrible at, so I was put in a special set with one other student, who was also rubbish. Weirdly, performing this routine alone means that I have probably made more practical use of my Anglo-Saxon poetry module than anyone else who studied it.

itself. And then I longed for a better time when not only were there no immigrants, but there was actually nothing, just a vast void. A void in which there was no crime. Obviously.

Because behind the practical critiques of immigration offered by the far right of today, there seems to be a more mysterious backstory, a kind of gaseous nostalgia for an imagined England that maybe never quite was, of warm beer, and old maiden aunts on bicycles, and the satisfying thwack of willow on a Gypsy's brown face.

The routine now bobs beyond my reach on YouTube, in a variety of different edits, some without the metaphysical coda about longing for oblivion, some with the removal of a burst of choice swearing, directed at an insolent prehistoric fish daring to come onto our land, which served crucially to leaven the polemic with ludicrous obscenity.

My showbiz friend Andreas Schmid, of krautrock legends Faust and Birmingham post-punks The Nightingales, even alerted me to a German stand-up whose verbatim translation of the routine had scored ten times more YouTube hits than my own original, for which the young comic has since apologised.*

The Ukips routine generated a flurry of oddly literal critiques, mistaking its intended effects for the writer's unintended errors, their blank analysis funnier than anything one could contrive. 'Lee is becoming so absurd', offers a contributor to a website called Western Defence, 'that one does have the impression the audience is laughing as much at him as with him. He adopts a (more) juvenile tone and begins singing a childish song, repeating himself all the time as usual. In an incredible display of

---

* Andreas Schmid's colloquial English is so good that he is able to use the Shropshire saying 'all round the Wrekin' with both accuracy and regularity. He is the Henning Wehn of post-punk.

40

immaturity for a 45-year-old man (perhaps befitting of the old children's television programme *Rainbow*), Lee continues his song. We are now supposed to laugh at the fact that Lee is really not making any sense at all. His arguments have been fully taken to absurd extremes.'

I am glad the bit has a second life and I hope it cheers people up, and perhaps takes away their fear for a moment or two. Maybe it will even sell me some tickets! But I don't know if I could write it today. Despite having been photographed hobnobbing with the EDL, claiming he wants to see the NHS dismantled, denying climate change, not supporting the ivory trade ban and refusing to quite disavow the BNP supporters he accepts the Ukips may have assimilated, the personable Paul Nuttalls of the Ukips seems eminently electable in post-fact, hate-fuelled Britain, even with his inexplicable loathing of elephants.*

It's not inconceivable that in a few years' time, former Labour supporters might be tactically voting Conservative to keep Nuttalls's far right out. Dancing around, singing childish songs and swearing at imaginary fish as a response to the Ukips seems to belong to simpler times, when Paul Nuttalls's avowed intent to ban comedians who did jokes about the Ukips from theatres seemed laughable. I don't know where I'd start a half-hour set on the Ukips today. I feel depressed, defeated, and often more than a little afraid for the future. This frog is now dead.

Try being amusing lad. That was what 'comedians' used to be paid for. No need to be afraid of the future. Our Paul is the future. He is made of much sterner stuff than you give him

* In the end it was pretending to have been in the Hillsborough disaster that finished Nuttalls's political career off. Everyone has a red line.

credit for. As befits a Hillsborough survivor. He will send seismic shock waves from Wales, the Midlands and the North that will reverberate through the Palace of Westminster. The price of sushi will be astronomical. Try having toast for brekkie instead lad. Kloppite

i don't get why people think stuart lee is funny. i'm a massive fan of stand up comics but i've never found him funny. much prefer a frankie boyle. wtfbollos

Stuart, why don't you get some loo paper and wipe your mouth. Mufc2014

More echo chamber stuff . . . yawn. Gravyring

Your whole act has been in the toilet bowl for years. Bobhelm

Beyond good and evil with
Gove and Trump

22 January 2017

In the Marvel Cinematic Universe, Scarlett Johansson's Black Widow is able to translate the grunting of Mark Ruffalo's incoherent Hulk into meaningful dialogue. Last Monday, *The Times* newspaper invited us to believe that the resentful foundling Michael Gove could do the same with the contradictory snarling of Donald Trump.

As a fellow adoptee I recognise Gove's irreparably damaged personality. Indeed, both of us were once published in the same vanity-pressed anthology of neurotic, self-justifying teenage poetry.* And as a member of the Gove-loathing metropolitan liberal elite, I thought we had seen the last of the self-serving nest-cuckoo and his hand-wringing wife.

Six months ago, it looked as if a stateless Gove and Sarah Vine were reinventing themselves as the amusing celebrity political couple for young millennials so jaded they no longer found Neil and Christine Hamilton quite sickening enough. Michael Gove

---

* Gove and I *were* both published in the same 1985 anthology of adolescent poetry by children attending fee-paying schools, *Independent Voices III* (but remember, I was on a charity bursary and then a part-scholarship, so I am free from blame). My poem was an innocuous and forgettable moan about gender identity. Gove's was a sinister attack on the sporty, non-adopted, posh boys who stole the girls that were rightfully the narrator's concubines, and it read like the sort of thing that would turn up in the personal papers of someone who went on to commit a high-school massacre. One could argue that what Gove has done in enabling Brexit is worse.

and Sarah Vine – a Neil and Christine Hamilton for the 2 *Girls, 1 Cup* generation.[*]

It had been Gove who, with David Cameron and Boris Johnson, sabotaged our children's futures in a doomed peeing war of competitive posh men.[†] As a student, David Cameron is rumoured to have put his penis into a dead pig. To outdo him as an adult, in an act even more bizarre and obscene, Michael Gove put his penis into a *Daily Mail* journalist. And to render both his rivals irrelevant, to do something even more disgusting and demented, Boris Johnson allowed himself to be put into the role of foreign secretary, a camp-guard punishment beating for the world.[‡]

But, in a plot twist worthy of an HBO box set, it is actually Johnson's old ally and enemy Gove who has made the first plausible contact with the new president of America. This journalistic coup goes some way to restoring the wounded pride of Gove, an adopted misfit masking his low self-esteem, afraid that his standing is an accident of administrative paperwork in infancy, desperate to assert his role in a world of entitlement to which he suspects he is not really entitled.[§]

---

[*] Do not google this Internet meme. Not safe for work.

[†] This whole para, scuffed up a bit, pretty much ended up as material in the *Content Provider* show, a rare example of prose material being directly transferable to the messier medium of stand-up.

[‡] Is it worth reminding everyone that prominent Leavers spent the last forty years comparing EU politicians to Nazi camp guards, Stalinists and Satan, and then threw their Union Jacks out of the pram when, in February 2019, Donald Tusk made the comparatively innocuous observation that there was a special place in hell for Brexiteers who had promoted their cause 'without even a sketch of a plan' of how they might do it?

[§] Obviously, the intentional subtext here is that this is my own assessment of myself. Below-the-line critics in the *Observer* merely

Encounters with Trump that appear calm usually suggest the school-bus driver in the film *The Enforcer* (James Fargo, 1976), interacting as politely as possible with DeVeren Bookwalter's vividly unhinged psychopath, in the hope that he won't massacre the kidnapped pre-teens on board. When Bookwalter forces the weeping children to sing 'Old MacDonald', the scene conveys the same air of forced jollity evident among Democrats at Trump's inauguration. But Gove's dealings with Trump were reported as relaxed, admittedly by Gove, in an interview he wrote, in a paper he works for, owned by an arse.

Everything you need to know about Gove's feelings for Trump, and for his previous paramour Boris Johnson, is contained in Nietzsche's 1887 book of essays, *On the Genealogy of Morality*. If you haven't read it, download Apple's Ask a Nietzsche app and question a tiny avatar of the dead philosopher, voiced by the German comedian and talkSPORT regular Henning Wehn. I first heard about the book on a radio show hosted by some-one called Melvyn Bragg, who I was surprised to find was a respected broadcaster, rather than a Siri-like app with a broken pitch control.

Now, I personally know nothing about psychiatry, philosophy, moral philosophy, psychology, psychoanalysis, psychological profiling, cultural history, politics, linguistics or the science of personality, but to me Gove would appear to exhibit all the char-acteristic traits of what Nietzsche calls the 'slave mentality', the resentful jealousy of the 'ill-born, meek' man, imagining that

---

assumed I had given away my own feelings about myself accidentally, thus: 'Jung pointed out that those who hurl insults invariably ascribe to others the failings that they fear they have themselves. This is a thoroughy nasty article . . . "an adopted misfit masking his low self-esteem" . . . do you recognise this person Mr Lee?' Earnestpipewhistle

one day the world will see that he was right all along.*

Boris Johnson and Donald Trump, however, fulfil the criteria of what Nietzsche names, in the same essay, 'blond beasts'. Not only are they both blond and beastly, but they are 'beyond good and evil', observing no law other than their own power. The Gove-slave needs to believe in deferred justice, as he is physically incapable of defeating the blond beasts on their own terms. Nietzsche sees this as the root of Christian morality.

Or alternatively, it would appear, the slave can canoodle with the beast, and if one blond beast doesn't take the bait, there's always another one over the Atlantic to cuddle up with instead.

But one doesn't need Nietzsche to understand Gove's relationship with Trump. Presumably you remember it from the playground, where Gove-like figures peeped over bullies' shoulders, urging them to violence from a position of cowardly safety, the Richard Hammond/Jeremy Clarkson dynamic, an eternal archetype, replayed in Trump's golden office, framed *Playboy* covers reflected in the smeared lenses of Gove's steamed-up spectacles. Is it just me or is it hot in here?

Gove may be a slave but he is not an idiot. He knows there is no point setting any store by anything Trump says. Trump's comments do not add up to any coherent worldview. Each emerges in the moment, suitable for that second, and that second alone. In his Gove interview Trump said he hoped to scale down his nuclear arsenal. But as recently as 22 December, in his famous 'Let It Be an Arms Race' series of 140-character treatises, Trump declared: 'The United States must greatly strengthen and expand its nuclear capability.'

* Yes, this is a rewrite of a joke I did about the Loch Ness Monster on *Comedy Vehicle*, a rare example of reverse traffic from stand-up back into print.

Trump's inaccurate pronouncements about NATO member states' financial contributions and the 'illegal' status of refugees in Germany were accepted and transcribed unchallenged by Gove. Jokes about farts that I perform on comedy DVDs are held to higher legal standards than Gove's *Times* piece on the then president-elect, but are not as funny.

After the interview's publication, Gove was deferred to uncritically on Radio 4's *Today* programme, a show currently so spineless in its questioning of government that it resembles not so much a news source as a stack of jellyfish piled up on top of one another and wrapped in an unbuttoned shirt and a Robert Redford wig, in the hope that someone will mistake it for Bob Woodward.

Gove is a desperate, disappointed man, staring into the murky dew pond of Trump's inarticulate pronouncements, looking for something that validates him. Hearing that Trump will do a trade deal with the UK 'absolutely, very quickly', Gove the emasculated Brexiteer makes this the focus of a *Times* interview so uncritical as to be as dangerous and dishonest as anything emerging from a Macedonian fake-news factory. This is not a game. Lives are at stake. You all need to do better. See me.

Play the ball, not the man. This kind of ad hom attack on Gove (and his wife too?) is very undignified. Yohdur

This seemed mean-spirited and irrelevant, for example: 'resentful foundling Michael Gove'. Lee being an adoptee does not make it right or excuse it any more than my father dying when I was 11 allows me to say 'half-orphaned Mr X was left wondering what his life would have been if his father had not choked his arteries to death prematurely in an effort to avoid his son's difficult teenage years.' DJS8

Usually laugh at this, but this is just vile. Hateful stuff today Stuart, just when we need the opposite. No doubt Hitler would have enjoyed it, with all your Nietzsche references you would be turning into his favourite comedian. Richyork

'I personally know nothing about psychiatry, philosophy, moral philosophy, psychology, psychoanalysis, psychological profiling, cultural history, politics, linguistics, or the science of personality' Then why are you writing this stuff? Is this the whinging libs version of 'I knows what I knows, guv, though I knows nuthink'? And I thought the *Daily Mail* was a bile filled garbage bin. Harbringer

Aren't comedians supposed to be funny? Poisonous hate-filled bile, and the rant of someone who is seriously disturbed. Mdebkk

What was the point of this pretty spiteful attack on Gove and his wife? Isn't it merely another petty grievance by some disaffected clod whose nose has been put out of joint somewhere along the line, causing frustration and an inability to shrug it off and learn from it like adults usually do? Juvenile name-calling not woth the space in the *Guardian* imo. Victormeldrew111

Several major errors. The film referred to is *Dirty Harry* – it's the 'Scorpio' serial killer who's on the School bus. Also, Nietzsche's 'On the Genealogy of Morality' is an interrelated sequence of essays which can't be read separately without distorting his intentions. Picking phrases at random to support a point is lazy and makes quoting from this source meaningless. Markfielding

You'd better keep the comedy coming, Stewart, because it's going to get a whole lot worse for your metropolitan liberal elite in the coming years! Happyhammer1982

As a self-confessed 'irreparably damaged personality' one might advise you to trial some sort of talking-therapy. It may prevent you making errors in 'analysing' other's personality defects. Carflosalbertos1970

Posh boys puts the boot into posh boy. Tony Griffiths

The champagne socialists had Ben Elton now they have Stewart Lee, funny how history is repeating itself. The Royal Oak

Another privately educated Oxbridge chap giving it to the great unwashed, make that man *Guardian* editor! Rainbownation

If it's real sexism you want – proper, vicious prejudice of the most misogynistic kind – allow me . . . to offer you [this]: 'As a student, David Cameron is rumoured to have put his penis into a dead pig. To outdo him as an adult, in an act even more bizarre and obscene, Michael Gove put his penis into a *Daily Mail* journalist.' Sarah Vine, *Daily Mail*

Roll over, Grandma, and tell
Robert Peston the news

26 February 2017

What would a *coup d'état* look like? Would you even notice if one was happening all around you? Should we even be allowed to use the phrase '*coup d'état*', now that we are leaving the EU? Should we return the very words themselves to the vile continent whence they came, and accept back in turn '*le weekend*', '*le camping*' and loads of leather-skinned racist pensioners currently dwelling in Spanish retirement complexes, to drain the resources of our imminently even more understaffed NHS?

My late father used to have a drinking buddy, Krtek, nicknamed the Mole, who claimed to have been caught in the crossfire of a hostile '50s coup in his east European homeland. Apparently, the Mole had been shot in the face in a street battle, leaving him with a permanent slit in his cheek, which he could open and close at will, like the oily perineal gland through which Michael Gove periodically oozes translucent globs of sincerity.*

---

* My father, who ran his own cardboard supply consultancy service from the spare room in his house in Featherstone Crescent, Solihull, and was hilarious, was inexplicably friendly with a man who had been something significant in Soviet-era Hungary. And this man did have a bullet hole in his face. And both he and my father had foreign wives, which may have been what drew them together in monocultural Solihull. The man was not called the Mole. *The Mole* was an animated Czech series about a hard-working Communist mole, which was shown on BBC children's TV in the late 1960s and early '70s. Even as a child I suspected it contained some subversive hidden message, and have since bought a Christmas ornament of the character from a Prague market.

The Mole first made my father aware of his face skill in the late '70s, at a family-run Italian restaurant, Da Corrado, on the then rural outskirts of south-east Birmingham. During dinner, in an argument about the veracity of the Dr Hook song 'When You're in Love with a Beautiful Woman (It's Hard),'* the Mole deliberately shot a compressed jet of masticated cannelloni out of the portal of his cheek wound into my father's hair, leading to a lifetime Da Corrado ban for the pair of them. This was particularly egregious for my father, who maintained that Da Corrado's deep-fried squid was the best in the immediate Cheswick Green area, if not the West Midlands generally.†

Nonetheless, as a child, the Mole's punctured face, and the exotic fables of street-fighting that accompanied it, defined my idea of a *coup d'état*. There'd be tanks, wouldn't there, rolling through redbrick squares, beautiful blonde Slavic girls putting

---

* My father was convinced that this Dr Hook song held the key to understanding all human relationships, and he would sigh sagely to the lyrics when it came on the radio. His father, in turn, thought that 'Atmosphere', by Russ Abbot, was, and I quote, 'a haunting melody'.

† In the '70s, Da Corrado's Italian restaurant was on the fringes of Solihull, where the Birmingham conurbation dissolved into the wild and mysterious *Midsummer Night's Dream* Warwickshire wilderness, though today the city has overtaken it and the land around it has been bisected by the M42 and the forthcoming HS2 atrocity. Back then, Da Corrado's provision of then-exotic dishes – cannelloni and carbonara, for example – and the fact that it seemed geographically beyond the law, created an outlaw vibe, as if what happened in Da Corrado's stayed in Da Corrado's. When, in my teens, my father finally allowed me to accompany him there, I was aware that he was allowing me into the secret adult world of sophisticated foods and swan-shaped napkins. Cheswick Green was a small newbuild '60s estate near Da Corrado's, made famous in a song on Napalm Death's 1985 *Hatred Surge* demo tape called 'Cheswick Green'.

hopeless blooms into gun barrels, and orders barked through megaphones by men with Nazi moustaches? And there'd be psychedelic bands, playing acid-polka music in mail-order Carnaby Street threads, driven underground by the military, awaiting respectable roles in the revolutionary government's Ministry of Culture, three decades later. Wouldn't there?

Well, roll over, Grandma, and tell Robert Peston the news. This is not your mother's seizure of political power. I suspect we Western liberal democracies may be in the middle of a very modern type of coup, namely an alt-coup. Look! I've used the hipster prefix 'alt', but in relation to reactionary politics, rather than in a phrase like 'alt-country', 'alt-porn' or 'alt-crochet'. How thrillingly twenty-first-century! This is what it must have felt like to have been Milo Yiannopoulos!!

(Sadly, it was only last month that I even learned of the existence of Trump-endorsed uber-troll Milo Yiannopoulos, who looked like a Tom of Finland pencil drawing of his Breitbart colleague James Delingpole. And already the boy has been dissolved in acid by his own suddenly squeamish paymasters. The news cycle moves so fast it's hardly worth finding out about anything any more as it's all sure to be irrelevant a week later. Note to self: that's what 'they' want you to think.)*

An American dictionary definition of '*coup d'état*' I found

---

* Yiannopoulos's comically abrasive alt-right columns were briefly useful to Breitbart, with some fascists thinking the boy might win over youth support, but they quickly dropped him in 2017, when he appeared to advocate underage gay sex in a 2016 interview on a podcast called *Drunken Peasants*. Our own parliamentary far right – Priti Patel, Jacob Rees-Mogg and Anne-Marie Trevelyan – made similar overtures to the alt-right youth group Turning Point in January 2019, a relationship which is sure to end equally badly, but for different reasons.

online calls it 'a quick and decisive seizure of governmental power by a strong military or political group . . . [which] arrests the incumbent leaders, seizes the national radio and television services, and proclaims itself in power'. So does our home-grown alt-coup fit the bill?

Well, undoubtedly, a coterie of far-right Conservatives are using the supposed Brexit mandate as an opportunity to pursue their extremist agenda, but the incumbent leaders weren't arrested, they just ran away. And the leader of our current opposition, if you'll permit me some *Daily Telegraph* blogger-type *Schadenfreude*, probably couldn't get himself arrested if he tried! (This stuff's easy! I'd be looking at a £250,000 book deal, if only I hadn't been such a careless and vocal advocate of non-consensual human–insect sexual relations.)

Unlike the classic coup, the new government hasn't seized the national radio and television services, as there has been no need to do so, Laura Kuenssberg in particular being essentially just a state-sponsored town crier who runs around the filthy lanes in a Theresa May tabard, blowing a heraldic trumpet in celebration of every government pronouncement. Snitch!

Indeed, earlier this week, the BBC chose to run a coincidentally timed documentary about the senile freeloaders in the irrelevant House of Lords, just as the honourable checks and balances were debating Brexit, the unelected peers intimidated from the sidelines by the unelected prime minister, sporting the face of a vicar's daughter who had eaten a whole bucket of spicy *huevos de toro* before being told which part of the *toro* they were made from.

Surely there must be at least a peerage waiting for the head of BBC scheduling, if the House of Lords isn't abolished? Here's hoping for an equally well-timed reappraisal of the professional/personal irregularities that led to expense-muddling Brexiteer and disgraced former defence secretary Liam Fox's now forgotten 2011 resignation.*

Sadly, the newspapers aren't up to policing the coup either.† When he interviewed Donald Trump for *The Times*, Michael Gove didn't even notice that Rupert Murdoch was in the room.‡ I'm not a respected journalist like Michael, I'm just a comedian, but to me Murdoch's presence changes the whole story, and makes it look as if the far-right coup is part of an international network of corrupt self-interested parties – a massive scoop for Gove to miss.

Unlike the coup that punctured the Mole's face, in our alt-coup not a shot was fired in anger. And yes, I am ignoring the shooting of Jo Cox, as Remainers have been asked not to 'politicise' it. And anyway, the gunman who shouted out 'Britain First!' during the killing has got the politicisation of that murder pretty much covered anyway.

* When he was defence secretary in 2010 and 2011, Liam Fox, it is now generally forgotten, took the tenant of his flat, the unaccredited Adam Werritty, around the world on MOD arms-deal trips, staying in economically shared hotel rooms. Would you trust this man to deliver 'the easiest trade deal in history'?

† I'm not a professional political journalist, but I nearly got this coup thing right. Two years after this piece, as moderate Tories started to defect to a new and then-unnamed independent group, it became clear that Jacob Rees-Mogg's European Research Group, and the UKIP members that joined the Conservative Party en masse to influence it from within, were organising a coup to take over the party, and thus the country. Old lefty Brexiteers that I know wanted out of the EU because Hungary and Poland had far-right governments, so it couldn't be any good. Here, leaving the EU was in danger of delivering us a fascist regime of our own.

‡ That's right! Rupert Murdoch was in the room when Gove interviewed Donald Trump, and he didn't think it necessary to write that detail up. What else has he failed to disclose?

Thirty years later, I wonder if the story of the Mole and his squirty face-hole, like so many of my father's tall tales, was true at all. It doesn't matter. It made me happy. My father had also claimed, repeatedly, to be a member of a secret society of European packaging-company reps, whose members met in various continental sales-conference venues, where they dared each other to place bets on how many small white plastic sticks were concealed in their clenched fists.* I don't care whether this

---

* I have since discovered that my father was indeed a member of such a club. The game was called Spoof, and the society was called the Spoof Club, and it met in Amsterdam and Brussels. I do not know if the Mole was also a member. My father is dead now. He wasn't the sort of father who would save sensibly to help you in later life, but once, when I was a student, he rang my shared house's payphone on a Friday night and, on finding that I couldn't go to the pub because I had literally no money and wasn't due any for weeks, he sent me £50 cash via the next post, though this was a figure I was subsequently to repay to him many times over, including, on one occasion, in the form of a substantial kidnapping ransom. There are a lot of things I didn't know and will never know about my father, both trivial and significant. Was his painting of two gun dogs by the sporting artist Roland Knight really damaged when his third wife tried to shoot him with an air rifle and missed? Who knows. His favourite book, and indeed the only book he ever expressed an interest in, apart from a pornographic novel set on a slave plantation I once saw him reading, was *The Autobiography of a Super-Tramp* (1908), by the Welsh poet W. H. Davies. He had read this book as a child and never forgotten it, and he bequeathed me his copy the last time I saw him, before he left the country. It was about a man who ran away for a life of gambling, smoking, drinking, telling tall stories and 'occasionally taking exercise or going out for a walk', which is essentially how my dad ended up living, in a land far away. And in so doing, I think, he won a kind of victory over the world on his own terms. I can relate. I read from *The Autobiography of a Super-Tramp* at his memorial service. It was, literally on this occasion, what he would have wanted. At my funeral, I would like my son to read from this book, because I am a narcissist.

club existed. Either way, it is now a useful metaphor for Theresa May's Brexit negotiating strategy. Thanks, Dad.

'What would a coup d'état look like?' I was in Ankara during the recent attempt, and it was pretty easy to tell cause of all the F16s buzzing the city, bombs being dropped on parliament, tanks rolling through the streets, gunfire all night long . . . Funnily enough a BBC documentary on the HoL and a dishonest Gove interview doesn't quite feel like the same thing. Dickapocalypse

Stu, I think Krtek means Mole. In Czech or Polish. Ajmb

Aaah. Da Corrado. Saturday lunchtime hangout for all the local politicians of the area. A dire eatery. Arthur Sternom

Puerile nonsense as usual. Tony35

Milo's articles are beautifully written with dazzling clarity rather than impenetrable verbiage. His book will find a publisher and will sell widely not least because his style is eminently readable and peppered with comedy gold. I can understand why he induces envy from lesser talented writers. AgnesMay

Is Stewart Lee supposed to be a comedian? AvenellRoad

One of us needs to check what is the definition of comedy as opposed to a bile filled incoherent unfunny rant. MikeHogger

Us normal people love to hear the hysterical rantings of the loony left. Lots of wailing and gnashing of teeth. The western world is moving swiftly and sharply to the right. Get used to it losers. Britainforbrexit

Well, that's 10 minutes of my life I won't get back . . .
Gruntymalunty

Ostracizing/demonizing Milo in this way is the direct equivalent of banning foreign people from entering a country. Oh, the hypocrisy! Even the most mighty moralists, like Lee, can fall into the mainstream medias' clutches. Deianera

'I'm just a comedian', no, you aren't. The requires being funny. Not just blathering on about your wierd political opinions. Marcus Wolfson

You're not a comedian, comedians should make people laugh not provoke a nervous embarrassed titter at best. A hangover from the alt comedian days maybe, though they all sold out in the end anyway. Birney

Krtek wasn't 'nicknamed' the Mole. It's his actual name. That's what krtek means in Czech. Not the most creative nickname. Cerealcat

Even stand-up has been
weaponised by fake news

30 April 2017

Last Sunday,* Le Pen was predicted a 92 per cent landslide; Serge Gainsbourg's zombie corpse, barely discernible from his living form, rose from the grave and endorsed the Front National; and, apparently, ten-hour queues meant it wasn't worth busy French metropolitan liberals turning up to vote, as they would not then have time to drink absinthe in Saint-Denis, dance with Moulin Rouge showgirls and pursue their extramarital affairs before bed.†

If you'd googled the word 'France' in the hours up to the first round of the French election, you'd have found fake news stories, skewed in support of the anti-EU far right, all over Twitter and Facebook. Writing in this newspaper in February, Carole Cadwalladr revealed how one-third of all traffic on Twitter before the EU referendum was generated by automated 'bots' programmed to trend pro-Leave topics,‡ a story that should have gained more ground except that, well, it wouldn't, would it, obviously.

Sometime around the weekend of 1 April, the comedian Marcus Brigstocke blogged that members of his audiences 'walked out every night' when he mocked Brexit. Within days,

---

* The 2017 French election.

† All these fake stories were placed on French social media in the run-up to the election.

‡ And this was only the first blast of an investigation that should have discredited the referendum.

the *Daily Telegraph*, the *Daily Mail*, the *Daily Express*, Breitbart, the *Spectator*, *ShortList* and *Spiked* all had fake stories suggesting Brexiteer audiences were also deserting en masse shows by me, specifically, and a subsequent host of unnamed 'far left London comedians' (Breitbart). 'It's nice of them to wait until the end and applaud while doing it,' my tour manager noted, drily. But by now, the fake-news tsunami was blowin' hard.*

The crappy male-grooming freesheet *ShortList* was among many sources that decontextualised self-aware jokes I had made about my perceived liberal impotence in the face of Brexit, even going so far as to congratulate me for 'substantial self-awareness'. Here and on stage, I parody the Right's expectations of liberal comedy, only to have them thrown back at me, free of their moorings, to confirm its ignorant assumptions. In Brexit Britain, we are post-fact, post-irony and post-nuance.

To its credit, the *Daily Express* changed its timid assertion that I was receiving 'scornful glances' from audiences to my suggested correction: 'Comedian Stewart Lee, in contrast, claims his career has only been strengthened by Brexit. He has been performing nationwide, with a set that includes twenty minutes of anti-Brexit material and describes Leave voters as "c***s".' Like my twin heroes Eminem and Christ, 'I am whatever you say I am!'

I emailed the first twenty-five stand-up comedians in my address book to ask them about any experiences of doing Brexit

---

* Surely somebody, somewhere along the chain of falsehoods, could have checked whether this news story was accurate in relation to what it said about me. If I was paranoid, I would think that the Leave machine and the newspapers that serve it wanted to emasculate comedy, because they saw it as some kind of threat to their false narrative. Whenever I am involved in a news story, I find it is usually inaccurate. Then I start to wonder about news generally.

material, which is perhaps the sort of thing you could do if you were a journalist covering the story for a newspaper as part of your actual real job.

Thirteen responded immediately, all but one of whom work nationwide, and all had done Brexit material. The survey comprised, to my tremendous satisfaction, only three heterosexual white English men, alongside a female Irish immigrant, a female white English feminist pensioner, a Northern Irish Catholic heterosexual man, a Jewish American immigrant, a bisexual Englishman, a British Baha'i man, a British Muslim woman, a Canadian immigrant heterosexual man, a white Scottish male Buddhist and a British Hindu man who has nonetheless been vilified for looking like a Muslim in an Internet meme.*

A majority of ten of the stand-up comedians took specifically anti-Brexit positions. 'I disagree that it's career-ending. Comedians have coped with massive political changes before and there's comfort in using your skills to meet new demands,' said the Irishwoman, philosophically. 'I've yet to see a reaction to a Brexit joke even ruin a gig, let alone a career. I know there's a huge change in the country's attitudes but I still think there's more non-cunts than cunts,' the Northern Irish Protestant man concluded, with characteristic regional ferocity.

'I had no idea my career was over if I did Brexit material. I thought things were going quite well. My experience is that audiences expect it,' reflected the Muslim woman. The Muslim-looking Hindu comedian, however, revealed that a fight had

* Obviously I tweaked the selection of people I emailed so that it was ludicrously socially diverse in order to parody and confirm the prejudices of people who hate me and post below the line on *Observer* columns accusing me of virtue signalling, which is exactly what it did, thus: '*Tremendously impressed with the diversity of Stuart's address book, and with his forthrightness in revealing it.* Freddy Starmer'

broken out in Leamington Spa during his anti-Brexit routine, but with shades of high-level UKIP meetings, it had been between two Leave voters who differed over whether he should have been allowed to make jokes about Brexit at all.

I looked at the Twitter identities that had driven the spread of the fake story. Was 'Brexpats' a real thing or a lie platform generated by a pro-Brexit data company such as Cambridge Analytica, which currently features in an investigation into whether it gave undeclared free cyber-assistance to Leave.EU? Was someone called 'Luca Saucedo' really interested in the supposed failure of Brexit comedy, when the rest of his Twitter timeline concerned beachwear and phone wallets? Did 'Luca Saucedo' even exist? Was he an anti-EU Kremlin bot, perhaps infected with some kind of sandal and swim-trunk virus?

By the end of the fake-news week, the anti-EU *Daily Telegraph*, as if to shore up its dubious story, ran a consolidating opinion piece by 'Brexit comedian Simon Evans'. But Evans immediately admitted on Twitter: 'The article as I wrote it is more about acknowledging nuance, perspective and not taking consensus in the room for granted. However, a lot of the nuance has, predictably, been stripped and I'm not entirely happy with how it reads .. Just wanted to distance myself from "Brexit comedian", which wasn't the point to me at all.'*

---

* It is always exciting to be asked to write something by a newspaper, and who can blame 'Brexit comedian' Simon Evans, who prefers 'Alexei Sayle's acerbic bile' to my 'nuanced pontificating', for naively agreeing to cooperate with a paper as dishonest as the *Daily Telegraph* without insisting on the proper checks and balances. But cool heads must prevail, and I always ask for approval over edits, and even over any photographs or illustrations, as these too can swing the way a piece reads. Even the *Guardian* has, on occasion, stiffed me with an editorialised photo caption. Fake news!

Bizarrely, the more moderate Twitter version of 'Simon Evans' was now in conflict with the hard Brexit 'Simon Evans' identity, created by the *Telegraph* through judicious subediting, misrepresentative headlines and manipulative captioning of irrelevant photo montages.

I emailed what I assume is the real Simon Evans, who likes to remind his Twitter followers that they are allowed to find me 'not particularly funny', nearly three weeks ago now to ask him if he had been solicited by the *Daily Telegraph*, with the brief of substantiating its position, but he does not respond. Does 'Simon Evans' even exist? Are he and sandal- and swimwear-loving Luca Saucedo different manifestations of the same algorithmically generated, Putin-backed, anti-EU mechanism, weaponising* falsehoods to destabilise Europe and crush the saboteurs?

Or am I the fictional entity, brain dead somewhere on life support, dreaming of nightly applause for my anti-Brexit witticisms as I pass 100,000 tour ticket sales, when in fact I made a failed suicide attempt weeks ago, sick of being booed off from Land's End to John O'Groats, just as the papers said?

And who are you, reading this and choosing to retweet it? Are you real? Would you even know if you weren't? Are you a program created to think like a person? Am I? Is this how it is now? For ever? Fake news all the way down?

---

* I was going through a phase of enjoying using the word 'weaponise' because, recently, while walking past a building site, my blind eyes had misread a sign that said 'We Apologise For Any Inconvenience' as the far more inspiring 'Weaponise Any Inconvenience'. I think Weaponise Any Inconvenience is a genuine philosophy for art and life.

This is a made up story. Susie

Virtue signalling. Cranky Mac

It does not matter what topic Stewart Lee talks about, Brexit or not, the sad fact he is just not funny. Northoflondon

Poor old Stuart Lee far to clever for his own good, he doesn't seem to realise that his time has come and gone It's there 1979 moment when the northern working class comedians became obsolete so to June 2016 marked the point when the metropolitan liberal elite became obsolete Looking forward to seeing Stuart Lee on a Home Counties version of *Bullseye.* Sheffield Monkey

Like most up themselves left wing liberal comedians they can dish it out but can't take it back. They seem to become easily offended when some members of their audience decide to walk out on them for not enjoying their material, actually its no big deal and certainly not worthy of a article when someone so sensitive starts crying, bellyaching and making a big fuss about it. Cyrilthewasp

Lefty comedian in not being remotely funny shocka! He is no jim davidson or bernard Manning . . . I will give you that. Marcus Wolfson

Lee seems to have forgotten that hes' a professional entertainer, whose sole job is to entertain, rather than offer political theory lectures. Soupdraggon69

Stewart Lee has more in common with Thatcher then even he knows! He is part of the Neo-liberal elite and he does not even know it. Or maybe he does as it seems good for

business? I hope he pays his full whack of income tax from all this money he makes? David Coalman

Perhaps Stewart Lee should do a double act with his tour manager. With Lee as the straight man. CM Rowney

Celebrity *Observer* columnist in 'telling his readership exactly what they want to hear in order to carry on feeling embattled yet superior' shock. Pete CW

I used to run a pub in Brighton and we had a regular comedy night to raise money for medicines sans frontieres. Simon Munnery was supposed to be headlining and pulled out last minute as he had double booked. Marcus Brigstocke was doing a show at the Dome/Corn Exchange that night. After he finished his gig he came up to the pub, did the headline set, refused to take the fee and got the train home. Proudsonofduck

Only Stewart Lee could have the most diverse, multi-cultural, liberal and progressive email address list in the UK. Youcantalk

Lee talks like a North London musher from a council estate when he's a public schoolboy who went to Oxford. Does that mean he's a fraud? I assume that since he's lived in London so long that when he's practising his 'working class' accent in the mirror every morning that he's unconsciously transformed himself from a phoney Brum to a phoney Cockney. What a geezer! Dropped 'h's and glottal stops all over the place from a 50 year old Oxbridge-educated public schoolboy were surprising and strongly suggested the type of left-wing pretension and phoniness that are so valued by rich socialists and their admirers. QuarkMusterMark

How a sex robot ended up
on the *One Show* sofa

14 May 2017

Artificially intelligent humanoid sexual partners are now commercially available. And indeed, I have often wondered if I myself am in fact one such 'sex robot'. My lovers always disengage from me in silently satisfied wonder, and rarely request second encounters, having had their expectations soul-shatteringly exceeded, their sexual futures rendered endlessly disappointing. I'm joking of course! I have been married for twelve years. There is nothing to see here.

But once, as a young adventurer, I crossed America by bus, arriving in Seattle in September 1994, three years after Peak Grunge, just in time to see the genre winding down with a local band called Peach, at the Crocodile Café. The ATM ran dry that night and a scenester at the bar bailed me out with the offer of his sofa. He seemed normal enough by the standards of the day – beanie hat, goatee beard and pierced nipples poking through a T-shirt bearing the legend 'Public Castration Is a Good Idea'.*

* I went to Seattle, grunge central, in 1994, on a road trip from Vancouver to San Francisco with my then girlfriend, on a £500 budget. We briefly witnessed a very late line-up of Moby Grape in a supper club, and an indie-pop band called Baby Snuffkin, along with a thoughtful group called Peach, at the Crocodile Café. Peach was made up of ex-members of The Posies, whom I liked, and they were nice to us. We drank exotic and mysterious Starbucks coffee and micro-brewery craft beer in rooms full of bearded hipsters and tasted the future of Western Civilisation. We didn't stay in a flat full of sex robots. In San Francisco, our motel was rocked by a minor earthquake, and somewhere in Oregon

To say that Matt's apartment was a surprise would be an understatement. The walls were lined not with Tad and Mudhoney posters, but with the suspended forms of life-size naked female dolls, of troubling anatomical accuracy, which he had made himself. 'Don't worry,' Matt said, 'I'm not crazy or weird. I hope one day to make these dolls into artificially intelligent sex robots. Imagine having your own erotic mechanical slaves! Nachos?'

Last month, I saw Matt for the first time in twenty-three years, this time in a *Guardian* feature about the ethical dilemmas created by a newly available luxury product he had developed: life-size, artificially intelligent sex robots. Then, suddenly, events here at home made me realise I needed to speak to Matt McMutton again, and not as a potential customer!

Last week, Sarah Vine, who is married to Michael Gove, opened the scab-encrusted blowhole of her *Daily Mail* column once more, this time comparing Brigitte Macron, the wife of the new French president, whom he met when he was her fifteen-year-old drama pupil, to the alleged child rapist Roman Polanski, and suggesting, not entirely unreasonably, that had the couple's roles been reversed their marriage would seem 'grotesque'.*

---

we met a man whose wife told us he had murdered a Mexican on their land and that she had seen The Quicksilver Messenger Service live, back in the psychedelic day. America obligingly became what we had hoped it would be.

* Boris Johnson, the Goves' former dinner-party guest, is also twenty-four years older than the woman he left his last wife for, though admittedly he was not her former schoolteacher. He was Boris Johnson. I am three years older than my wife, but once, when we went out for dinner on our wedding anniversary, it was clear the waitress thought she was my daughter, or perhaps even my carer. We played up to this idea, and when we asked the waitress to take a photo of us, I stayed seated and my wife stood behind me with her hand on my shoulder, as if she

But Sarah Vine is married to Michael Gove. And Michael Gove is, in turn, married to Sarah Vine. And the thought of either of them being married to anyone, let alone each other, is also grotesque, despite Vine being an acceptable four months her adopted husband's senior.

And, uniquely, the notion of the Goves' union remains equally grotesque, even when their ages are reversed to be more in line with those of a normal partnership. The image of a cluster of toads spawning in a dew pond is more pleasing to the mind's eye, for unlike the dissembling Goves, the assembling toads are merely following their own natures, in accordance with the watchmaker's perfect mechanism, amphibian messengers of Christ's majesty eternal.*

Of course, I appreciate that the previous four sentences are unpleasant. They are deliberately so, as a mirror image of the Vine sensibility that inspired them. The cultural theorist James Naughtie explained to me on the *Today* programme, while screwing up his stupid red face like a baboon eating a thistle, that an earlier column of mine about the Goves and their ilk was 'poisonous'. But to say a column about the Goves is poisonous is unnecessary, like saying that a slow-motion film of a cat vomiting is nauseating.†

---

was there out of a sense of duty. How we laughed later. It is laughter that keeps marriages together, I think. That and simply running out of other options.

* I have been fixated on the image of 'a cluster of toads spawning in a pond' ever since a friend who had been a customer of an Old Street gay sauna used it to describe his experience of activities in the venue's swimming pool in the 1980s. Does mentioning this gay friend count as 'virtue signalling'? I do hope so.

† James Naughtie had me on some literary review show on BBC News. He clearly hadn't read my book and tried to bluff his way through the

It is foolish of politicians and their guff-trumpets – and this is what Vine is here – to score points off their rivals' choice of spouse, especially if you are Sarah Vine. And it is even more foolish to do so when Theresa May parades her husband Philip before the cameras of *The One Show*. The poor banker came across not as strong and stable, but like a tortured hostage forced at gunpoint to tell the people at home how kindly he is being treated.

Eighty-two kidnapped Nigerian schoolgirls are free! But when will Philip May be free?* And will he have any strong hope of readjusting to a stable life, where he is spared the endless repetition of the words 'strong' and 'stable'?

And why is Theresa May's lower jaw permanently locked into the same sort of jutting/munching shape Eric Morecambe's made when theatrically sucking a pipe? She has no pipe. How will Mrs May's imaginary pipe face play with the Europeans? They will say, '*Ceci n'est pas une pipe*.'†

---

interview, using stuff he, or his producer, had gleaned in five minutes from Wikipedia and the *Daily Mail* website. At one point, the question J. Naughtie was asking me made so little sense, and bore such little relation to anything I had ever said or done, that I asked him if he wanted to start the interview again, so he did, and then just did it equally badly, while I sat there making a bemused face. It was like I was still at school, and he was the impotent and resentful dad of a girl I was taking to the fair, trying to get one over on me for some inexplicable reason that I didn't understand, interrogating me in the kitchen while she waited on the sofa with a video of *The Return of Martin Guerre*, which we simply had to watch. I look forward to being allowed to behave equally badly to some young man.

* In the interests of full disclosure, on reading the sentence back I realise it is rhythmically indebted to the superior and more nuanced joke the comedy genius Simon Munnery wrote in the late '80s, in his Alan Parker Urban Warrior guise: 'The Birmingham Six are free! When will the rest of Birmingham be free?'

† *The Treachery of Images*, René Magritte, 1929.

I am no international trade negotiator (who is?), but can it be prudent, as we enter into talks with a newly united EU, determined to reaffirm its Enlightenment values, for Sarah Vine, one of our chief Brexiteers, and the spouse of a former cabinet member, to compare the French president's wife to an alleged child rapist? How will this affect barista visas, roaming mobile-phone charges and the future dimensions of Toblerones?

However offensive the French first couple's relationship, it at least seemed genuine. But, to me, there was a strange, haunted, empty quality to both Michael Gove and Philip May, the latter having vouchsafed to *The One Show* that he 'quite liked ties, although I'm not wearing one this evening'.* This indefinable absence of the flame of being makes the idea of a relationship involving either Mr Gove or Mr May oddly implausible.

Troubled by a mysterious worry, on Thursday I called Matt. 'The project stalled soon after we met,' he recalled. 'It was initially too difficult to replicate the unpredictable workings of the complex female brain. But men's brains were easy. They just thought about sports and neckties, so I turned out a couple of male dolls as practice. I only make the female dolls now, but for a few months in the mid-'90s I had a small client list of successful rich women who wanted compliant partners. They didn't mind if their sex robots had no real personality to speak of, as long as they'd take out the trash and eat the occasional tuna taco way down south in Dixie, if you get my drift. Mumble in the moss, man, mumble in the moss!'

'You don't still have that list, do you, Matt?' I asked. 'Sure.' The two names from the old customer base that shocked me most

---

* Imagine being able to just say such hilariously banal things naturally, as Mr May does here, without spending hours, like I do, trying to think up hilariously banal things on purpose.

meant nothing to Matt McMutton. But then he wasn't a follower of British politics. When and where and why, I wondered, had the sinister switches been made? 'So,' Matt continued, five thousand miles away in the Pacific Northwest, as the realisation dawned and I sat down in stunned horror, 'you in the market for a sex robot? Or are you still dating humans, old school? Faggot!'

This isn't the first time I've seen this in the *Guardian* – pointing out that Gove is adopted. It's not relevant to anything and needlessly offensive to keep doing so. Alastair T

What an unbelievably vicious and small minded article. It is like a distillation of Frankie Boyle, except for the fundamental difference that Frankie Boyle is actually funny. Presumably the perpetrator of this sick juvenile filth feels justified in his unmitigated hatred of the Goves and the Mays because he does not approve of their politics. Keep it up, all the better to show the world want hateful unthinking spiteful petty morons you leftists are. Peter Grimes

Stewart, I'm guessing you know that pipe in French is in common usage. Now I can't get the image of May and her screwed up expression out of my mind. ID873852

'progressive' comedy about as funny as cancer. JoePublic247

If a right wing writer had written an article like this about, say, Diane Abbott, they would rightly be pilloried. Hypocrisy by Lee. GruntyMalunty

Typical snowflake misogynistic bullship. If a powerful woman wants to have a sex robit who is Stewart Lee to criticise them? We can't all have the winning personality of Mr. Lee, if we did have what would he write about? Obscure 80's bands and Jazz most likely and what's worse we'd let him because we'd all have his personality as I stated before. Jonty101

I'm all for articles like this. The trouble is that if Milo or others had written something similar there'd be incensed outrage and 'how dare anyone be so offensive'. Ubermensch1

Read this article and then had to check who Stewart Lee is, apparently he's a comedian.. Derek Strange

Wtf IS this Lee twerp? He's as witty as herpes and without its charm. Allan Friswell

Hate is hate. What you are experiencing here is exactly the same emotion people who crucify the looks and mannerisms of a less than attractive feminist feel when they spill their bile over, say, gamergate – I disagree with your opinions so therefore it is ok to attack you personally. Don't think for one second you are better than them – you're the same. Self-assured, bullying and vile. Can't stand the May's – but I'm not so devoid of self-awareness that I'd turn myself into the exact thing that I'm claiming to be 'against'. maybe have a moment of reflection and ask yourself if you're any different to the people you slag off, or if you're just doing the same thing from a different position. MrSiegel

Anyone who read this article and enjoyed it needs to re-appraise their attitudes and think whether they are a fully functioning human being. Catu11u5

'And eat the occasional tuna taco way down south in Dixie.' Will they get it without 'way down south in Dixie'? I suspect the author agonised over this. The addition makes the sentence a little too long for mine and though the use of over-emphasis

71

has a precedent, Basil Brush as an example, I believe the writer was trying too hard for his laugh. It may have been slightly more obvious, economic, and shocking if he had said 'stimulate the clitoris with their tongue', but I suppose the comedy is in the euphemism. PerryW

When Boris Johnson's inner monster goes on the rampage

21 May 2017

Last Wednesday,* our chief Brexiteer, Boris Johnson, dressed up in a Sikh costume to visit a Bristol gurdwara. There he told the alcohol-abstaining supplicants to take bottles of Johnnie Walker to Indian relatives to speed up post-Brexit booze exports, leading one to comment that had he made that suggestion in India, the foreign secretary would have been killed immediately. Another successful Boris Johnson PR exercise.

That said, I don't think Boris Johnson was seeking to pique the Sikhs. Indeed, Boris Johnson's own wife, Marina Wheeler QC, is half Sikh, though it is not clear which half, so it is difficult to deduce anything from this.† It might be just her leg and some bits of one of her arms. I don't know. This notion is a minefield of potentially explosive cultural sensitivities, both gender- and faith-based.

Personally, I think the Sikhs' reaction is a perfect example of that Political Correctness Gone Mad™ that they have now. In respect of his pernicious Brexit lies, it is not necessarily wrong that Boris Johnson should be punished indiscriminately by the full force of whatever belief systems are most unforgiving, but he shouldn't be slain for saying 'whisky' to a Sikh. No one should.

* 17 May 2017.

† Boris Johnson and Marina Wheeler split in 2018, after she became bored of his infidelities. You can't have your cake and eat it after all, it seems.

Nonetheless, an expensively educated hominid like Boris Johnson, doing the sensitive job he does, should have a sub-liminal awareness of cultural taboos. The Sikhs' offence is Eton College's failure. Perhaps fewer soggy biscuit competitions after lights out, and more comparative religion, headmaster!

And gurdwara-gate definitely calls into question Boris Johnson's fitness for the role of foreign secretary, a position he is unlikely to occupy after 8 June anyway, especially in the event of a Corbyn win.*

But Boris Johnson's biggest cultural cringe happened earlier in the week, in faraway Newport, South Wales. The Conservatives consider Wales invisible to mainstream media, which is why they sent Boris Johnson there in the first place. But my friend, the Welsh mystic Carlton B. Morgan, sent me the following email.†

---

* Well, I was wrong about that.

† Carlton B. Morgan, the Welsh mystic, is a former *NME* cartoon-strip scriptwriter and ex-member of both The Immortal Invisibles and The Supernormals, and my annual hook-up with his magic band in Cardiff, Swansea, Bristol or Newport is one of the things that makes touring tolerable. Carlton in Cardiff, Anthony and Linda Frost lighting up Cornwall, Richard Dawson and formerly Rhodri Davies in Newcastle, Andy Miller and his forensic mind in Canterbury, Dan Rhodes writing great novels and delivering the mail in Buxton, The Nightingales drinking late in Wolverhampton dive bars, Peter 'Trotsky' Edwards still furious in Yorkshire, The Aberdeen Knitting Circle weaving their woollen magic, and a whole bunch of psychedelic seers and record collectors down in Brighton – there are little beacons of companionship along the otherwise lonely way: a stolen hour in a pub with a late licence after the show has been packed up and driven out of the venue, and a pint of something local – Brains or 80 Shilling or Ghost Ship or Tribute – to make you feel human again, not inadvertently famous or exhaustingly presidential to the people in the merch queue, or forcedly cheery to tonight's theatre staff, making sure you leave everyone with a pleasant

'Apparently, Boris Johnson came to Newport market yesterday. I had sadly just vacated the place having ate a vegan breakfast with Fakin' Bacon, so there but for the space–time continuum goes a smart-alecky remark I could have made to the odious sap.'

'Anyway,' the vegan punk visionary continued, 'this have I gleaned: BJ approached the Negative Zone comics stall and said to the comics man, "Oh! When I was a youngster I wanted to be the Incredible Hulk™. The madder Hulk gets, the stronger Hulk gets!" I thought you might like to know. *Nos da*.'

Sure enough, Wales Online was now reporting the story of Boris Johnson™'s disastrous visit to the Gwentish market. Apparently, Boris Johnson™ declined to eat a suspected hash cake; said, 'This is one of those cakes that you can both have and eat,' but then, illogically, did not eat the cake that he had; painted some concrete letters that spelled out his name, like a clever fat baby; placated a weeping Nigerian; was booed about the miners; and having told the Negative Zone man that his favourite character was the Incredible Hulk™, was met with the response, 'You're halfway there, if you don't mind me saying, Boris.' Pow!

In less than a minute, I found four interviews, from 2009 to 2015, in which Boris Johnson™, each time citing the comic-book quote 'The madder Hulk gets, the stronger Hulk gets', said he would like to be the Incredible Hulk™.

Perhaps quoting a comic book is one of those little tricks clever Boris Johnson uses to appear down with the normal people, irrespective of his actual feeling for the work itself, having long

---

memory. Carlton, an original Welsh punk scenester and expert on both Arthur Machen and Captain Beefheart, is one of my national network of ears and eyes on the ground, which keeps me one step ahead of The Man, and he squats at the centre of a vast network of counter-cultural contacts, outsider artists and *flâneurs*, like a psychoactive spider. His flat could do with a tidy-up, though.

since made the concepts of truth and expediency indivisible in his own mind.

Johnny Marr told David Cameron he wasn't allowed to listen to The Smiths; Bruce Springsteen disavowed Ronald Reagan's absorption of 'Born in the USA'; and '80s anarcho-punks Flux of Pink Indians were privately dismayed by the Countryside Alliance's misappropriation of their album *The Fucking Cunts Treat Us Like Pricks* to soundtrack its campaign against rural post-office closures.

And likewise, Boris Johnson™ absolutely cannot have our Incredible Hulk™ – no way, man! You've taken our future. At least leave us our comic books, dude.

I emailed various comics creatives to solicit their opinions on Boris Johnson™'s desire to actually be *the* actual Incredible Hulk™, the most succinct coming from exiled Hulk artist Gary Frank.

'I can't help feeling that Boris Johnson™ slightly missed the point of it all,' wrote Frank, 'in that Hulk's alter ego, Bruce Banner, doesn't actually want to get angry, become stupid and then smash everything to fuck. Do you think Boris Johnson™ misread the Hulk comics as a sort of Tony Robbins self-help guide to fulfilling your potential?'

But dig a little deeper into the Hulk's genesis, and it seems Boris Johnson is right to identify with the creature, but not for the reasons he imagines. The early American comic-book super-heroes were authored almost exclusively by liberal Jewish vision-ary autodidacts, who reluctantly Americanised their Jewish surnames, and leaned heavily on Hebrew mythology.

Hulk was created by Stan Lee (Stanley Salmon-Bagel) and Jack Kirby (Jacob Matzoh-Balls) in 1962, and though influenced by *Frankingstein* and *The Strange Case of Dr Jekyll and Mr Hyde*, the character is best understood through the sixteenth-century tale of the Golem of Prague, as, indeed, is Boris Johnson™ himself.*

Having made a man-monster from magic mud to protect his community, Rabbi Loew soon finds he, like Bruce Banner after he unleashes his inner Hulk, loses control of the creature, which heads off on a psychotic rampage, destroying everything, though stopping short of telling Sikhs to buy whisky.

Finally, the golem is subdued and stuffed back into the attic, leaving the rabbi – like Theresa May or Donald Tusk, depending on your politics – to clear up the mess the deranged creature has made.

At the end of the second issue of *The Incredible Hulk* (July 1962), Bruce Banner wakes from the fever-dream of a night spent as the monster, dimly aware of his responsibility for the destruction around him. In torn rags, he says, 'Tell me – quickly – what happened? I – I can't remember – it's like an ugly fading nightmare!'

Banner's haunted face recalls nothing so much as the face of Boris Johnson, as he emerged the morning after the Brexit vote, in denial of the destruction that his own inner Hulk had wrought.

Boris Johnson was always the Hulk, all along. And he always was the golem. The ancient legend claimed him at birth, and it knew Boris Johnson better than Boris Johnson knew himself, as legends are wont to do. And now his attic awaits.

Wow. I guess most posters here would have sided with the attackers of *Charlie Hebdo* too. Wow – Boris said a word that – by the way lost on Stewart Lee – only 1 haughty dumbass took

* It's the golem again. My metaphor bucket overflows!

offence too. No one else did. But hey its Boris so who cares right? And Mr Lee where the f is your condemnation of those who think it's alright to kill someone based on an off the cuff remark? Haven't got one? Shock. Londonrob68

Sikhs love beer and johnnie Walker is regarded with veneration. Sikhs are not like Muslims in their attitude to alcohol. Why the racist assumption that all brown people eschew alcohol? Boris actually knew a thing or two about Sikh culture more than the hand wringing Guardianistas. Ever been to a Sikh wedding? Not much abstinence there. Nidoc10

A papal encounter with a bat-faced duck-lion

28 May 2017

Beelzebub, the gluttonous emperor of hell, master of calumny, foremost in wickedness and crime, is a fallen angel who presides over the Order of the Fly. Some say he is as high as a tower. Others say he has the figure of a snake, but with the generative organs of a young woman and the face of a bluebottle.

Consequently, the god of Ekron's first ever official visit to the Vatican last week was fraught with difficulties regarding imperial protocol, dietary requirements and appropriate toilet usage. To which facilities were the Swiss Guard to direct a pert-breasted snake-fly?*

Pope Francis is a normally cheery man, but on seeing photos of his haunted visage on Wednesday, it seemed to me that a great sadness, a coal-black fear even, had seized his holy heart. At first I was confused. Had the Pope, like me, read Morrissey's comments on immigration and terrorism and realised that after years of trying to make fanboy allowances for the singer's pronouncements, he was finally going to have to throw away all his Smiths records?†

Perhaps the pontiff had learned that Russell Howard was going to be replaced as host of Comedy Central's *Stand-Up Central* by

---

* The Trumps visited the Vatican, OK? That's what this is about.

† Morrissey had been quoted earlier that week linking immigration policy, and a politically correct fear of speaking the truth, to the Manchester Arena bombing. Allowances were made by loyal fans. But there was worse to come.

the less experienced Chris Ramsey, a source of anxiety not only to the Pope, but to the brightly lit show's hundreds of non-papal fans? Or was the leader of the world's Catholics saddened by the death of Roger Moore, star of his favourite film, the 1980 marine insurance-themed thriller, *North Sea Hijack*?*

(Though Moore was cast against type as the boorish misogynist marine insurance expert Rufus Excalibur ffolkes, Pope Francis is known to have admired the way Moore beatified the gruff, no-nonsense and decidedly politically incorrect character by making him a lover of cats. At the end of the movie, foulmouthed ffolkes accepts only a litter of kittens as payment for thwarting Anthony 'Psycho' Perkins's perverted oil-rig hijack, snubbing grateful dignitaries to nurture the newborns with a saucer of milk.)

Sad-faced Pope Francis had my sympathy, whatever ailed him. I am not a religious or a superstitious person, despite having once been given a wedgie in a Paris mausoleum by the ghost of Napoleon,† but like many atheists and agnostics, I find in Francis

* In 1980, I queued up outside Solihull cinema with Richard Hougham to try and get in to see *North Sea Hijack*. We were twelve and it was an AA certificate, so you had to be fourteen to get in. We thought we might pass for older, and Richard was excited because, as it was an AA, there should be 'some good swearing' in it. We got in. And sure enough, there was good swearing aplenty, my friends, and we loved it.

† I suspect this was some kind of mad hallucination brought on by baby-driven sleep deprivation, but at Les Invalides, in April 2009, I felt myself lifted off the ground by the back belt hook of my jeans and pushed up over the balcony, just for a second or so. There was no one else in the building, and I emerged ashen-faced into the *plein soleil*. My wife insists Napoleon was punishing me for calling his self-aggrandising mausoleum 'arrogant and ridiculous'. She is jealous because, although I am an atheist and don't believe in the afterlife, I have had three ghostly experiences. A week after my mother died, and when I had to bite the bullet and fulfil

much to admire, at least in comparison to all the evil popes that preceded him.

Pope John XII raped pilgrims and drank toasts to a Satan; Pope Alexander VI had an incestuous relationship with his daughter and made naked boys leap from cakes; Pope Benedict XVI wore

---

tour dates that couldn't be rescheduled, she appeared to me in the foyer of Wolverhampton Civic Hall, looking totally alive in her favourite puffa coat and holding her handbag in front of her, smiling encouragingly, indicating she was OK and it was OK for me to go back to work. For a moment, I forgot she was dead, gave her a wave and, mouthing to her that I'd be with her in a minute, bowed my head back to sign the punters' books in the merch queue. But then I realised she shouldn't be there and snapped my gaze back to where she had been standing, but she was gone. I felt happy, not afraid or saddened in any way. But I know this was a hallucination, as my mum didn't really like Wolverhampton and would not have come to see me there under any circumstances, even to communicate an important message from beyond the grave. My brain needed to jolt me into rejoining the flow, I think, and so it spun this little farewell scenario for me without my knowledge. When performing the routine about seeing dead comedians all around me, night after night for a year, which ended up in the fourth series of *Comedy Vehicle*, it was the feelings I experienced during this encounter with my mother's ghost that I dredged up every night to try and perform it convincingly. It was emotionally exhausting, but cathartic on some level too.

As well as being sexually assaulted by Napoleon, I have also, momentarily, seen hundreds of medieval monks bent in prayer in Fountains Abbey, the ruined walls around them suddenly reassembling themselves and then disappearing again. It was a beautiful experience, and I'd love to see those crazy monks again, but I don't think it was really happening. Is this sort of stuff interesting or do you feel embarrassed for me? My wife thinks I may have mental health issues and that I should talk to someone. I can keep it professional, if you like, in these footnotes – just politics and comedy theory, yes? It's just I've not been terribly well this year, and if I don't get some of these stories down, well, who will remember them? Does it even matter? We are all just dust in the wind.

extravagant Prada shoes, sported a decadent red hat and was a notoriously unenthusiastic member of the Hitler Youth, adding laziness as well as dressing as a young Nazi to his list of crimes.

But Pope Francis has never made naked things leap from cakes, worn prideful footwear or drunk toasts to Satans, or indeed to any demons for that matter. Until now. And perhaps this explained the stunned horror that had spread across the usually illuminated fresco of his face on Wednesday.

Writing in his 1536 treatise *Zodiacus Vitae*, Marcellus Palingenius Stellatus described the monarch of hell as a menacing being of prodigious size, with a swollen chest, a bloated face, flashing eyes, large nostrils and raised eyebrows, capable of changing his appearance into ever more terrifying aggregations of horror at will. And Pope Francis, it appeared, had broken with papal tradition to host Beelzebub and his entourage, for the first time ever, in Rome.

First, the Lie-father and his caravan of infernal harlots were given a tour of the Sistine Chapel, the Lord of Flies now choosing to manifest himself dressed like a bee, with two dreadful ears and his hair painted in all colours, with a dragon's tail.

His retinue coiled around him in obedience, Beelzeboul stood before Michelangelo's *The Last Judgement*, which depicts souls weighed in the cosmic balance. But if Pope Francis had been intending to intimidate the White God into contrition by presenting him with the painting, he failed. Instead, Ba'al, having asked if this Michelangelo guy was available for hotel-lobby work, immediately took the form of a pile of dung, beset by flies, and slithered away.

The tour over, the historic summit between Pope and Filth Lord began. As is customary, the two exchanged gifts. Francis gave Ba'al Zebûb a large medallion that depicted an olive, a symbol of peace. He also offered the Prince of Demons, who by now had become a goat-tailed calf with the face of a hornet, some of his latest writings (encyclicals), including his work on the need to protect the environment.

Belzebuth offered the Pope a large box filled with novelty condiment dispensers. Pope Francis's advisers had warned him that the Father of Lies might test him with an offering of unimaginable horror, which he was to accept unflinchingly, but Francis was taken by surprise. 'This is a gift for you. The ketchup comes out of an asshole and the mustard is a shaved pussy,' the demon was overheard saying. 'I think you will enjoy them. I hope you do.'*

As the demon, now in the form of a bat with duck's feet and a lion's tail, moved towards the exit, he expressed gratitude to the man he once called disgraceful for questioning his beliefs. The dispute was related to Beel d'Bobo's proposal to destroy all that is good and drag Christ down to Hades to subject him to eternal torment – a policy the pontiff had said was not Christian. The library door opened and the bat-faced duck-lion could be heard braying, 'What's done is done, Frankie. Now how about that mustard pussy?'

By the end of the half-hour private meeting, Pope Francis seemed forcedly jovial. He asked a wizened homunculus, swinging from the pendulous, bald testicles of the beast – who now appeared as a howling wolf with a lion's head – what it gave its master to eat. It was unclear whether the being understood the remark, and it seemed to say, 'Pizza?' before smiling and answering, 'Yes.'†

Pope Francis knows evil. He knows the contents of the demonic tracts chained in the Vatican's secret library; he has

* Trump actually gave the Pope a set of books by Martin Luther King.
† Melania Trump and the Pope had some kind of small-talk exchange. No one is sure exactly what was said, but at one point she was heard to have replied, 'Pizza.'

read the suppressed internal reports his predecessors abandoned unresolved; and he has spent a lifetime fabricating plausible theological excuses for the cruelties of man and nature. But he has never had to confront, until now, corruption in a manifestation so blank and uncomprehending and unapologetic.

In short, Francis's visitor this week forced him to acknowledge evil in a different form, evil at its most banal. And his own impotence before it was written on his defeated papal face.

I stopped believing that the *Guardian* was a serious publication some years ago. This is why. Grandmechanteloup

Obviously Stewart Lee thought this was very funny and clever. Buttercups

Evil? This is not the definition of evil. The left has become the great intolerant. Any and all who do not agree get the evil, fascist, monster, buffoon, demon tag. Mr Trump is not Beelzebub. He is a man out of his depth who cannot accept criticism and seems to be existing in the Land of Bewilderment but he is not the great evil. Stewart Lee was once a comedian of great charm who offered his acerbic observations with effortless style. He's floundering here (not unlike the north sea drama that lasted about 3 seconds and then disappeared without a trace). Sean1976

I was busy concentrating on a young lady's particularly complicated bra fastening when *North Sea Hijack* was on the telly in the early 80s. Never did see the end of the film. Never did get the bra fastening undone either. Repeatandfade

This tries so hard it is pitiful. Joss Wynne Evans

Keep on calling Trump lots of stupid ugly names. It's only inflames more people to vote for him. This name calling just shows how childish the media are and what utter rubbish they will write to get viewers. It's no wonder *Guardian* Journalists cry like sissies when they get body slammed.* Bad Drivers

* At his campaign headquarters in Montana, in May 2017, Republican candidate Greg Gianforte grabbed *Guardian* reporter Ben Jacobs by the neck, body-slammed him to the ground and hit him.

It will take more than ceramics and cheese to unite our divided country

4 June 2017[*]

Wake up and smell the covfefe and tell the spinning corpse of Robin Day the news.[†] The old politics is over. This election is no longer a choice between left and right, between traditional working-class or middle-class allegiances, between self-interest and concern for others. It is a new kind of choice. It is a choice between bastards and twats.

It was half-term, and like Theresa May, I began the week appearing before prearranged crowds of people who loved me, the throngs applauding my arrival and clapping at everything I said. Then, after leaving the Wells Comedy Festival, I crossed the nation honouring familial obligations and projecting my own electoral anxieties onto obliging British landscapes. Who knew that the gaping gash of Clutter's Cave in the Malvern Hills, when viewed from the footpath, looks exactly like the prime minister's open mouth?

On Monday, I made my annual visit to the Cooper's Hill Cheese-Rolling competition in Gloucestershire. The uninsurable

---

[*] This column was uncommonly personal and revealing in a way I didn't intend it to be. There is no overarching comedy concept, no satirical through line. The insults to Leavers are largely witless. It's just me travelling listlessly around south-west England feeling depressed about politics and resentful of people who I feel have sabotaged the country, and as such it is probably the most accurate representation in this book of my actual state of mind over these last three years.

[†] On 31 May, shortly after midnight, Donald Trump sent a tweet saying only, 'Despite the constant negative press covfefe.'

million-year-old-produce-pursuing event sees heroic drunks leap suicidally down a 2:1 slope to chase a 9 lb wheel of Double Gloucester, which they have no chance of ever catching. Foreign observers need look no further to understand the peculiarly British mentality that drove us as a nation to embrace the vertical cliff of Brexit, our nostalgic visions as elusive as a speeding cheesy wheel.

The cheese-rolling over, I arrived in Gloucester (Leave) and sat down to watch the evening's bastard/twat face-off on Channel 4. But even the biggest bastard, even the most feckless twat, I decided, deserved better than to be interviewed by Jeremy Paxman, an embarrassing and punch-drunk old prize-fighter now, decades past his best, fit only for satirical election-night specials, keen to land one killer blow to prove he once had it, before soiling his concealed Conservative Party Y-fronts in public and stepping down to endorse aftershave or a range of fat-reducing grills. He could have been a contender.

I went into Gloucester to buy a pork roll from a van and carry out a mobility-scooter census, but when I came back, Paxman was still snarling and growling, like a senile attack dog who had mistaken his own flaccid penis for a dangerous snake.* 'Mr Corbyn, if you were asked to shoot a fluffy kitten through the head with a bolt gun, could you do it? Could you do it? Could you? Answer the question!' 'I could do it, Jeremy, but I would have to be fully aware, from the intelligence agencies, of the facts that supported the cat's supposed guilt first,' answered an unflappable Corbyn. 'What if the fluffy kitten had a ribbon tied in its hair and a tinkling bell, Mr Corbyn? Could you shoot it then? What if its name was Twinkle? Answer me!!'†

---

* Gloucester had both pork-roll vans and mobility scooters in abundance.
† During the election campaign, Corbyn's accusers became fixated on

The debate seemed less like a news programme and more like an ancient, traditional, ritual humiliation, still played out to this day, of would-be mayors in the square of a Pyrenean commune. During her wobbly TV appearance, trembling Theresa's jawbone began all but flapping loose of her skull on its right-hand hinge. If May were a gunfighter in an Italian western, this familiar phenomenon would be the 'tell' that revealed her cracking under pressure, and Sergio Leone would zoom in on ever tighter close-ups of her gradually dislocating mandible.

The southern regions of May's visage now seem to be held in place only by skin and saliva and fear. I wonder if she didn't attend Wednesday's debate because part of her face had actually worked loose. On Monday, it seemed almost inhumane of the Conservatives to expect her to continue to front out a shoddy manifesto she clearly found quite literally jaw-dropping in its inadequacy.

On Tuesday evening, in Worcester (Leave), in the company of elderly relatives, I watched the artist Grayson Perry on Channel 4 fashioning two healing pots, depicting Leavers and Remainers respectively. My family are not Perry's natural fanbase, but they were nonetheless delighted by him, though they thought his twin sister in the dress was strange.

It seemed that Perry had used a glazed image of my face as the sort of thing trendy Remainers like.* Luckily, no one in my

---

whether or not he would be prepared to press the big red nuclear-war button, a possibility Theresa May had embraced with disturbing enthusiasm.

* We saw this pot *in situ* at the Serpentine Gallery. I moved through the crowd, just like a normal person who wasn't on some top Art, and I didn't point it out to the kids – I didn't want any fuss from bystanders. 'Is that you?' my six-year-old said, finding my face for herself, unbidden. 'Yes,' I said. She didn't know enough about the world to know that it was

family noticed, as they would have been utterly baffled by how a man they regard as having wasted his educational opportunities to become a kind of travelling Gypsy-clown could have possibly symbolised anything other than failure and tragedy.

Perry's pots aimed to show that we have more in common than that which divides us. I would have put Peter Stringfellow in a thong on the Remain pot and Nick Griffin's funny eye on the Leave one, but I am not an artist. At the end of the show, Perry united the two different groups of white people depicted on his ceramics, and they all cried and hugged like a bunch of dicks. If I had been there, I would have kept the angry flame of despair burning and called all the Leavers arseholes to their stupid Leave faces. Not only have they ruined the future, but they also get a lovely pot commemorating their stupidity, made by a top artist. Where is the justice in that?

On Wednesday, I drove back to London (Remain) across the Cotswolds at dusk, listening to the leaders' debate on the radio. The children couldn't believe it – loads of supposedly responsible adults just shouting over each other and screaming. It was just like being at home.* Corbyn stayed calm, and I found myself pitying Amber Rudd, press-ganged to defend the indefensible, to audible audience laughter.

We stopped at the Bronze Age Rollright Stones to eat pizza, bananas and home-made cake. Don't you wish I was your dad? The sun was sinking over the horizon as we made our usual votive offerings of lavender and brown pennies.† Some dreadlocked

---

weird for your dad to be on an exhibited Art pot, and moved off, suitably unimpressed by the subject of Perry's daub.

* Ka-boom!

† I always do this at ancient sacred sites, but I don't have any kind of belief system. Like Dylan said, you gotta serve somebody!

young people, sitting in a ring, were smoking and drinking and setting the world to rights. I remembered being their age, here in this exact same place, in a summer twilight thirty years ago,* and doing the same, blissfully unaware of just how bad things were going to get.

Given the vast areas of humour that are off-limits for someone PC, Lee does quite well. LePharaon

Christ – this shit doesn't work as satire, doesn't work as humour, doesn't work as political commentary. Just anaemic bile. Pete CW

* We'd get the bus from Oxford to Chipping Norton and walk the last three miles down lanes lined with hedgerows, alive with insects and birds, buzzing and fecund in a way that our children will never experience, as the world dies around them. Back then, an old lady owned the site, and she sat in a wooden cabin collecting money for a cat charity. I still plot my course around the country via prehistoric sites, if I can. It gives otherwise meaningless processes an imaginary sense of purpose. I read a book called *Mysterious Britain*, by Janet and Colin Bord, when I was eleven or so, and it set me on the path. The weekend before my final exams at university, my friend Doug and I slept in sleeping bags at Wayland's Smithy, a burial chamber on the Ridgeway, before such places were so rigorously policed, to clear our mental pipes. On the actual day of my fiftieth, I was in the Maes Howe tomb, shining water on all sides, in a suddenly sun-drenched and cobalt-blue Orkney, weeping over runes, and it was the best birthday I ever had. But I walked with Robert Lloyd, lead singer of '80s Birmingham post-punk band The Nightingales, to a snow-dusted Mitchell's Fold stone circle, on the border of Wales and Shropshire, last month, and he clearly found the whole process pointless.

Nothing like those cutting edge references; Peter Stringfellow, Nick Griffin. What about Chas and Dave and *Bullseye*? Glad you've got this covered Stewart. Arriestotle

Foul and nauseating prejudice for haters. I'll be surprised if you are not ashamed of this article within a decade. Mustapha Mondeo

What a pile of poo. Ive read it twice now and it got worse. Lanhar

Brexit has brought a revelation of the pompous, sneering attitudes of Remainers. It makes their pain a guilty pleasure for the rest of us. Freddy Starmer

It pretends to offer insight and analysis while being just another string of cowardly attacks on easy targets who aren't allowed to fight back with the same weapons. Stringvestor

Got anything else to talk about other than brexit? Youcantalk

Even Brexit has it's up side. Given you now mention it most of your columns, there's been at least 20 minutes in it for you. Paul Lambert

From the Cotswolds to London. Could there be a more middle class journey in the world . . . The Talentless Mr Exile

Chronicle of May's fiasco
foretold in a urine stain

11 June 2017

It's 8.29 a.m. on Friday now, and I have to file this column in two hours, thirty-one minutes. I awoke at 6 a.m. to watch the bloody election results coagulate, in a hotel room in Tunbridge Wells, a town so solidly middling it has been twinned with a branch of Carluccio's.*

But last Sunday, I had seen Chris Martin from Coldplay cavort before a global TV audience of more than ninety nations with a visible urine stain to the right of his fly. Evidently, a poorly self-milked penis, presumably his own, had made damp contact with the inner side of his trouser.†

In the run-up to the election, commentators used polls to

---

* Theresa May had called a snap election, thinking that Labour was now so unpopular it would consolidate her majority and enable her to push through a version of Brexit unopposed. Increasingly now, I found myself writing columns that were about the very act of trying to write a column against the backdrop of Brexit. At this point, I was about halfway through the 250 or so dates of my tour, and I was surprised that the show, assembled a year previously, had not fallen completely apart in the face of events. Surely this snap election was going to kill it off, and propel the story forward in a way that rendered it irrelevant? And yet, the following morning, Theresa May's slim victory only deepened the Brexit inertia and made even more of the material depressingly relevant. Nearly two years later, as I write this, the same personalities and the same situations remain ridiculous and awful in all the same ways.

† Martin was appearing on TV in live coverage of a benefit for the victims of the Manchester Arena bombing.

predict the future. But I felt I had divined something of the un-expected flavour of our forthcoming fate from my own little set of signs and wonders. On Friday of last week, I found a mummified newt beneath a Frisbee in the nook where I store rakes, betokening woe.* The following day, I saw Tom Stoppard staring hungrily at soup in Norfolk, prefiguring a light lunch.† And on Sunday, I saw Chris Martin from Coldplay with a urine stain on his trousers.‡

Mark E. Smith of The Fall appeared at Glastonbury in 2015 in apparently urine-soaked slacks,§ but I believe this was a deliber-ate piece of stagecraft, designed to provide fans with a comical anecdote, and detractors with confirmation of their prejudices. Such is Smith's commitment to his shaman-clown persona.

Chris Martin from Coldplay's urine stain, however, was all too real, and indeed it was hard to imagine how a liquid so base

* This was true.

† This was also true. It was in the café of a stately home in Norfolk called Houghton Hall, which was exhibiting the sculptures of Richard Long. I took the kids there to see the abstract land art. Don't you wish I was your dad? I first saw a Long sculpture in a gallery in, I think, Lucerne, on a school trip to Switzerland in 1983, and have loved his work ever since. I was in the school Mountain Walking Club, with some of Napalm Death, and I ended up running it. Long made it look like walking was a work of art, and there was a pig-headedness about what he was doing that appealed to me, as if the works would be completed anyway, with or without anyone's approval. He's the one artist I will travel to see, and I suppose there is a certain primitivist megalithic vibe to his oeuvre that chimes with lots of my other obsessions. Much of Long's art is about the journeys that complete the finished work itself. The process is indivisible from the end product, and he often makes technique and theory explicit within his pieces. Come to think of it, I've really ripped him off, but just done it really badly, in a worthless medium.

‡ This was also true.

§ So was this.

as urine could mark the garments of a man who seems almost angelic, as if woven from lamb's wool and light.

The stain was an omen, certainly, but what did it mean? Was the urine stain of the Tories going to remain on the Chris Martin from Coldplay's trouser of British politics for some time yet? Or did Chris Martin from Coldplay's spreading urine stain portend a spread of hope and sunshine? Either way, it was all yellow.*

Yesterday morning, Thursday, I took a massive diversion from a Wednesday-night stand-up show in Colchester (Leave) via my North London Metropolitan Liberal Elite home (Remain) to vote in my safe Labour seat, a typically British odyssey involving multiple cancelled trains and a bomb scare in Trafalgar Square, where I understand there are now plans to fill the fourth plinth with an uplifting effigy of Chris Martin from Coldplay in urine-stained trousers.

I arrived at my Tunbridge Wells (Remain) hotel at 5 p.m. The young woman on reception said she wasn't voting at all, as 'they are all as bad as each other'. But they aren't. Boris Johnson, for example, himself a lying columnist for the lying *Daily Telegraph*, is currently the worst one of 'them' all by some distance.

At 6 p.m. on Thursday night, a world away now, I ate a soggy salad and found myself thinking about *The Medusa Touch* (1978), arguably Richard Burton's finest movie, in which he plays a tortured writer of fiction whose ability to imagine terrible disasters convinces him he may actually be willing them into being. Lee Remick plays his psychiatrist. And the newsreader Gordon Honeycombe is, cruelly, cast as an actual piece of honeycomb named Gordon.

For the last nine months, like Burton's paranoid novelist, I have been selling the same stand-up routine nightly to

* And they say I can't write jokes.

audiences, advancing the idea that the secret Tory steering committee always intended Boris Johnson to be leader of the party, and that Theresa May had been put in place only as a kind of palate cleanser, a nasty-tasting mouthwash that you swill around your gums before being forced to eat actual human shit.*

While he himself is doubtless clean as a whistle, Johnson's renewed public appearances these last few weeks have displayed the violently belligerent and incoherent sweatiness that people with a cocaine problem take as a sign that it's time to stop partying and seek help.

And at 7 p.m. on Thursday, remembering Boris rampant and evidently ambitious once more, a frothing jackal circling the expiring wildebeest that is Theresa May, I found myself fearing my own Medusa Touch. Do my jokes make these awful things happen? Who am I? Should I take this minibar corkscrew and trepan my own brain to stop my worst fears becoming reality?

Alone in my Tunbridge Wells hotel room at midnight, snorting a snowdrift of uncut Dimbleby in my post-show adrenaline high, a storm raging over the multi-storey car park, I wondered what kind of fudge of an *Observer* column I could concoct to file on Friday morning, when everything was uncertain and it now looked like a hung parliament was in the offing. Luckily, I had seen a urine stain on Chris Martin from Coldplay's trousers the previous Sunday and imagined writing about that might fill a few hundred words near the start.

Long after midnight, I ate my Marks & Spencer Harissa Spiced Roasted Almonds and weighed up a half-bottle of champagne in the minibar, which I eventually chose to ignore. I was, literally, if not a Champagne Socialist, then at least a Harissa Spiced

* This sentence became stand-up material. I said it 250 or more times in the end. It appears a second time later in this book. Look out for it!

Almond Anarchist, alone and on the loose in a hotel room in Royal Tunbridge Wells as the arrogant presumptions of the Conservatives turned to tatters. And it felt good.

I have a show tonight in Basingstoke (Leave) and I'm mentally ticking off lines that are invalidated or changed by the shock result, but I expect the audience will be in a state of hysteria. And look at this joyful chaos! Laura Kuenssberg looks like her cat just died. It's 11 a.m. on Friday and there's apples all over the road. Emily Maitlis is scrabbling around to pick them up. And in a red dress, of all things.

What was this supposed because I certainly hope it wasn't supposed to good. Gtardkgb

Dear me, what a typical show of nasty arrogance. P4451d

When Coldplay performed at the One Love concert for victims of the Manchester bombing, you mean? Chris Martin is a very easy target at the best of times, but like you say, you had a deadline to hit. ID3122d

Utterly puerile. Hexagon Nipples

One thing for sure is no one will have pissed themselves laughing reading this. Youcantalk

Repulsive piece and utterly unfunny as ever. Tony35

What on earth is this tripe published for, surely it can' t be normal, milking penis's, what an awful picture that paints! Old Franky

'Oh, Jeremy Clarkson.' Is that any better as a Glastonbury chant?

2 July 2017

Jeremy Corbyn appeared at the Glastonbury CND festival, as part of an ongoing comeback more surprising than Dylan's 1997 *Time Out of Mind* turnaround. Like Dylan, a contrary Corbyn refused to give his enthusiastic new fans what they wanted. A last-minute set amendment pledging to block Brexit would have displaced even The Wombles* from all-time Glastonbury CND festival top fives. But Corbyn didn't deliver. Once he had Islington in the palm of his hand, the New River ran through every day. He must have been mad. He never knew what he had, until he threw it all away.

Nonetheless, Nigel Farage, a stateless Twitter golem,† its task complete but still rampaging around the Internet with a torn-up

---

* The Wombles were the first band I ever saw live, with my mum, at Birmingham Bingley Hall, circa 1974, and one which I now realise probably included, inside the furry suits, Chris Spedding (Colosseum, Geoff Wayne's *War of the Worlds*, Sex Pistols), Stoke Newington's Clem Cattini (drums on all 1960s and '70s British records), Ray Cooper and maybe even Robin Le Mesurier, son of John Le Mesurier and Hattie Jacques, although he was kicked out of The Wombles at some point for marijuana possession. (This book's editor, Andy Miller, adds: 'The Wombles was my first concert too, at the Fairfield Halls in Croydon. The support act was pianist Bobby Crush. Someone on Twitter told me that it probably wasn't Spedding etc. in the suits because there was a legally questionable rival bunch of Wombles on the road at the same time. Maybe it was The Pretty Things.')

† That golem image again!

Daily Express between its teeth, was instantly furious about the BBC coverage of Corbyn's set. And rightly so. It is wrong of the BBC to use the licence fee to give airtime to politicians, and Farage has proven this more convincingly than anyone.

Suddenly, cross Conservative commentators nationwide all knew what the Glastonbury CND festival was supposed to be, and who should be allowed to be on there, despite never having expressed any interest in attending it ever, because it obviously isn't for *Daily Telegraph* readers, bastards and people who hate humanity.

It would probably have been better, apparently, if the Saturday mid-afternoon slot had seen Dan 'Dan' Hannananananan, dressed as a pound note, introducing Mike Read singing a racist calypso in a Jamaican accent,* over footage of migrants being beaten back into the sea with rolled-up copies of the UKIP conference brochure. I am sure the audience reaction would have been memorable.

Personally, I think the Henley Regatta, instead of having loads of boats in it and being by a river, would be better if it featured Napalm Death, Kunt & the Gang, Yoko Ono and some Grayson Perry plates that mocked sailing, and took place in a landlocked desert full of ferocious wolves. I suppose it's not aimed at me.

Know this! There is a genuine photo online of Jeremy Clarkson and David Cameron shooting the breeze at the cheese bloke from Blur's cheese and music festival in Oxfordshire in 2011. This image, more than any other, which should never have happened, told us that the '60s were finally over. Did Free Festival founder

---

* Former BBC Radio 1 DJ Mike Read recorded a funny song in a Jamaican accent to raise money for UKIP. It was political correctness not gone mad.

Wally Hope die so Jeremy Clarkson could eat a Groucho Club cheesemaker's pop cheese?*

Tories like Cameron and Clarkson should not be at rock festivals. If two such turds had turned up at Glastonbury in the '80s, they would both have been fatally stuffed face-first into a deep trench latrine by hordes of psilocybe-crazed convoy-dwellers, the sound of Black Uhuru's *Youth of Eglington*† growing ever more faint as their fat pink ears filled with festival-goer faeces.

Ironically, Clarkson would have then escaped the far more ignominious fate of spending his twilight years manufacturing bespoke controversy to an ever-diminishing audience of impotent Level 42 fans who think ice cream is gay, like a failed dictator awaiting arrest, yet still making futile proclamations, in his supermarket denim-lined Amazon firestick bunker.

You! You awful people! You cannot have our festivals! You have taken everything else! Our health service! Our libraries! Our very air! Even our future! Leave us our filthy fields! We will always have Glastonbury! No pop music for you!

But what do I know? I attended the Glastonbury CND festival a dozen times or so, usually as a performer, from the mid-'80s to the mid-'00s. Every year, the late Malcolm Hardee would host

* Wally Hope, aka Philip Russell, was the founder of the Stonehenge Free Festival and died under mysterious circumstances in 1975. Penny Rimbaud says he inspired him to form the anarcho-punk band Crass.

† In my early teens, if ever I had a high temperature at night, I would suffer hallucinations in which I was crushed by falling rocks, dead animals or human bodies, and the visions would always be accompanied in my mind by the song 'World Is Africa', from Black Uhuru's 1980 album *Sinsemilla*, or the instrumental bit from the end of 'Youth of Eglington'. My mum would come in and have to pretend to move all the dead bodies and rocks off me until I was all right.

the comedy tent and open by observing, 'I remember when this was all fields.' It never got old.

In 1992, still awake, I saw the sun rise over a misty morning meadow, profoundly empty except for Jimmy Pursey from Sham 69, sitting high on an upturned wheelie bin, heroically topless, dragging on a cigarette and staring blurry-eyed into the distance, as if searching for an answer that had always eluded him. Either that or he'd forgotten where his tent was.*

But eventually, rather than being a cut-and-paste Shangri-La of freak rock and folkies and topless hippy chicks, the Glastonbury CND festival came to feel to me like it was full of music I didn't like any more, squares taking ironic pictures of themselves in front of Lionel Richie, and privileged young people wandering around eating expensive street food, while looking at their phones and saying how funny they thought Hayseed Dixie were.

The crusties were cleared out and the hipsters had moved in to gentrify their abandoned haunts. To be fair to the Glastonbury CND festival, I now feel the same about much of London, which I once loved beyond all reason, the city redeemed in comparison to the festival only by the quality of its toilet facilities.

The Glastonbury CND festival was changing. And I was changing too. At least we parted as friends.

Maybe I'm romanticising things. The festival movement was always, if not middle class, then at least more bohemian than

---

* I did actually see Jimmy Pursey doing this. He looked amazing. I can't help thinking that on some level, he was consciously creating an iconic punk-rock image for the benefit of any stray early-morning passer-by, offering me a memory and an anecdote to keep for life. And here it is. The first time I interviewed Julian Cope, he stood over me on a chair, leaning down towards me with one booted foot up on a work surface, dressed in First World War flying ace uniform. And he was in his *own kitchen*! He was giving me an anecdote. It's all showbiz.

Bolshevik. After my Glastonbury CND festival sets, I was paid in food vouchers by the festival's co-founder, an ex-debutante philanthropist called Arabella Churchill, granddaughter of our national icon, who still oversaw the circus and cabaret tents on what were now the site's fringes, her death in 2007 severing a seam that ran back to the sensibility that first shaped the event in 1970.*

Each year, as I signed my chit, I amused myself by trying to sneak Churchillian rhetoric into our perfunctory conversation. 'How was your show?' 'We've all been finding it hard, Arabella, with the flooding this year, but you know what it's like. We will never surrender.' Arabella Churchill just smiled wryly, stubbing out her massive cigar as she petted her poodle.

In the London *Evening Standard*, a weak anti-Corbyn humour piece by a man called Nick Curtis mocked the Glastonbury CND festival's 'perfect spread for ordinary, young, working-class music fans who can afford £238 for a ticket plus the cost of transport, organic falafel, and reiki sessions'. In the same awful paper, there are restaurant reviews for dinners for two that cost more than that, and they don't come with thousands of different acts over hundreds of different stages. They come with some bread. And the tip doesn't go to Greenpeace.

This year, Jeremy Corbyn's logical appearance at the Glastonbury CND festival seems to have reminded people that '60s and '70s festivals emerged from an actual un-co-opted counter-culture. Maybe they, and their attendees, will now re-embrace the radical spirit that spawned them, alongside the apparently unavoidable twenty-first-century follies of glamping, Goan seafoods and selfies with Jack Whitehall.

* It was Arabella who ran the cabaret and circus fields. I am really glad I met Winston Churchill's actual granddaughter.

Oh, the times they are a-changing. Jang jangy jangy jang jangy jangy jang jangy jangy jang!

Lee occasionally slips in something quite funny, but mostly he slips in dog shit. Freddy Starmer

More left wing chip on shoulder rubbish. Johnnyboy

When in Europe, dress like a
walking apology for Brexit

9 July 2017

In the 1980s, the pornographic bookshop (bad) where we bought amyl nitrate was opposite the women's bookshop (good), where we hung around skim-reading *Spare Rib* and Shulamith Firestone's *The Dialectic of Sex: The Case for Feminist Revolution* (1970) to try to get dates with the clever feminists, who saw through us immediately.

The women's bookshop (good) had a camera set up in its window to covertly photograph male fans of pornography (bad) coming and going from the pornographic bookshop. If this seems a depressing state of affairs, look on the bright side. In 1986, a small provincial town could still support two independent bookshops!

Our purchases complete, we would stand opposite the feminists' camera position, waving our bottles of amyl nitrate around, so the feminists would know we only wanted to get high in a shared flat in the middle of the afternoon, and not degrade women by looking at pictures of them nude. How did they resist us?*

Ten years ago, I inherited a vintage Singer sewing machine from my mother. During my childhood, she became expert at hand-making perfect costumes of whatever character was my current favourite. When I was five, in 1973, her Hartley Hare from *Pipkins* costume was perfect, functioning alcoholic eyes and all; in 1977, my mother's Captain Britain tabard was unique,

---

* I didn't actually do any of this. A man I knew well did. I stole his story. He now runs a floating bookshop and has won the game of life.

the obscure Marvel superhero being resistant to official merchandising; and I doubt there were many boys lucky enough to attend their tenth birthday party in a one-piece zip-up costume of the Welsh experimental film-maker and poet Iain Sinclair.*

This summer, I had planned to take the children, Six and Nine, to the United States on a once-in-a-lifetime pilgrimage to pay homage to the unmarked paupers' graves of my forty-seven favourite significant pre-First World War blues harmonica players. It was to be a journey I am sure they would have looked back on with some fondness, or at least tolerance, in later life at least.

But I imagined a difficult American situation, where a delightful pea-soup restaurant waitress, who has been nothing other than charming this last hour, asks us in parting what we think of good ole Donald Trump, kickin' Muslamic ass.† My daughter, Six, would

---

* This paragraph is mainly nonsense. I did wear a Captain Britain tabard and mask to our Silver Jubilee street party, but it had come free with an issue of Marvel UK's *Captain Britain* comic. My mother did make me a lot of soldier, sailor, Native American and traffic cop costumes as a child, however, which enabled me to do a one-person Village People show for the family at Christmas, though it was admittedly slowed down by the multiple costume changes. When my mum let me go to the Birmingham Comics Convention in 1979, when I was eleven, a tiny affair by today's geek-fest standards, she sat in the café of the Metropole Hotel, while I went to watch Jim Steranko give a talk. When I came back to the café, Chris Claremont, who created Captain Britain and rebooted the X-Men, was sitting with my actual mum having a coffee. I expect she was the only person in the building who wasn't a smelly fanboy, and he probably liked hanging out with someone who didn't care who he was. He introduced himself to me. 'I'm Chris Claremont. I write *The X-Men*. Do you read *The X-Men*?' It was the first time I was star-struck. I could barely speak. Of course I read the fucking *X-Men*.

† I imagine this incident taking place at Pea Soup Andersen's Inn, Buellton, California, where I had pea soup while on a road trip with the

doubtless say, 'Donald Trump is a smelly poo-poo head.' It is her habit to regurgitate wholesale the adult discourse she overhears around our dinner table, without necessarily understanding it.

In the ensuing conversational difficulties, we would then be gunned down by aggrieved onlookers and hung naked from poplar trees, as a warning to any other visiting snowflakes considering casting doubt on the composition and cleanliness of the forty-fifth US president's head.

So instead of being murdered in a roadside diner, we are going on a self-guided tour of major European cities, before the administrative gates that make our access to them so easy are finally lowered in 2019, in an elaborate star-studded ceremony featuring Elizabeth Hurley, Ian Botham, Public Image Ltd and a racist calypso from DJ Mike Read.

Last year, when we visited France, I made sure the children always wore lapel badges, which I bought on the Internet, of the EU flag. No one would be in any doubt of our political affiliations. Any awkwardness could be immediately abated by enthusiastic lapel-gesturing.

At the French holiday camp, Six and Nine made friends with some Belgian children of similar ages, Zes and Negen. And though, being English, we were unable to speak any foreign languages, least of all Belgian, we made our feelings about the complex pros and cons in the argument for European political and economic unity understood to the Walloons by pointing at the badges and pretending to cry, over and over again.*

Of course, twelve months later, the situation is much worse, and the British, or more specifically the English, have gone from

---

actor Kevin Eldon and the performance artist and writer Ben Moor in September 1995.

* I know 'Belgian' isn't a language. I did this on purpose for comic effect.

being regarded by the Europeans as the cool kids who gave the world The Beatles, James Bond and football to being a kind of embarrassing, weird family of angry and confused hooligans, whose garden is full of used nappies, old, wet copies of *Fiesta Readers' Wives* and rusted tricycle frames.

Last summer, a man on a second-hand record stall in the street market of a Pyrenean village pretended he was not going to sell me a first pressing of Catherine Ribeiro's 1972 classic *Paix*, despite my EU badge, due to assumed political differences.* 'Ah, Brexit,' he said, 'no seminal stream-of-consciousness Parisienne street-poet space rock for you, monsieur!' But the tension was palpable. We needed to raise our game.†

I realised I could use my mother's sewing machine to clothe my very family itself, this summer, in unambiguously pro-European Union garments, exactly the sort of bespoke outfits we would need to ensure safe passage across the continent in these troubled times.

The McCall's Patterns M5500 Children's Knight, Prince and Samurai Costumes kit, which I found for $8.91 on the Internet, had the basic shapes I needed for my pro-European Union suits. And while European Union-patterned dressmaking material is not available in and of itself, European Union flags 15 ft square are available for about £1.50 each online. These were the tools!‡

---

* Ribeiro is a superb cross between Patti Smith and Nico, backed by early Pink Floyd – pure spirit of May '68 made flesh. The man didn't have any of her records, but should have.

† The man was selling French psychedelia in the weekly market at Mirepoix. We got on fine. It was in fact the organic rose ice-cream seller who said we couldn't have any ice cream because of Brexit. But he was laughing. I wonder if he is still laughing now.

‡ Again, this is a Simon Munnery rhythm, from his Alan Parker Urban Warrior act. 'These are the tools. The tools for a better tomorrow!'

By upscaling the size of the patterns I was also able to provide templates for my wife and I, and by the end of June I had cut and stitched four perfect medieval-style European Union two-pieces for us to wear as we make our way across divided Europe. For headgear, I copied our clearly pro-EU queen, and wove yellow plastic daisies in European Union star formations into the brims of four blue wickerwork hats.* Four pairs of blue-and-yellow trainers set off our ensembles perfectly.

In Germany, the still extant *Wanderjahre* tradition sees young people wander the country for a fixed period, dressed in stove-pipe hats and bell-bottoms, singing for their sausage suppers in inns and bars.† This, I realised, could be the model for our ritual journey, our pilgrimage of contrition.

Six plays the French horn, Nine is a skilled oboist, and I own a theremin, while my wife can shriek. I have arranged a version of the song 'I Apologize', by the 1980s Minneapolis hardcore punk band Hüsker Dü, for our family quartet, and I plan to spend the summer performing it in our pro-European garb at a succession of significant European sites.

And when their children, standing in the ruins of ravaged Britain, ask my children what they did to try and sabotage Brexit, they can answer, 'We stood outside the Stasi Museum, and Notre-Dame, and the astronomical clock, clad in European Union costumes that our father stitched himself, and used our oboe and our horn to apologise.'

* Having been co-opted into the anti-EU argument against her will, when a lie was leaked to the *Sun* in August 2016 saying she supported Brexit, a sneaky trick assumed to be the responsibility of Michael Gove, Her Majesty staged her own small act of rebellion by wearing a clearly EU-themed hat for the June 2017 opening of Parliament. I love the Queen.

† I encountered this tradition in a bar in Hannover in 2004 and, not knowing what it was, found it delightful.

Yawn! Get over it! A Balrog Has Come

Thanks stu after reading that cloying sentimental self indulgent middle class twaddle. Oh boy do I now no why I voted leave. Left Of Stalin

I was very surprised to hear that a six year old could play the french horn. Fake news, surely. Samsssss

Virtue-signalling, par excellence! Paulilc

There is no language called Belgian . . . Aintmuch

Zes and Negen are Flemish (Dutch) words, Belgian is not a language and Wallons speak French. No Bugger You Know

I am Belgian myself, and I can't even speak Belgian. Furthermore, I don't know anyone here in Belgium that can speak Belgian. Maybe it is because the official languages here are Dutch and Flanders and in Brussels, French in Wallonia and in Brussels, and German in the east, near the German border. Sendoake

Not sure if this is intended to be ironic. Likely not. In which case someone ought to point out to the writer that the self righteousness, gesture politics, snobbery and complacency of wealthy progressive politics are core reasons political opposition has been so easily hi-jacked by the ideological fruitcakes of Brexit and the racist and regressive Alt-right. Promoting more of the same is hardly likely to help. Dr Wibble

'By upscaling the size of the patterns I was also able to provide templates for my wife and I' It should be 'templates for my wife and myself/me' without context 'my wife and I' is sound

but in the context of 'able to provide templates for', well one rule is it has to sound right if you remove your wife so choose between 'able to provide templates for I' or 'able to provide templates for myself' or 'able to provide templates for me' and pick whichever is right. In this case as the sentence refers to the self at the start then 'myself' is the right answer. To use 'I' in that sentence smacks of someone trying to sound grammatical without the knowledge of grammar to back it up. BigJohnFX

The trolls from Olgino are already out in force. Have you noticed that they are now swapping a single account between trolls rather than just creating new accounts? A worthwhile reminder that the rise of nationalism in the West is funded by Putin who wishes those pesky EU-sanctions and that cohesive NATO would just go away and let him get on with the business of annexing Eastern Europe. AnnONeymous

I couldn't even get to the Brexit bit. Had to give up after the fawning over feminists. Virtue signalling at its finest. I'm sure many people had many different reasons for voting remain, the fact that some did it just because they're virtue signallers leaves a little taste of sick in my mouth. RodneyM72

When will the complaining cease? It's happened. We are leaving. Deal with it. B R Foulkes

Lee has a child with the same name as jacob rees mogg new child.? Seriously, more drivel, badly written and just ridiculous, do you get paid for writing this kind of stuff?.As least you are not the only one who can't speak Belgian, no one can. Derek Strange

What a deranged load of twaddle from this multi-faceted Britain hating jerk. I fear for his children, being brought up by such a right on PC filleted humanoid. Taff2

That the phrase 'Donald Trump is a smelly poo-poo head'. passes for adult conversation around the writer's dinner table more than explains the childish tone of the article and the even more childish approach to Brexit. Nomad Scott

Political turmoil has left humourists with nothing to aim at

16 July 2017

Last summer I wrote a comedy drama script, currently 'in development with a major broadcaster', concerning a charming, confident, clever and Machiavellian politician. Named Horace Thompson, he manipulates popular culture to consolidate support for a controversial referendum that he narrowly won, intending to further his own self-interest. And he was in the Bullingdon Club. And he lives in Islington.

(I don't know where I got the brilliant idea for this character from. Sometimes I think I am a genius, or some kind of unwitting god, forcibly exiled to Earth, his memory of his own divinity erased by jealous members of his former pantheon.)

But like Liam Fox and David Davis and all the bullying Brexiteer shitbags, the charming, confident, clever and Machiavellian politician the character of Horace Thompson is inspired by no longer seems quite so charming, confident, clever and Machiavellian.

The problem for me is that the average high-profile Brexiteer now looks like a once-powerful man who thought he was playing a rigged party game of pass the parcel, aiming to win a prize he had previously wrapped himself, but who has suddenly realised he is sitting with an unexploded nail bomb in his lap, right next to his shrivelled nut-sack.*

---

* In the end, despite the promise of a payment from Channel 4 for the finished pilot script, I had to abandon this project. Boris Johnson no longer seemed charming enough to be a plausible anti-hero, and the full

Still, as long as there is some way to hold on to the closing scene, in which Horace Thompson's head is sliced off by the rotating blades of a ceiling fan and then eaten by his own guard dogs, I will feel it has all been worthwhile. My final rewrite will consciously uncouple the character from specific details.

It may have been folly to hitch my story wagon to a character so clearly inspired by Boris Johnson, even though his future once seemed secure. Boris Johnson will be a forgotten casualty of the crisis his own lying *Daily Telegraph* columns created; the mad scientist, raging at his own now-murderous monster, at the end of some black-and-white B-movie, 'But no, Brexeeto, I am your master! I created you to serve me. Noooo. Brexeeto, aaaaa-ggggghhhh! My nut-sack!'*

Pity the professional humourist. It has become a cliché of opinion pieces that the news of the past twelve months has been so absurd, unpredictable and fast-moving that it is beyond satire. Only the infinite keyboard monkeys of Twitter, trapped on the inhospitable concrete island of their moated social media platform, and lobbing the wet simian excrement of their viral memes and gifs into the hair of curious onlookers, can respond to news stories with the speed required to land a blow.†

---

horror of the extent of Brexit's failure overtook the project. I'd had a high blood pressure diagnosis in the week of the Brexit vote and was worried I'd have to quit live work, so it was reassuring to know I was good enough to get a comedy drama commission. Three years and 250 shows later, I'm still alive and well enough to start writing the next tour, so I don't need to cash that goodwill in yet.

* I think that via the conduit of B-movies, this is another golem comparison. V. poor.

† An orangutan threw its excrement into my gran's hair from its moated island in Dudley Zoo in 1972, having been wound up by hundreds of horrible kids making monkey noises at it all day, the cruelty encouraged

Then the roulette wheel of events spins again and makes the carefully conceived conceits of slow-moving professional humourists immediately irrelevant, leaving us spluttering through our long-winded set-ups as the gas cloud of poorly thought-out policy our punchlines aimed to ridicule evaporates in a fog of central-office plausible denial.

The trick to being a champion clay pigeon shooter, my violent and weaponry-obsessed wife tells me, is to aim for the space you anticipate the clay fool moving into, not the space where it appears to be.

(My advice for any clay pigeons reading is to avoid being shot by moving forwards into a space you didn't anticipate being in. Then perhaps your decimated numbers will recover in the wild, flying idiots.)

Lawyers and nervous TV producers pore over contributors' jokes, while the politician they concern is already in the process of being sacked, resigning, performing a blatant policy U-turn or saying something so stupid and racist that their valuable contribution to the mildly amusing Teignbridge Business Buddies scheme is swiftly eclipsed.*

---

by their foul parents. My mum cleaned it out and told my gran it was just mud, but later on that night she told me it was orangutan excrement after all, but she didn't want her old mother to know that, and I wasn't to tell her. I hope my kids are as kind to me when I am old and covered in the filth of a simian.

* Earlier that month the Conservative MP for Newton Abbot, Anne Marie Morris, the founder of the Teignbridge Business Buddies scheme, was suspended for using the phrase 'nigger in the woodpile' to describe a no-deal Brexit, for which she subsequently apologised unreservedly, raising a bar for ill-advised public pronouncements which it would take a talent like Liam Neeson to vault. In the interest of full disclosure, I should reveal that I played the butler, Tom Rogers, in our 1983 school

The successful modern satirist must enter a Zen-like state, where all possible outcomes take shape in his third eye, each in turn satirised in advance of its existence, in the event of it becoming a reality.

(When I wrote for the BBC radio satire *Week Ending* in the early '90s, the writers' room smelt of excrement and BO, and was full of filthy ashtrays, empty crisp bags and overflowing spittoons. Nobody there was in a Zen-like state, although some functioning alcoholic visionaries were asleep under the desks, which is the next best thing.)

Satirists are supposed to comfort the afflicted and afflict the comfortable. Stand-up comedians, all of their professional metaphors involving violence and death, call this 'punching up'. But which way is up?

Is it 'punching up' to poo your comedy pellets onto a severely weakened prime minister with a randomly flapping lower jaw, whose desperate over-reliance on a small repertoire of endlessly repeated and ultimately meaningless statements indicates she is clearly on the verge of a nervous breakdown, and who has

---

production of a dramatisation of Agatha Christie's novel *Ten Little Niggers*, in which one of the original members of Napalm Death, Daryl Fideski, played a fisherman called Fred Narracott. Usually now called *And Then There Were None* or *Ten Little Indians*, the play of *Ten Little Niggers* doesn't appear to have been produced under the name *Ten Little Niggers* anywhere, apart from my old school, since 1959, though the last publication of the novel under that title was in 1977, only six years prior to our production. There were black and Asian kids in our school. Nobody on the staff gave this any thought, which seems appalling in retrospect. All the female parts were played by fourteen-year-old boys dressed up as women in tights and dresses and false breasts and make-up, all singing a rhyme about niggers. It was insane, transphobic and racist. It was sick karnival of hate. It was showbiz!

sacrificed her future career and hard-won credibility on the altar of her ungrateful party's best interests?

I don't know. But when a woman was filmed putting a cat into a wheelie bin, everyone thought it was awful. Theresa May is that little cat. History is that wheelie bin. Am I that horrible woman, putting that miserable cat into that horrible bin? I need a clear clay pigeon villain to aim at. All I see, everywhere, are victims and losers.

I'm halfway through my current two-year tour, but I'm taking the summer off because my towering stage set, made entirely from the smashed DVD cases of other stand-ups' shows, is too high, and my show is too long, to fit any Edinburgh Fringe venue. And I hate all comedians under forty, so I don't want to spend a month trying to act presidentially around them.

About a quarter of my current near-three-hour run-time uses topical material as feeder routes into the main narrative thrust. For simplicity's sake, I could do with Boris Johnson and Donald Trump still being around in September, as the similarities between them dovetail the two acts together neatly, but every night in the interval I have to go online to check Trump hasn't been assassinated or impeached.

Just over twelve months ago, I declined a role in a promising new topical satire TV show, which, though green-lit now, still hasn't made it to our screens. By the time it airs, the government under which it was conceived will have been replaced at least twice. If the news roller-coaster ride of the past twelve months were a real roller-coaster ride, it would long since have been closed down. People like excitement, but no one wants to emerge from every brief perusal of a daily newspaper covered in spilt Diet Coke and the vomit of other people's children, while a showman makes off with all the change that fell out of their pockets.

Unfortunately i have seen your show and was the loser, luckily i was given the tickets and was able to escape. Genghis223

The current political climate calls for Charlie Brooker, not Stewart Lee. Mr Daydream

There could have been a good article here, with some incisive and valid points. Unfortunately this is a piece of unilluminating shit. Gene Marcus

I wonder how Mr Lee feels performing as a stand-in stand-up sit-down writer to Frankie Boyle? I don't know why Mr Boyle is no longer writing for the *Guardian* but I suspect he wrote something that offended their 'liberal' sensibilities and so Mr Lee was brought in off the subs bench to write stuff that will be 'not too offensive' while giving off a reek of his 'intellect'. Mr Lee is extremely clever, talented in many areas, very, very, successful but just not funny most of the time. Minotaur

Kim Jong-un's happiness is just a weekend mini-break away

10 September 2017

At the beginning of the current decade I was often mistaken for the then North Korean dictator-in-waiting Kim Jong-un, which led to an embarrassing incident in a pet shop on Dalston High Road in February 2009. Needless to say, I was unable to convince the Polish lady behind the counter that I was merely looking for a canine companion for my elderly aunt and did not in fact regard labradoodle puppies as a 'superfood'.*

But it was worse for Kim himself, who once ended up accidentally and uncomfortably appearing in my place on a December 2006 edition of *8 Out of 10 Cats*, alongside Sean Lock, Jason Manford, Liza Tarbuck and Nightcrawler from *The X-Men*. A comment he made about the production company, Endemol, was described during the recording by host Jimmy Carr as the single joke 'least likely to make the final edit of the show in the programme's history'.† Needless to say, due to

---

* My father, who at home mainly ate pork scratchings, frogs' legs and Maltesers, would come home from visits to the Far East boasting about the foods he had consumed there. He claimed to have eaten dogs, lizards, handfuls of fried beetles hot off street-market woks and, incredibly, monkeys' brains direct from the animals' skulls with a spoon. In this last instance I suspect he may have been confusing his own life with that of Indiana Jones. The last time I saw him, all he would eat was Indian food and digestives. Is it any wonder I struggle with my diet?

† This is true. I think Jimmy was genuinely trying to help me, and the show, out of a hole when he said it.

Kim's poor performance I was not asked back.*

Fans of unusual celebrity–dictator friendships with long memories will recall the physical comedian Norman Wisdom's odd 1950s relationship with the totalitarian Albanian leader Enver Hoxha. In between mass executions of dissidents and incarcerations of anti-Communists, Hoxha even found time, in 1951, to accompany Wisdom and his family on a week's holiday to the Isle of Wight amusement park Blackgang Chine.†

Beside the English Channel, the curious pair cavorted between the open legs of a giant fibreglass smuggler and frolicked in a fairy glade, all the while crying out, 'Mr Grimsdale! Mr Grimsdale!!' and 'Have you, Albanian peasant brothers, ever sought the reason for the poverty, misery, hunger and

---

* Appearing on *8 Out of 10 Cats* in the autumn of 2006 was probably one of my worst, and most misjudged, professional experiences. I was pretty broke and needed the £600 fee, and even though I had never seen the show, I thought, 'How hard can it be?' I assumed that you just sat on the panel and riffed in a supportive atmosphere, but it gradually dawned on me at the studio in the afternoon that the other panellists were working all day on prepared material with their own paid writers. Within moments of the show starting I realised it absolutely wasn't going to work for me. I gritted my teeth, got my head down and waited for it to end. In his autobiography, *They Called Me the Grocer and I Wore It Like a Hat*, the comedian Lee Mack disparages comics who can't 'cut the mustard' on panel shows, and it is true that their regulars develop special skills to survive them. But imagine if they had used that time instead to do something of value or worth?

† Britain's oldest, and perhaps most bizarre, amusement park, as featured in the psycho-geographic travel book *Bollocks to Alton Towers*, by Robin Halstead, Jason Hazeley, Alex Morris and Joel Morris, which is a far more thoughtful work than the stupid cover of its paperback edition would suggest. Seek out the hardback on eBay.

gloom which have been your lot for centuries?"*

In a modern echo of Hoxha–Wisdom, the American basket-ball player Dennis Rodman sees himself as the unofficial peace-broker between the US and North Korea. Having befriended Kim in 2013, and with whom he claims to go horse-riding, ski, sing karaoke and generally hang out, Rodman claims, 'I just want to try to straighten things out for everyone to get along together.'†

Since Kim took power in North Korea in 2011, the stress of the top job has relieved his friendly round face of much of its puppy fat, whereas I have slid into a porcine middle-aged spread of repellent aspect, meaning Kim and I are now rarely confused with each other.

---

* Hoxha was a huge fan of Norman Wisdom, who became an unlikely star in post-war Albania, where, like the Czech mole, he was viewed as a symbol of the ordinary worker lost in the faceless machine of society. I held a door open for Wisdom in Liverpool in 1991. As a five-year-old, off sick from school and watching daytime television at my gran's, I was very taken with the unnamed band that appeared in the 1969 comedy *What's Good for the Goose*, in which Wisdom goes on a road trip with some young hippy chicks. Skiving off school in the '70s you would see the weirdest films on afternoon television, so strange that you would think you had imagined them. I have a memory of seeing a Spanish film about a man getting trapped in a phone box and then being taken to a cave full of dead men in phone boxes, and it turns out it was real (*La Cabina*, Antonio Mercero, 1972). Years later, after I had become a Pretty Things fan and seen them live, I found out that the band in Wisdom's psychedelic sex comedy was The Pretty Things, appearing under their soundtrack pseudonym of The Electric Banana. The German version of *What's Good for the Goose* is twenty-seven minutes shorter than the British original, but the sex scenes in it are considerably longer and more explicit, with topless shots inserted into them. Is it any wonder we voted to leave the EU?

† Rodman really said this, and is genuinely Kim's friend.

119

That said, when one of my critically acclaimed stand-up specials from 2005 aired on Netflix in the US last year, I did notice a tweet from Dennis Rodman which read, 'Yo! My bro Kim Jong-un on TV right now slaying the Scotch people at the Glasgow Stand! Tell it like it is! Braveheart was a fag!!'

At the risk of sounding arrogant, I do feel the many occasions upon which I am still addressed as Chairman of the Workers' Party of Korea, Chairman of the Central Military Commission, Chairman of the State Affairs Commission, Supreme Commander of the Korean People's Army and Presidium Member of the Politburo Standing Committee of the Workers' Party of Korea by shocked North Korean expats have given me some insight into the dictator's mindset. Needless to say, Trump's approach to dealing with Kim Jong-un is entirely the wrong-un.

I understand Kim, certainly more than Donald Trump, and perhaps even more than his hoop-bothering friend Dennis Rodman, who has all scribbles all on him. I am the most consistently critically acclaimed male British stand-up comedian of the century, while Kim is the most dictatorial dictator in the world today, and let me tell you, like little Kim, I know that it is lonely at the top.

I wonder if, like Kim, many of my life's achievements (winning six Chortle Awards and an edition of *Celebrity Mastermind** in my case, developing a nuclear arsenal in his) are simply attempts to gain the attention of an absent father figure. Instead of rattling his atomic sabre and sticking his flaccid orange penis into the heart of the wasps' nest of south-east Asian geopolitics, Trump could choose to be that father. What Kim needs is love from a big daddy, and Trump could be that big daddy, bear-hugging and play-wrestling us out of the impending apocalypse.

* I answered questions on the improviser guitarist Derek Bailey.

Donald Trump sees the world as a set of business deals. Business is not moral. It is about results. Trump is alleged to have done alleged financial or publicity deals with people allegedly worse than Kim – dodgy Russian oligarchs, Italian-American mafia families and Michael Gove. All Kim wants is Trump's attention, so why can't Trump, in the interest of global security, simply invite Kim to the US for the holiday of a lifetime?

Kim and Trump in Long Beach, Washington, marvelling at the world's largest chopsticks, laughing as they act out the futile attempts of normal-sized men to use them; Kim and Trump in Topeka, Kansas, at the Evel Knievel Museum, bonding as they hold hands in silent, humble admiration; Kim and Trump in San Luis Obispo, California, comparing notes at the Madonna Inn's famous waterfall urinal, laughing as their twin torrents cross streams, *Ghostbusters*-style, in the soft subterranean lighting. You cannot make nuclear threats against a man whom you have urinated alongside in the beautiful waterfall urinal of the Madonna Inn, San Luis Obispo, California.*

My mentor, the former comedian and failed recluse Roger Mann, recently befriended a goat near his Pyrenean hermitage in an experimental attempt to understand the nature of relationships.† Were Trump to engage paternally with Kim, he himself may learn something, something that might cure the emptiness inside him that threatens to suck all human history into it like a black hole made of nameless need. For Trump, like Kim, is also lonely.

* I used this urinal alongside the writer and performance artist Ben Moor and the actor Kevin Eldon in September 1995, soon after we visited Pea Soup Andersen's Inn. We are all still friends today.

† It's perhaps worth pointing out that since the time of writing, Roger has even given up on the goats.

You can own New York, but you can't make it love you; you can execute hundreds of North Koreans, but you can't make North Korea love you. To be feared is not the same as to be respected. A father whose children obey him only through fear is a failed father. When we think of fathers, they paint Airfix models with us and wrestle in the summer meadow of memory. They do not threaten us with warheads.

Kim Jong-un pleads to be disciplined. Donald Trump is desperate for love. If diplomatic channels could be opened to enable the gaping maws of these two desperate needs to meet, they would engulf each other with a flood of unrequited love, and we would all sleep easy again.

Kim is a mass murderer whose state run concentration camps trade in child sex slaves and whose government have eliminated all forms of free expression. This jokey equivalence between him and Trump is an indirect apology for Kim's fascist regime. Making out that they are both as bad as each other shows a remarkable ignorance about what is happening in the North and the danger Kim represents. Midland

North Korea is in North-East Asia, Stew! Okayama Man

When is Frankie Boyle coming back? Wintermute99

'The North Korean leader needs discipline; Donald Trump needs love.' Please, tell us the author is kidding us? Comic book psychoanalysis. Fred Budtz

So your view of the ethnic world is that all Poles think all Koreans eat dogs. How very modern. Sisterraysays

My futile attempt to sell satire
to the *Daily Mail*

26 November 2017

Pasting together doctored drawings of the *Daily Mail*'s long-running cartoon dog, Fred Basset, I'm creating the mother of all monetisable Christmas cash-in books.*

In the first of a typical three-frame strip, Fred defecates insolently on a pavement. Then Fred's owner scoops up the excrement before – and this is the twist – popping it through the letterbox of an immigrant family and saying, 'Merry Winterval, my coloured friends! You're in England now!!' It's hilarious, no?†

---

* Fred Basset is a cartoon basset hound created by the late Alex Graham. His suburban dog adventures have run in the *Daily Mail* since 1963. Fred's male owner travels to work in the City of London each day and plays golf. His female owner is a stay-at-home housewife. The strips contain minimal topical references, and each three-frame story is unrelated to the next. While charming, they explore few of the possibilities offered by the medium, apart from a strange period in the mid-'70s, when Fred fantasised about killing his owners, a series of dream sequences depicting their deaths in a variety of ever more lurid and sadistically sexual ways.

† Winterval was the catch-all name for a series of pan-denominational events held in Birmingham in November and December 1997, which gave rise to the pervasive alt-right foundation myth that politically correct killjoys have banned Christmas. In 2011, the *Daily Mail*'s Melanie Phillips agreed to a correction, noting that Winterval was not intended to replace Christmas. The myth of Winterval was even cited in the Leveson Inquiry as an example of the press's lack of responsibility.

Was it possible to work the lucrative adult Ladybird book market, using a similar level of ironic self-awareness of the *Daily Mail* brand, across a range of self-parodying *Daily Mail* products, without necessarily undermining the integrity of the loathing-ridden opinion sluice itself?* After all, Lego's funny children's Batman, Adam West's liberal gay Batman and Christian Bale's fascist asthmatic Batman all coexist commercially. And Paperchase were already interested in an exclusive stockist deal.

But now the whole thing is ruined! And all thanks to that Political Correctness Gone Mad brigade that they have now!!

As a proud member of the 'metropolitan liberal elite'™, I would normally have been delighted that a tiny minority of 'left-wing bullies'© had forced the high-street card shop Paperchase to dump an advertising deal with the *Daily Mail*, fearing the negative association of Paperchase's wholesome family-card retail values with the *Mail*'s conduit of poisonous hate, sudoku and Sarah Vine.†

Usually, I am the sort of person who thinks that anyone who has ever worked for the *Daily Mail* is worse than Adolf Hitler, even the temps and the tea lady.‡ And I'm not alone.

* . . . as exploited by Joel Morris and Jason Hazely of *Bollocks to Alton Towers* repute, who first explored the idea in their *Framley Examiner* local newspaper parody in the early 2000s.

† It's such a thin line between people power and left-wing bullying.

‡ When I met my wife, she was temping, between acting work and stand-up gigs, on the showbiz section of the *Daily Mail* and had also been working as an unofficial aide to one of the paper's former star writers, who was now unwell (she appears uncredited in a photo of him visiting a Catholic shrine that appeared in an authorised biography). Wisely, my future wife realised she could not tell me she worked for the *Daily Mail*, as the paper had, at that point, been instrumental in

So disgusted are youth voters by the repellent newspaper, it's now clear that the *Daily Mail*'s increasingly hysterical attacks on Jeremy Corbyn, the coddled egg of British politics,* may even have helped secure his triumphant loss in the last general election.

I find that a damning *Daily Mail* review can attract hundreds of thousands of paying punters, precisely because they assume that anything hated by the hated *Daily Mail* must be worth seeing, while anything it likes must be awful.

My current tour poster proudly boasts the following *Daily Mail* quote from the 2001 Bad Sex Award-winning novelist and *Daily Mail* columnist Christopher Hart: 'Clever-clever, oh-so-fashionable and deeply unfunny "anti-populist" comedian

---

sabotaging my career, such as it was, and essentially rendering me destitute. Because she was so cagey about the source of her income, I assumed it was derived from amoral earnings (which it was, ironically, but not in the way I imagined), and yet I still loved her, and was prepared to accommodate this. The upside of this is, fifteen years later, if they ever come for me, I know where the bodies are buried, and who buried them.

* I had never heard of coddled eggs until Jeremy Corbyn said he liked to eat them, when he was a guest on a 2017 edition of *Celebrity Gogglebox*. I googled 'coddled eggs', liked the sound of them, and whenever we were on our travels subsequently, we kept our eyes skinned for egg coddlers in charity shops. Our first were a pair we picked up in the town of Coleford, in the Forest of Dean, and now we have five egg coddlers, including two in a velvet-lined presentation box. Coddled eggs are not the kind of fast food you can whip up on a schoolday, but at weekends I like to experiment with adding different ingredients to the basic egg – mushrooms, leeks, hot chilis – before submerging the egg coddlers in boiling water, and now coddled eggs are one of the family's favourite breakfast treats. And all thanks to Marxist firebrand and terrorist sympathiser Jeremy Corbyn, who should perhaps think about fronting his own coddled egg-based reality TV show, *Celebrity Coddlebox*!

Stewart Lee is an exceptionally well-trained lapdog of the Brexit-hating establishment."*

Ker-ching!!!! Thanks, Christopher! The ticket-buying public's hands are, as you might once have written, 'moving away from my knee and heading north. Heading unnervingly and with a steely will towards the pole. And, like Sir Ranulph Fiennes . . . will not easily be discouraged' (*Rescue Me*, Christopher Hart, 2001).†

I understand, from a purely business point of view, Paperchase's need to disassociate itself from the elderly and expiring racists that read the *Daily Mail*, to court instead the affections of the growing market of tomorrow's mixed-race, polyamorous avocado-coveters. But on this occasion, I was on the verge of sealing a three-way creative partnership with both Paperchase and the *Daily Mail* that would have made me millions.‡

Sitting across the desk from the editor, Paul Dacre, last week, I gave him my pitch. 'The *Daily Mail* is already adept at working contradictory markets simultaneously,' I flattered the hate magnate, as he sucked hard on his fourth Calippo of the morning. 'The print edition pretends to despise the very ephebophiliac swimwear sleaze that the *Daily Mail* website thrives on, for example.

* I don't think the bad-sex novelist Christopher Hart even believes the things he has written about me. He's just a hack who has to fill space in the style he imagines his current employer expects, a process I attempt to parody, while also fulfilling it to the letter, in the *Observer*.

† This is a genuine example of Hart's sex writing. Oddly, thinking of Ranulph Fiennes during coitus is, for me, a tried and tested method of delaying ejaculation.

‡ Less than a year after this column was written, anti-Brexit editor Geordie Greig was put in charge of the *Daily Mail*, presumably in order to detoxify it. If Brexit turns out to be as bad as experts think, then it would be wise for the paper's shareholders to put some clear water between the *Daily Mail* and the catastrophe it helped cause.

'But imagine if, Paul baby, as well as profiteering from the hateful scaremongering that is your vile newspaper's *raison d'être*, you could also empty the pockets of those who claim to despise your organ, by selling them irresistible satires of your own sickening values.' I emptied my sample sack. Dacre's two eyes exploded in hot greed. Greetings cards. Christmas cash-in books. Sex novelties. And all with an ironically arch *Daily Mail* flavour.

'These greetings cards are sure to be top-sellers,' I told Dacre. A photo of columnist Quentin Letts disgorges the opinion, 'Middle-class parents are middle-class because they have learned what it takes to succeed. Happy Birthday.' Sarah Vine opines, 'Jacob Rees-Mogg is worth far more than the flaccid consensus of the commissars of political correctness. Merry Christmas.'*

And a sepia-toned card of the first Viscount Rothermere, the paper's 1930s proprietor, declares, in *Daily Mail* font, 'I urge all British young men and women to study the Nazi regime in Germany. There is a clamorous campaign of denunciation against "Nazi atrocities" which consist merely of a few isolated acts of violence, but which have been generalised, multiplied and exaggerated to give the impression that Nazi rule is a bloodthirsty tyranny. Congratulations on passing your driving test.'

In order to annoy politically correct prudes and killjoys, I had arranged for the darkest recesses of Paperchase to showcase a range of naughty, but saucy and harmless, adult *Daily Mail*-themed items. The paper's star columnist and author of *50 People Who Buggered Up Britain*, Quentin Letts, had agreed to lend his image to a fun range of used female sanitary products, Quentin Lil-Letts.

Meanwhile, the vibrating head of the *Daily Mail* royal columnist Robert Hardman crowns the novelty 'Hardman' Sphincter

* Real quotes, obviously.

Stimulator; and a special brass hammer, designed for nailing your own penis to a table, was to be called the Paul Dacre Nail Your Own Penis to a Table Hammer.

Dacre actually laughed himself silly at the final few strips in my Fred Basset book. In the end, the beagle just looks on bemused, while his squatting owner simply scrapes his own human foulness directly from his own bottom himself, to deposit through the offending immigrants' door; until the climactic strip, where, perching atop a brass bust of Jan Moir,* Fred Basset's owner defecates directly into the immigrants' letterbox, with a triumphant cry of, 'Brexit Means Brexit! Now get back to Bongo Bongo-land!'†

'We're looking at a massive hit,' said Dacre, his Calippo melting

---

* For years, Jan Moir was the *Mail*'s most reliable sluice of calculatedly provocative opinion, making up a load of stupid wank about me, for example, in 2011, but she seems to have lost her mojo of late and has manufactured little real outrage since around 2013. Suggesting, without any proof, that Boyzone's Stephen Gately's death was due to his 'lifestyle', in 2009, was probably her career highpoint, the equivalent of my 'Paul Nuttalls from the Ukips' routine, and Moir has found it hard to maintain that level of uncut hate since. The trick, as the former pop star Julian Cope once told me, is to push through being a has-been and onwards into being a legend. You go, girl!

† UKIP's Godfrey Bloom put Bongo Bongo-land back on the map in August 2017, the country having been forgotten since it was last mentioned by the columnist Taki, in a 2004 piece for the *Spectator*, obviously. Ironically, in the decade or so that it was off the radar, Bongo Bongo-land had thrived, mining a powerful mineral called vibranium and evolving into a democratic state that combined traditional values with cutting-edge technology, in a style best described as Afro-Futurism. Bongo Bongo-land's King T'Challa invited Godfrey Bloom to stay in the country and have his prejudices confounded, but he, of course, declined to visit.

in his excited hand. And then the phone rang. The Paperchase partnership was off. 'Sorry, son. You get yourself a coffee, and I'll tidy your samples away,' said Dacre, kindly. When I came back, my novelties were bagged, but I could hear Dacre in his private bathroom, squealing and using an electric toothbrush, so I left.

When I got home, I unpacked my futile creations. All present and correct, except the Robert Hardman probe. Never mind. It's not like this deal is going anywhere fast.

Reading this piece reminded me of the time I was driving along a winding road in Malaysia and was suddenly confronted by a local tribesman wearing his native clothes, carrying some small dead animals and armed with a blowpipe. Sitting in my air-conditioned car it was hard to imagine how he must live his simple if precarious lifestyle. So it is with the type of humour which leaves me absolutely straight-faced but apparently packs them in to theatres in London and elsewhere. It belongs to another civilisation and I can't begin to relate to it I'm afraid. Lurking Class Hero

'As a proud member of the "metropolitan liberal elite"™' Translated: Lives in London, enjoys virtue signalling and was educated at private school and Oxbridge. Summary: middle class tosser. Jaunchito

Just watched this virtue signaller on Youtube. Totally UNFUNNY! Political Correctness is just so pass. Weary Wanderer

I think it's terrific that the *Guardian* has one of their standby Oxbridge comics always ready to rip the piss out of *Mail*/ Trump/Leavers etc., but it all seems to be getting a little bit desperate now. Perhaps if there had been a little less sneering from the 'clever' types, the *Mail* would have less readers, Trump less votes and we might still be in Europe, too late now, carry on sneering. Simba's Dad

The pure hate this man exudes of everyone who has a different opinion to him really is rather disturbing. Hala123

Lee has always confused smarm with satire, which is why he plays so well to the echo-chamber and its right-on readership. And let's face it, smarm in this context, is little more than gentrified hate, an opportunity to sneer at the unsophisticated thinking of the masses and their choice of media. Knockdownginger

Can Harry and Meghan make Britain whole again?

3 December 2017

In 2005, the then twenty-year-old Prince Harry appeared as a Nazi at a fancy-dress party. Perhaps the uniform had been inherited from his great-great-uncle, Edward VIII, who was not averse to a spot of recreational *Sieg Heiling*.

But next year Prince Harry is to marry the mixed-race descendant of a black American slave, his wedding garments scrupulously stripped of any stray swastikas. Cosmic order is restored.

Has the prince nobly taken upon himself the symbolic role of a healing force in our rapidly unravelling world, which is suddenly riven with the sort of open racism and fears of nuclear annihilations that we had assumed had been laid to rest? I'm all for '70s and '80s revivals, but these aren't the parts of my childhood I feel nostalgic for. A Fab lolly, an Altered Images twelve-inch remix and a vibrant trade union movement would have done.

Today, we need the hope that the forthcoming royal nuptials offer more than ever. Prince Harry and Meghan Markle's marriage could be a healing ritual for our ruined land, a joining of races that fascists would have us divide. But of course, the racist writing has been on the wall for years.

In 1965, during Eric Clapton's tenure in John Mayall's Bluesbreakers, the phrase 'Clapton Is God' began to be grafittied around London. But in 1966, Jimi Hendrix arrived in the city, and Clapton was usurped, a seething Salieri to Hendrix's soaring Mozart.

Ten years later, on stage in Birmingham, a drunken Clapton praised Enoch Powell and declared, 'Get the foreigners out, get the wogs out, get the coons out. Keep Britain white.'* The Rock Against Racism movement was formed soon after his pronouncement, and The Stranglers brought cavorting strippers on stage with them to smash racism at a Victoria Park RAR concert. Different times.†

Today, western world leaders openly praise neo-Nazis, but instead of forming a grass-roots rock'n'roll resistance, young people remain passively plugged into their PS4s playing *Pac-Man Go*, waiting for their brain-dead fuck-buddies to come round with some pacifying bong-weed, I expect, while laughing at You-net films of people gobbling down more cinnamon than is necessary, squandering bakers' dwindling spice reserves.

There's currently a cynical viral marketing campaign for Clapton's forthcoming Hyde Park show that sees the ancient phrase 'Clapton Is God' sprayed all around London once more by paid PR vandals. I have prepared a stencil saying, 'Clapton is an alcoholic racist,' but getting it out there doesn't, at the moment,

---

* To be fair, lots of people said much the same thing in Birmingham in 1976, but they weren't making a living playing a music derived from the culture of the people they wanted deported. A major '80s breakthrough with my elderly relatives was their attempt to use the word 'coloured' to describe black people, rather than more traditional epithets. Today, one rarely hears the word 'coloured', although it is still used accidentally by the *Windrush* scandal's mortified Amber Rudd, herself the sometime lover of a 'coloured' man.

† Crazy days! The objectification of women was used to battle discrimination against racial minorities. Fourteen years later, Kim Gordon of Sonic Youth explored the same dichotomy in 'Kool Thing', a duet with a sporting Chuck D of Public Enemy.

seem like a great use of time. There are worse people to worry about than Clapton or, to give him his blues name, Mississippi Nigel Farage.

We should have seen all this coming, but I thought the culture wars were won when New Order got John Barnes to do a rap on their 1990 World Cup single. I expect I was too busy being ironically racist in a Shoreditch bar, drinking Grolsch from a pop-top bottle and toasting Tony Blair. It's not only Eric Clapton who has a shameful past.

Alarm bells should have been ringing. Somewhere around the turn of the century, in the perineal period between the ubiquity of email and the pervasive idiocy tsunami of Twitter, my BNP-voting auntie sent me an attachment, typical of the era, designed to melt my snowflake mind.

It comprised a supposedly scientific study, using history and genetics, to prove that all Muslims were demonstrably culturally and morally inferior, and downright dangerous. Of course, a quick google showed that neither the academic who wrote it nor the institution he worked for had ever existed, a discovery that one would have thought would discredit the piece.

But confronted with this evidence, my auntie just said, 'All the same, I think it makes a lot of good points.' How pleased she would be, were she alive today, to know that her research reached the same exacting standards as that of the president of the United States of America.

This morning, on LBC radio, the professional wasps'-nest-poker Nick Ferrari was audibly rattled. Ferrari, a man who is 85 per cent wazzock, and who has made a living out of inflaming the unstable passions of the 'political correctness has gone mad' brigade, realised the monster robot he had reared on raw opinion meat and a vapour of Facebook hearsay was now beyond his control and he'd forgotten to install its emergency-stop button.*

Cautiously describing Trump's Britain First-endorsing missive† as 'a tweet too far', Ferrari suddenly found his white-knuckled listeners largely disagreeing with him and retorting that these videos needed to be aired, whether they were verifiable or not. Could straight-talking Ferrari smell the smoking torches of a previously loyal mob approaching his own mountaintop castle, his Jaguar F-Type aflame on the brick-paved driveway?‡

On Monday, as Theresa May cautiously accepted that we will have to pay for EU schemes we were already signed up for, and the inevitable impossibility of the fluid Irish border was at last made flesh, it seemed to me that the wheels had finally fallen off the lie-encrusted Brexit battlebus. But the quiet coup currently enacted by the billionaire tax-avoiders behind Brexit continued its forward motion, as cognitive dissonance drove their brainwashed Leave-voting serfs to misdirect their ongoing anger towards everyone but themselves.§

But Harry knows the power of symbols, and he begins the enactment of a healing ritual. Has Harry, ever the self-aware

* Curiously, I avoided comparing Ferrari's listenership to some kind of golem. I must have been having an off-day.

† Trump had retweeted Islamophobic tweets from the far-right group Britain First, which used video clips of random violent images as examples of unrelated Islamic extremism, mere days after the organisation's deputy leader, Jayda Fransen, had been arrested over a speech made in Belfast. Jo Cox's murderer had shouted 'Britain First!' as he killed her.

‡ This is the golem idea again, surely? The golem and I should get a room.

§ I do appreciate now that sentences like this are why people voted for Brexit.

134

prankster, chosen the tiny St George's Chapel, Windsor Castle, as his wedding venue in a coded satirical message every bit as meaningful as the clearly pro-EU hat his grandmother wore at the opening of Parliament last June?*

In a comic pantomime of self-immolating isolationism, our next National Royal Ceremony will be performed in a room too small to accommodate all those who might have been expected to attend, in a building named after our national saint, a man famous for fighting something that didn't exist: a dragon as unreal as Boris Johnson's *Daily Telegraph* vision of a banana-hating EU. The chapel's roof is decorated with heraldic animals. Guests might find themselves staring up at a unicorn, which canters away into the mist of myth, as gaseous as an NHS promise, the porous Irish border, the cake that can be eaten and had.

And here come the prince and his scion of slaves, to make us whole again. Meghan Markle. Her name even sounds like 'Mrs Merkel', and she symbolises an America far better than Trump's, a virgin new land coming into conjugal union with a grizzled Britain that, like the prince himself, could still choose to divest itself of its unattractive fascist garments and begin again.

We went to a Stewart Lee gig on our honeymoon. Never laughed so much in my life. The woman next to us was really funny. We stopped laughing when Stewart came on. Weary Wanderer

* Michael Gove and his fellow Leavers had falsely ascribed assumed pro-Brexit sentiment to the Queen, who, not allowed to address politics directly, responded in the only way she could: through millinery.

This man, apparently some form of comic, is a poseur, and his form of humour one that appeals only to people like you. I read the article 3 times, and found no value in it at all, nor did it even once cause me to smile. Maciver

A prince symbolising a feudal system of inherited title and privilege and a celebrity actress . . . I think our problems run deeper than that lol . . . is this article for real? The Thoughtful One

St George is the patron saint of England, not Britain. Another columnist who is unconsciously exclusive of the other countries making up these islands. Disappointing how fundamentally these entitled attitudes still thrive. Barbara C McLuskie

'Alcoholic' you really want to attack Clapton over that one? I paid good money to see you in Birmingham a couple of years back, you were a little tired and emotional yourself. RobindraJayaJaya

It's extremely difficult to tell, but apparently, Stewart Lee is a comedian. Druadh

Can Harry and Meghan make Britain whole again? Yes, as long as the progressives doff their caps in deference and know their place and stay firmly in it! A Balrog Has Come

'Her name even sounds like "Mrs Merkel", and she symbolises an America far better than Trump's, a virgin new land' Wow.. Opinion writer, put these magical rose-tinted glasses for sale on eBay and you'll make a fortune quickly. Groniady

Can the *Guardian* please be a little more intelligent than other newspapers and stop writing such drivel. Who the hell cares if two banal and uninteresting people are falling in love, getting engaged and then married? I'd rather see a good film. I think us loyal *Guardian* readers need you to move on from the most boring subject of the year. Thank you for a future free paparazzi journalism . . . CFJGaillard

How Toby Young got
where he isn't today

14 January 2018

The grindingly algorithmic controversialist Toby Young was always painfully and obviously in the oedipal shadow of his socialist intellectual father, Michael Young. Each of his desperately politically incorrect tweets was an attempt to cuckold and castrate his progenitor.

Toby Young has wasted his life spitting cold mucus at a ghost and throwing clumps of his own hot excrement at a shade, a raging zoo monkey.* Toby Young was at war with a phantom cloud of semen, long since turned to dust motes, bobbing on the west London thermals. But because I am kind and good, I take no pleasure in the slow-motion farce of his downfall.

On Wednesday night, the probable reason for the sudden twin resignations of the self-styled 'right-of-centre maverick' from both the spurious universities regulator and the Fulbright Commission became clear. Despite having survived last week's cataloguing of his hastily concealed career of context-free, non-character-driven, monetisable offence, on Monday evening Toby Young finally ran out of options and fell on his own cucumber spiraliser.

Even though he was defended by his chum, Boris Piccaninny Johnson, as being a 'caustic wit', the maverick self-styled 'Toadmeister' had to go. Because while the national media slept or commissioned supportive think-pieces from Young's wealthy

---

* An orangutan threw its excrement into my gran's hair from its moated island in Dudley Zoo in 1972. I think this had a big impact on me as a child as I keep mentioning it.

and powerful celebrity friends, the *London Student* newspaper was about to reveal that the Maverick Toadmeister had attended a secret conference on 'intelligence', featuring notorious speakers including, in previous years, white supremacists and a weird far-right paedophilia apologist called Emil.*

Of course, attending a secret conference alongside white supremacists does not amount to endorsing their ideals. I once attended a performance of *We Will Rock You*, the Queen musical by Ben Elton and Queen, and if anything, it made me despise the dreadful group even more than I did before, from a position of greater understanding.† The Maverick Toadmeister, by his own admission, attended the secret event only for a few hours, only sat at the back, didn't inhale any of the Nazism that was being handed round, and nor did he supply any to anyone else.

But on Monday night, the Maverick Toadmeister realised that even declarations of love from his greatest champions – the environmental opportunist Michael Gove, the *Daily Mail* hate-funnel Sarah Vine and the napkin'n'knick-knack guru Kirstie Allsopp – would not overwhelm the taint of his incidental association with genuine white supremacists.

For God's sake, that's what paranoid community activists in '70s blaxploitation movies thought white folk were doing – having

* Emil Kirkegaard.

† I don't know what it is about Queen. 'Bohemian Rhapsody', which is genius, apart, everything about their sound and sensibility just makes me feel queasy, like choking down an incredibly rich dessert. It's so arch and insincere and knowing. I don't have such a visceral reaction to any other music really, and the time I was sent to review the Queen musical was one of the most uncomfortable nights of my life. And I was aware that I was alone in that massive room in not finding it transcendental. I think I must, without knowing it, associate the band with some buried childhood trauma. I am sorry.

secret meetings about how to stop them breeding – and it turns out we are! In fact, that's the plot of the martial arts and black power musical *Three the Hard Way* (Gordon Parks Jr, 1974), but now with Toby Young as a curious bystander watching the evil Dr Fortrero plot to wipe out the black population and claiming it's research for a forthcoming speech.

If Boris Watermelon Smile Johnson's brother, Boris Johnson Junior, intended the appointment of the Maverick Toadmeister to the universities regulator to counteract the influence of the Political Correctness Gone Mad brigade, it's fair to say he may have overplayed his hand somewhat.

The Maverick Toadmeister's fellow secret conference attendee, Richard Lynn, for example, advocates that predominantly white American states secede from the Union, making them danger-ously likely to sink into the sea under the excess weight of the massive arses, and brains, of their remaining inhabitants.

The question presupposed by the title of the Maverick Toadmeister's best-selling book *How to Lose Friends and Alienate People* had been fairly comprehensively answered.

Asked last week to comment on his attendance at a second intelligence jamboree, this time in Canada, a clearly discombobu-lated Maverick Toadmeister said he had been giving the 'Amanda Holden Memorial Lecture'.* Amanda Holden? Les Dennis's ex-wife? Was the Battersea Dogs & Cats Home's celebrity ambas-sador now a eugenicist? And also dead? Thank God Dustin Gee didn't live to see the memory of *The Laughter Show* tarnished so.

I knew that there had been a famous science writer called Constance Holden. Had the Maverick Toadmeister, as no one is calling him ever, suffered a slip of his toad tongue? There wasn't time to check the facts, sadly, as the witch-hunt countdown

---

* The Maverick Toadmeister genuinely said this.

clock was ticking. Needless to say, I immediately mobilised my massive bullying Twitter following of furious politically correct snowflake hypocrites to have Amanda Holden, eugenics apologist, erased from history.

By Wednesday, public pressure had seen Holden lose her role as the face of Alpen, the colonic-cleansing breakfast dust. And on Thursday, Holden was digitally erased from every episode of *Britain's Got Talent*.

Then I realised the Maverick Toadmeister *had* made a misspeak. He *had* meant Constance Holden. Amanda Holden was not a Nazi (nor, it turned out, was Constance Holden), and she was not dead.

I don't know the Maverick Toadmeister and I have never met him, though he did once make a winsome face at me across a corridor at Heston services, Britain's worst services, on the M4.*

---

* Toby Young did make a funny face at me as he walked past me at Heston services, Britain's worst service station, about a decade ago. I had met him for about five seconds four years previously, at some theatre awards, where he asked me if I would appear on a reality TV show about rowing, and I said no. The face he made at Heston services was neither friendly nor unfriendly. It was just kind of weird and superior, as if he knew something that he thought made him better than me. But I don't think it was personal; that's just what his face is like. Similarly, I can't help having a naturally sarcastic-sounding voice. A few years later, the Maverick Toadmeister was asked to review a book I wrote on Radio 4, and he said: 'I've always thought of Stewart Lee's comedy as doing the opposite of what really good comedy should do. He essentially uses comedy to browbeat people into agreeing with his rather dogmatic left-wing political points of view. It's as though he's essentially taking what is the sort of prevailing politically correct dogma of his generation and aggressively ridiculing anyone who doesn't sign up to it, using comedy as an instrument to enforce conformity, not as a means of subversion. He's a red-faced man jabbing his finger in my face because I don't agree with him. He may as well be playing to an empty room, for all the concessions

I recognised him from somewhere, but something about his curious smirk and his strange gait made me assume he was a lesbian, dressed as a homosexual, who had assumed I was a lesbian dressed as a heterosexual man and was trying to pick me up. What a tangled web we weave.

But where now for the Maverick Toadmeister? Can even vile jam-rags like the *Telegraph* and the *Daily Mail* employ him now? Who calls themselves, as an adult, the 'Toadmeister' anyway? And 'maverick' is what the commissioner shouts at Dirty Harry. It's not what Dirty Harry tells the commissioner he is himself. That would be very uncool. Who does these strange and desperate things? Someone in search of an identity that has eluded them.

Sometime around twenty years ago, Toby Young started being nasty about people less fortunate and privileged than him, and like a shit Clarkson, he found it was easy to do and paid good money; and then the wind changed, and Toby Young was stuck with the horrible face he had made. And now people all over the Internet will be drawing foreskins on his bald head. For ever.

---

he makes to the audience. His refusal to concede to the audience is part of an ongoing desire to be taken seriously, but someone who wants to be taken so seriously is quite hard to take seriously.' Only a few years previously he had opined in print that I was a 'genius'. Make your mind up, baldy!

The reference here to dressing as a lesbian relates to an article Young wrote in 2004 about how he pretended to be a lesbian to get into lesbian bars. He probably didn't even do that. I mean, I feel sorry for him, to be honest. What a corner he has backed himself into, with all his stupid cheap shit.

Hooray! Thank god we live in an age when no man who has ever made a filthy joke, or admitted to being sexually attracted to women, or repelled by gay sex can ever hold down a public post again. (Unless he comes from a protected 'minority, natch!) Yes, he was an obnoxious, unfunny little Tory toad, but at least he had one thing going for him – he was funnier than Stewart Lee. Offshoretomorrow

'vile jam rags' is too far to go *Guardian* – please have the article withdrawn until it is rewritten at least without that, which was where I stopped reading. Tolkny

Lee has got his thesaurus out to prove nothing. A pointless article. Lee is like a left wing Bernard Manning . . . a throwback way past his sell by date. Marcus L

Lee appeals to a narrow base who like his formulaic predictable humour. Fair enough everyone has different tastes. But his too-cool-for-school bashing of Queen is surely a bit tired now. Does he really think he matches them for talent and memorable work? Think about it – anyone could have written this article or Lee's output. It written to a formula. You would not know it was Lee's if his name was not at the top – it could have been any left wing comedian. Now go and see how easy it is to write 'Bohemian Rhapsody'. BobMcGhee

Why use 100 words, when one can get paid for a few thousand? Possibly accurate, but oh so boring Mr Lee. Yorkyman

At least some of Young's tweets were humorous. He gets bonus points for his ability to enrage the hysterical PC brigade. MarkB35

It is possible to agree with every word of Stewart Lee's takedown of Toby Young and yet wish it hadn't been printed. I've started to think that all this normalized abuse just leads to everyone thinking that abuse is the new journalism. I wasn't a fan of the 'jam-rag' quip (nothing to do with Young, and normalizes misogyny). Or the nudge-wink-iness of the 'homosexual-dressed-as-a-lesbian' bit. Or of the fact that it tells us nothing we didn't already know, in a style already overused by Young himself. I'd like to see something elegant and excoriating for a change, instead of just reading a series of journalists calling each other cunts. I'd like it if we could be better than this, not as nasty, but somehow still funny and not smug or self-righteous. Piece of piss, I reckon. JoAnne Harris, Twitter

Much as I hate Toby Young this is just the usual thing: a predictable, polite middle-class person talking to other predictable, polite middle-class people like himself. In fact, Stewart Lee is not really a comedian, he's more of a smart-arse, something else altogether. Mike Spilligan, Twitter

My desperate bid to match Boris Johnson's colossal lies

28 January 2018

When Boris Johnson announced in a press conference on Thursday his intent to fly to the moon in a basket carried by enormous swans, as part of an ongoing quest to seek out new post-Brexit trading partners outside the EU, it seemed the logical end point of a political career characterised by the propagation of elephantine falsehoods. And yet no lie is too big, it seems, and Johnson endures.*

Any half-decent journalist would have destroyed Johnson's moon-swan lies immediately, but his Friday-morning interview with Nick Robinson on Radio 4 displayed the feeble

---

* The previous week, Boris had claimed to be planning to build a bridge across the Channel to France, an obvious propaganda distraction from the Brexit disaster he helped cause. About a decade ago, I was walking the Offa's Dyke path with my friend, the poet, gardening expert and confectionery historian Tim Richardson. A church we stopped at, in Llandaff, I think, had been the seat of one Francis Godwin (1562–1633), subsequently Bishop of Hereford. His proto-science-fiction fantasy *The Man in the Moone*, published five years after his death, concerns a man who flees to the moon in a basket drawn by swans, where he meets the moon king, Irdonozur. On a North Devon trek we visited a hut and a remote cave, once inhabited by the poets Ronald Duncan and Robert Stephen Hawker respectively, and in Pendeen we crawled through slurry in the farmyard of the antiquarian William Borlase to get into a prehistoric ceremonial chamber. I miss our walks, but I am fat and slow now and my knees have been Clarkson'd to bits. Now, I already can't even do the thing I thought I'd spend my retirement doing, and I am only fifty.

indulgence we have come to expect from the gumless *Today* programme.

Johnson told Robinson he was looking forward to meeting the moon king, Irdonozur, who he thought was 'exactly the sort of person we should be in business with', and Robinson didn't even feel the need to point out that no such lunar monarch exists.

Robinson didn't even intervene when Johnson declared that he wasn't 'the least bit scared of moon-piccaninnies or moon-bumboys for that matter', and that he would be taking his friend, the convicted fraudster and gold smuggler Darius Guppy, to the moon with him, and that Darius would have any disobedient moon-piccaninnies and moon-bumboys 'knocked to the ground' and covered in horse manure.*

Footage on CBBC's *Newsround* later, of Johnson standing by a bus emblazoned with the legend 'Let's fly to the moon in a swan-drawn basket and knock the moon-bumboys to the ground and cover them in horse manure', barely even a raised eyebrow from presenter Ricky Boleto,† who seemed stricken with a terrible ennui beyond his years at the very thought of more of Johnson's colossal and time-consuming lies.

Meanwhile, predictable newspaper cartoons slung the familiar image of the crash-helmeted Johnson, waving flags while

---

* This paragraph is a mixture of comments Boris Johnson has made about homosexuals and black people and mangled quotes from a transcript of a phone call with his friend, the convicted fraudster Darius Guppy, during which the latter outlined how he would exact violent revenge on a journalist who had wronged him, with Johnson's help. Guppy's mother, Shushā, was, bizarrely, a purveyor of the kind of '70s Iranian folk rock now prized by crate-digging collectors. Personally, my favourite psychedelic Iranian is Kourosh Yaghmaei.

† I don't really know anything about Ricky Boleto. It just felt right to name him here.

suspended from a zip wire, beneath a flock of soaring swans.*

Even seasoned political observers finally find themselves asking: what on earth is Johnson playing at? Some think the answer lies in the Dead Cat Strategy, pioneered by the Tories' former attack dog, Lynton Crosby. Crosby's main contribution to political discourse has been the idea that a massive distraction, such as throwing a dead cat on a table or announcing your intention to fly to the moon with Darius Guppy in a swan-drawn basket, will divert public attention from some ongoing political disaster, such as the entire last eighteen months.

Some cynics even suggest that the public disgrace of Johnson's crony Toby Young was actually dead-cat driven. Did the Conservative media machine maintain Young's implausible career only so as to have a dead cat ready to fling on the table when they needed one? Was Toby Young the Lee Harvey Oswald of the failing Brexit negotiations?

I'm not sure that Johnson's pathological dishonesty is quite that calculated. I suspect he liked the attention that his lies got him. But suddenly he is being trounced in the funny-toff stakes by Jacob Tree-Frog, and his Brexit lies – the £350 million a week for the NHS, the fabled 'cake and eat it' trade deal – are dissolving like David Davis in a hail of hot facts.

So Johnson is having to mouth ever more vast lies to get the attention he once earned from lesser falsehoods, like a veteran motorcycle stuntman, long past his peak, incrementally driven towards an audience-maintaining jump over a massive lake of sharks that he knows will finally kill him.

On my desk is a stack of commemorative Brexit coins, price £4.99 each. I ordered them from a Brexiteer on eBay in a moment

---

* Like all the cleverest villains, Boris Johnson conceals his evil nature with absurd theatrics.

of mean-spiritedness, because they are emblazoned with the misspelt slogan 'I voted to get back our sovereign independance'. The tragedy of it, the black, black comedy of the thing.*

But the coins made me remember the act I did on the fledgling comedy circuit, back in the 1980s, and how it related to the nuclear escalation of Johnson's weaponised lies. Older comedy fans may remember the early days of 'alternative' comedy, when bills weren't simply twenty-something stand-ups in trousers remembering recent cultural ephemera. Back then, those pub-back-room bills featured a host of absurd 'spesh' acts: the Amazing Mr Smith, who sang satirical songs with his head in a birdcage full of actual birds; Steve Murray, who dismembered teddy bears while doing an impression of Tommy Cooper; the Iceman, a favourite of mine, who stood on stage with a big block of ice, describing how and why it was melting; and the late Malcolm Hardee, who, among other things, could make his testicles look like various British wartime politicians.†

* These exist. And I have one.

† All the above acts were/are real, and how I miss those days. The longing makes me ache. Every night I left our shared house in Acton to play unpaid try-out spots, in 1989, '90, '91, I felt like I might catch the end of some punk-hippy novelty-comedy aesthetic that was on the way out as the men-in-T-shirts steamroller lurched forward. I saw the Amazing Mr Smith only once, at the King's Head, in Crouch End, and he is dead now, as is Malcolm Hardee, whose funeral I spoke at. What a privilege to see these people, what an unalloyed privilege. And I sound like my own grandparents, saying how the past was better. I know, I know. I'm drinking wine and it's late. In the last eighteen months, we have lost lots of fifty-something comedians whom I knew from the early days, including Sean Hughes, Jimmy 'Jim Macabre' Miller and Jack Russell, all of them restless souls who found some sort of home in the comedy community, even if only temporarily. The terse Scot Jimmy Miller wrote the following joke: 'If an infinite number of

My own spesh involved me stuffing, or giving the impression of stuffing, a succession of coins of various foreign currencies up my back passage, while dressed in a tutu and playing the bodhrán. 'And now, ladies and gentlemen, the Icelandic 50 krona coin, the 50 krona. Here we go . . .'*

---

monkeys were given an infinite number of typewriters, eventually they would write, "Hey, hey, we're the monkeys."' He hadn't done a gig for twenty-five years and died under reduced circumstances, but was fondly remembered. At his wake, the only evidence that remained of Jim's comedy career was the photocopied flyers we used to advertise gigs in the '80s. Handing them round in the room above the Camden Head was like time travel. Jim set up the 'New Material' night that ran there, and at the Market Tavern down the road, from 1988 onwards. It was the circuit's first new-material night – until that point no one thought anyone would ever need new material – and in 1990, the biweekly team was Jim, me, Jo Brand, Hattie Hayridge, Mr Nasty, Simon Munnery, Mark Lamarr, Geoff Green, Eddie Izzard and the future playwright Patrick Marber, who at the time was heavily influenced by the unsung alternative clown Andrew Bailey. Both Jim and Sean Hughes were very kind, and also sometimes calculatedly cruel, to me at various times. You could argue that even though he betrayed his early promise by becoming a TV panel-show regular, Sean's 1990 Edinburgh show invented long-form stand-up in the UK and Ireland as we know it, an approach that is finally even influencing the less substantial form of American stand-up, via Hannah Gadsby's watershed *Nanette* hour on Netflix. Jim, in turn, saw alternative comedy as a branch of punk rock, and was terminally disappointed by the failure of its practitioners to live up to those standards. At his wake we found out that his cousin, who emigrated from Glasgow as a child, had just written the new Warner Bros animated comedy *Smallfoot*. It all made me feel very old, and very mortal, and very lucky. My act is still made from bits of Sean and Jim and many of the other comics whose sets seared themselves into my brain during my first three years or so of seeing stand-up.

* I didn't do this.

I was starting to make a name for myself, although admittedly that name was Roger Rectum Currency. Then suddenly, some-time around 1985, along came the uber-clown Chris Lynam, who launched actual lit fireworks from his actual anus, and now a man pretending to put yen into his wasn't impressive any more. I soon switched to straight stand-up, as it happened a more lucra-tive, but arguably less dignified, art form.

Suddenly, his lies no longer igniting the public imagination like they once did, Johnson himself is Roger Rectum Currency in his managed decline, needing to draw the public eye with ever more extravagant lies.

And maybe I am facing a similar dilemma. The political situ-ation has been so stupid now, for so long, it seems beyond satire. In print, and on stage, I reach for ever more desperate methods to mock it. And then my eye falls on that pile of commemorative British 'independance' coins. And I realise I may have stumbled across the answer. I'm sure I have that tutu somewhere.

I think Frankie Boyle would have said it better, funnier and in half the number of words. Dunkeldog

'. . . no such lunar monarch exists.' Of course not. Irdonozur is President of the Moon. Another woeful misunderstanding by our so called Foreign Secretary. Smallbones

Typical lefty luvvie quisling talking down the Lunarian trade deal. Feral Prole

Was this article supposed to be funny? Birkenhead90210

On my first night at Uni I watched Chris Lynam blow his own bollocks off when his firework went off prematurely. We thought it was immaculately-timed comedy. He ended up in Preston Royal Infirmary. Shakey Dave

I enjoyed that so much that I'd love to read more. Please let me know from which first form school magazine you copied it, I would like to see the occasional copy just to check whether or not the authors have grown up. Ricmondo

Satire only makes Jacob Rees-Mogg stronger

11 February 2018

Take heed, the metropolitan liberal elite! Cower, all you Conservative moderates!! Weep, environmentalists, and prepare your online petitions!!! Jacob Rees-Mogg is upon you, a black darkness over the shire, a shade upon your allotments. And your ancient weapons will not work upon his impervious hide, their keen blades blunt upon the armour of his cruel certainties.

This Rees-Mogg is no Boris Johnson, the blowhard balloon animal who eventually blew himself up, spattering onlookers with a residue of sticky lies. It's impossible to imagine now that once, only mere months ago, those who would enslave us regarded this gluteus oaf as their strongest asset; this blundering liability, whose greatest supporters now buckle under the heavy arse of his incompetence manifest, even as Johnson himself clings for survival, the cleverest piglet in the flooded farmyard, to the unexpectedly buoyant rubber ring of the suddenly viable Jacob Rees-Mogg.*

Neither is Rees-Mogg a Gove, that cunning twig, nursing ambition beyond the scope of his tiny wooden body, buffeted by the river currents, hoping to drift towards the distant shore of victory and blown along the surface by the storm breath of his giantess troll. These two – the tiny twig and his fair-weather friend, the burst balloon animal and swimming pig – may yet be remembered as nothing more than the twin Ikea mini-stepladders upon which Rees-Mogg raised himself as

---

* I have compared Boris Johnson to a piglet again. Poor.

he reached up towards the blown forty-watt lightbulb of Tory leadership.

Journalists and wits! TV panel-show satirists!! And all the historic enablers of *Have I Got News for You*, unwitting celebrity engineers of the Boris Johnson golem!!!* To rankle Rees-Mogg you need a charm word even more powerful than John Crace's 'Maybot', which damned an already doomed leader in two conjoined syllables. But you have nothing. Your arrows of satire are blunt before him and your broken spears sleep in your hands, which are clawed uselessly into the shape of decades of lunchtime pints.†

You call Rees-Mogg 'the honourable member for the eighteenth century', and Rees-Mogg ingests the insult and owns it; he takes it as the highest compliment, and it makes him stronger. He is Stan Lee's Absorbing Man, and even the Norse gods are no match for him.

Rees-Mogg acts as if all his political positions are the result of nothing but quiet contemplation of the facts, with no visible emotions to betray the idea that they may be anything other than totally objective. You cannot hurt his feelings. He admits to none. You may as well stand in an aquarium hurling insults at an eel or swear at a chutney.

(Long ago, in my capacity as Britain's most consistently critically acclaimed stand-up comedian, I learned to treat all heckles, however aggressive, as if they were genuine inquiries made by people who were not fortunate enough to have recognised my

---

* That fucking golem thing again for, what is it now, the eighth time or something? Why don't I make myself out of clay and go and live in medieval Prague if I love golems so much, that's what I say to me.

† I do feel, controversially, that satire has failed to reckon with the lying Brexiteers.

genius. Rees-Mogg affects to regard all outbursts of noisy protest as the babbling of people sadly too foolish to realise that he is right, appearing to pity those who hate him for their lack of understanding. It may be that he is doing this consciously. Or it may be that the machine of privilege and entitlement that has fashioned Rees-Mogg has done its work so well it is simply impossible for him to believe otherwise. Either way, it's an impregnable strategy.)

'The honourable member for the eighteenth century!' You will have to do better than that. For Rees-Mogg is upon us, his cold breath on our heels. Eventually, as Boris Johnson has shown us, even a public raised on *Britain's Got Talent* and tomato sauce-flavoured crisps tires of empty novelty, and the allure of Rees-Mogg will fade. But by that time, what damage may already have been done?*

But as all around us crumbles, a plucky band of little folk nonetheless stands firm against the wraiths of the government's far right: old Bilbo Ken Clarke Baggins, upon the road to Rivendell with Sonny Rollins's *Freedom Suite* bopping on his Walkman; little Frodo Soubry, stepping forward in grim determination with her loyal follower, tiny Samwise Greening; all under the protection of ancient Treebeard Heseltine, a speaking and often incoherent tree of indeterminate vintage. This brave band sets off to save the Tory party and, by association, the nation from itself.

* As I write these notes, in February 2019, it seems Rees-Mogg's stealth strategy has paid off. Boris Johnson has blown himself out, but Rees-Mogg's European Research Group is a powerbroker in the Brexit clusterfuck.

'. . . the honourable member for the 18th century.' How fresh. Marc Adams

'The honourable member for the 18th century!' This was not really that amusing the first million times it was parroted. Now that is has been repeated more times than there are atoms in the universe it really is starting to pall just a little bit. Any chance of reaching for a bit of originality some time soon? HogarthOpines

Lee, of course, was at Oxford with Johnson, Ree-Mogg and many other influential people who have developed media careers on the strength of the contacts they made. I left 'laughable' out of the description of Lee. I didn't think it appropriate because he has seldom made people laugh. Rowlocks

What is a 'gluteus oaf?' Maybe you mean 'glutinous'? or maybe your vocabulary is as imprecise as your rather woolly mind and you just fire off adjectives for the sake of it. Claire Brittain

What a load of febrile tripe. 'Gluteus' isn't even an adjective. KevinK

It's very gratifying to see public school toffs like Stewart Lee and Rees Mogg turn on each other. Maybe they will wipe themselves out and we won't have the ultra privileged filling the political, entertainment and media arenas by promoting 'chaps like us'. Morrisseysmiff

Stewart, if you want to know how to write a funny and pointed article read ANYTHING by Marina Hyde . . . JohhnyV321

Possibly the worst and most bizarre article I've ever read. Mikemills2016

I think he's trying to be funny – 'edgy': the entire piece sounds like Lee's hero and mentor, Russell Brand. Ronniestorrs

What an evil article. A pompous and self satisfied diatribe against one of the few honest and honourable members of Parliament. JRM certainly has the lefty illiberal Corbynista worried. What an eye opener this article has proven to be! It has brought the nasty party and remoaner rats swarming out of their sewers into the light of day! If anyone was in doubt as to who the true vermin in our society are, this extraordinary outburst of hate against an honourable man, who has done nothing more than publicly state his honest opinions, has really shown what sort of people support the EU and Momentum. Thank you Stewart Lee. Pongoid

I very much doubt the *Guardian* would allow articles which described women as swimming pigs. Peter Wizard

Stand-up comedians are part of the problem; they have been since Thatcher. Since then, all you have to do is say how superior you are to this or that reactionary bogeyman/woman's supporters, how much less racist, sexist, etc., you are. The Radio 4 audience have a good laugh, then troop off home to get on with their private, and privatised lives. Failed

What a vile piece! If I wrote stuff like this online the cops might show up . . . Nathan Alexander

I live in hope of the day when Lee chokes on his own bile. Rowlocks

Is a sci-fi-style dystopia such a bad outcome for Brexit?

25 February 2018

For nearly eighteen months now, the increasingly frustrated European liberal fat-cat elite has been asking for some clues as to what we brave British Brexiteers imagine Brexit will be, the pastry edifice of Theresa May's monumental 'Brexit means Brexit' statement having already crumbled last year, when a moth's tear fell near it.

Unable to say what Brexit is, a strategically and heroically vague David Davis last week chose instead to tell Brussels what Brexit isn't, promising, definitively, that Brexit will not be 'a *Mad Max*-style world',* despite evidence to the contrary commissioned by his own department.

Andrea Leadsom, meanwhile, has clarified that Brexit will not be 'some ham', Jacob Rees-Mogg has stated categorically that Brexit will not be 'a drawing of Alain Delon',† while Dan 'Dan' Hananananan has further elucidated that Brexit will also not be 'a kind of thing with all stuff on it, and brown stripes, going up and down, like humbug mints on an escalator or some hot bees'.

---

* David Davis, speaking to Austrian business leaders, 19 February 2018.

† Alain Delon, along with Sylvie Vartan and Johnny Hallyday, is part of a raft of 1960s French celebrities who remain at the forefront of my mind, as they featured in the patronisingly youth-friendly French textbooks that we were issued with at school in 1979, by which time they were already fifteen fast-moving cultural years out of date. Presumably there is a fifty-year-old Frenchman somewhere, similarly puzzled by memories of a textbook featuring Simon Dee, Sharon Tandy and The Applejacks.

In the light of Davis's assurances that we will not be 'plunged into a *Mad Max*-style world borrowed from dystopian fiction', I wonder how much worse the post-Brexit dystopia could be anyway? Would the air of the capital remain technically toxic? Would there be nuclear power stations abandoned in danger-ous disrepair? Would the oceans choke on plastic? Would secure housing be a pipe dream for millions? Would Boris Johnson still be free to scatter his lies at midnight into sleeping children's eyes?

For many of the disenfranchised and disenchanted Britons who voted for Brexit, being plunged into a *Mad Max*-style dys-topia would represent an improvement in their living condi-tions! Perhaps being plunged into a *Mad Max*-style dystopia is one of the few tangible benefits of Brexit!! Especially if it was sunny and featured Tina Turner as an Amazonian cyber-punk!!! And anyway, better to live one day free in a *Mad Max*-style dystopia than a thousand years as a slave in the world's largest single-market area!!!!

I worry that the idea that we will be 'plunged' into a *Mad Max*-style dystopia is a little optimistic. The word 'plunged' suggests events would unfold with a speed and decisiveness so far absent from the Brexit process. After a few years of sliding slowly and painfully into a *Mad Max*-style dystopia, with no clear end to the plunging in sight, Leave voters will look back at the suggestion that we were to be plunged into anything at all as just another example of the lying betrayals of their feckless and apparently unaccountable Brexit cheerleaders. Where was the plunge into a *Mad Max*-style dystopia we were promised?

But what do I know? I have not even seen any of the *Mad Max* movies, though last year Brendan McCarthy, co-writer of the recent reboot, *Mad Max: Fury Road*, described me as 'an archaic leftwing relic', adding: 'Milo Yiannopoulos is more on the zeitgeist.' But where is the discredited alt-right provocateur

Milo Yiannopoulos now? Nowhere. And where am I? I am in a three-star hotel room in Stratford-upon-Avon, eating a bag of humbug mints, which are what gave me the idea for the closing sentence of the third paragraph. I win.*

And anyway, the best dystopian sci-fi film is not *Mad Max*, but the straight-to-video *Mad Max* rip-off *World Gone Wild* (Lee H. Katzin, 1987),† which I bought on VHS from a shop called Rimpy's Fags, Foods and Non-Foods on Horn Lane in Acton for 50p in 1989.‡ (*World Gone Wild* was, of course, filed in the

---

* After finishing and filing this article, I went for a walk in the town and saw the actor who now plays the first doctor in *Doctor Who*, William Hartnell having died, wandering around the shops.

† The reason *World Gone Wild* is a better dystopian sci-fi movie than Brendan McCarthy's stupid *Mad Max: Fury Road*, for example, is because it doesn't have a colon in the middle of its title like what a idiot would do; and because it stars Adam Ant as a man called Derek Abernathy, who, in a plot copied off Kurosawa's *Seven Samurai*, harries a plucky village of survivors in a *Mad Max*-style dystopia; and because it co-stars the bewildering actor Alan Autry, who played a gay footballer in the controversial gay *Cheers* episode 'The Boys in the Bar', but went on to become the anti-gay mayor of Fresno, California; and because I've seen it and you never will. I win. Again.

‡ How thrillingly afraid I was at 32 Hereford Rd, off Horn Lane in Acton, for the first eighteen months I lived in London, from September 1989, with two would-be actors and the future pod-king Richard Herring. What would become of me, this boy adrift in the city? Within a few weeks of arriving, our front room was commandeered for police surveillance of a drug den opposite. Mr Chaudhry, the uncommonly fair landlord, dealt with the wasps' nests by putting plastic bags over his hands, and he gave us horrible wine at Christmas, free. And we bought all our food and fags from Rimpy's. I became a professional comedian while I lived there, and was soon making twice my £50 a week rent from gigs in rooms above pubs. The first weekend we lived in Acton, the four of us won the Sunday meat raffle in the Duke of York, Steyne Road. It

non-foods section of the store, along with the wood, a fossilised coelacanth and Terence Trent D'Arby.)*

David Davis rightly became the immediate target of the high-speed satire sausage machines of social media's infinite monkey treadmill for his foolish *Mad Max* metaphor, but imagine if he had been just a little more pop-culturally literate, in the way that Tories just never are.

Imagine if, instead of saying Britain would not be 'plunged into a *Mad Max*-style world borrowed from dystopian fiction', David Davis had said Britain would not be 'plunged into a Derek Abernathy-style world. You know? Derek Abernathy? The Adam Ant character in *World Gone Wild*? Haven't you seen it? Steve Jones from the Sex Pistols' forgotten '80s hair-metal band Chequered Past do the theme tune.' The confused corrupt Eurocrat fat cats of Brussels would have immediately sent their researchers off to score copies of *World Gone Wild* to decode Davis's latest opaque clue as to what Britain imagined Brexit was, thus buying Davis more time to invoke ever more obscure dystopian sci-fi movies in his quest to hide the dispiriting truth.

'I tell you what Brexit won't be. It won't be like that one set two years from now, where Christian Bale and a group of bedraggled

---

was a good omen. London would provide for us hopeful provincials, as if it were our mother.

* Credit here is due to my friend, the ex-comedian and Pyrenean goat enthusiast Roger Mann, who realised as long ago as 1992 that the name of the '80s pop star Terence Trent D'Arby, in comedy terms, sat at the perfect mid-point between obscurity and recognition, and was blessed with an inherently comic rhythm. I forget which of Roger's routines it was that included the phrase 'my mother, my father and Terence Trent D'Arby', but I know it was something to do with the narrator eating 'a fine plump capon'.

survivors hide in a desolate English wasteland attacked by giant dragons. *Rain of Fire*, wasn't it? No, *Reign of Fire*.

'Well, whatever, it won't be like that. Or Enzo Castellari's *The New Barbarians*, where the American footballer Fred Williamson* is a kind of Jedi ninja in a desert ruled by lawless bikers. Brexit won't be like that. Or a drawing of Alain Delon.'

Dear Stewart, In a democracy, you have the right to express your opinion. Which is that you'd rather die free tomorrow than live 'a thousand years as a slave'. All to the good and well. But your right of expression is balanced by others having themselves the same right to an opposite opinion. That is to freely choose to stay 'slaves' if they find this condition satisfying. Tell you what, if you really believe your quoted opinion above, please go live free in any war torn country for a full satisfying free day. And then depart this sad world. That way your wish will be fulfilled without impacting the lives of other people by removing the rights they use to live their daily lives 'as a slave in the world's largest single market area'. Dragon Jade

From edgy to Establishment in a few *Guardian* columns. Shame. That's how the *Guardian* neuter change on behalf of the Establishment. They commandeer threats to write columns and in no time at all they are repeating the tired old Establishment lines as if they thought of them themselves. Now you are thinking of all the times it happened. Keeps us in line,

* Ex-footballer Fred 'The Hammer' Williamson also appears in the 1974 blaxploitation movie *Three the Hard Way*, mentioned earlier in this book.

I suppose, plus the mouthpiece gets a fat Czech.* Maybe I'd sell out with all the riches they dangled before me. Like carrying a fun at a high school, you don't really know what you would do until it happens. Minutehands

'The confused corrupt Eurocrat fat cats of Brussels'. Neither funny nor accurate. Ratujone2

Rimpy's in Acton. They did Airfix models too. A veritable cornucopia of interesting artefacts. John O'Donnell

There goes 5 minutes of my life I'll never get back. Eyepatch

The Brexit Dystopia will be a bit like the late Dave Bowie's *Diamond Dogs* where rats the size of cats eat hats the size of gnats. What it definitely won't be is like the late Mark E Smith's dystopia where all England is a university town and all you can get is wine. Clark Gwent

I'm at Stew's Dartford show right now. It's the interval. He's handling it quite well, fair play to him. He won't be back though, you can tell. ID224110

---

* I hope this 'fat Czech' is some kind of obscure joke about Rupert Murdoch, or is this post more rushed troll-factory piecework?

The Brexit culture wars are driving me bananas

4 March 2018

On 10 May 2016, in the closing days of the Brexit campaign, during an impromptu speech in Cornwall, lying Boris Johnson again invoked the Brexiteers' foundation myth that the EU sought to ban bendy bananas. But voters who backed leaving the EU in order to get back the bendy bananas, which had not been taken off them anyway, must surely now be wondering, privately, if it was all worth it.

Last Monday, Jeremy Corbyn reluctantly declared his own 'bespoke customs union' Brexit fudge, with all the enthusiasm and conviction of a man held at gunpoint saying how well he is being treated. 'The option of a new UK customs union with the EU would need to ensure the UK has a say in future trade deals,' he mumbled. 'Also, I am allowed to coddle an egg on alternate Tuesdays.'*

---

* As I believe I wrote earlier, I had never heard of coddled eggs until Corbyn said he liked to eat them, when he was a guest on a 2017 edition of *Celebrity Gogglebox*. Suddenly, coddled eggs are one of those things which, once you are aware of them, seem to be everywhere! Not in Swaffham, though. Last February, driving through the Norfolk market town and noting it was full of charity shops, I assumed it would be easy pickings for egg coddlers. Well, how wrong I was. There were a lot of people on heroin, though. In a related incident, only yesterday (31 March 2019) I found two egg coddlers in a Cancer Research charity shop in Marlborough, Wiltshire. I bought them, for £3.50 each, and then went to meet my wife in Boots. I asked her if she had been in the Cancer Research shop, which she had, and then I ridiculed her for having overlooked the

Apparently, Corbyn's Own Brexit Fudge™® was offered to preserve the soft Irish border with Northern Ireland, as it will be impossible to re-bend a straightened Euro banana should a straight Irish banana need to cross into British territory, perhaps as part of an Irish child's snack box, an Irish chimp's dinner or as an Irish clown's comedy prop.

Some Tory Brexiteers have an almost blind faith in the idea that there may be some form of as-yet-non-existent techno-logical solution. Bernard Jenkin, interviewed by an increasingly scruffy Dobby the House Elf* on *Newsnight* on Tuesday, said Wilf

---

coddlers. She explained she had seen them, but as there was all old egg congealed into the rims, she hadn't bought them. I saw that she was right and realised I had to get rid of the coddlers. I went over the road to a dog charity shop and gave them to the man behind the counter there as a donation. The egg coddlers had travelled a few hundred yards at a cost to me of £7. I rang up the writer and performance artist Ben Moor to tell him what I had done, because it was like something the life-coach guru Jackson would have done in Will Adamsdale's brilliant comedy theatre piece *Jackson's Way*, which had inspired both of us. Jackson believed a form of enlightenment could be achieved by the performance of pointless acts, such as moving small amounts of litter from once place to another, i.e. from London to Melbourne. (Fifteen years ago, I sat in a café in Melbourne and saw Adamsdale, thinking no one was watching him, taking British litter out of a bag he had brought with him from London and putting it into an Australian litter bin. Superb!) While I was on the phone, a man recognised me, despite the fact that I was bearded and in a woolly hat, and asked for a selfie, so I wandered off. I sat on a bench by the river on my own. Another old man with a beard and a woolly hat came and sat next to me and started talking about his drug and mental-health problems and his bipolar girlfriend. He thought I was the same as him and would understand.

* I think I must have been thinking of Evan Davis here, but I don't remember.

Lunn,* the extravagantly moustachioed novelty-bicycle inventor from *Vision On* and *Magpie*, was already working on a bespoke Border Banana Detector and Straightener™®.

Lunn's Borderbananandetecto-straightorbendomatic™® would detect and straighten, or bend, any bananas crossing the border, so they would be the right banana type for the segment of the Irish island they were bound for. Jenkin's attempt to demonstrate a prototype Borderbananandetecto-straightorbendomatic in the *Newsnight* studio backfired spectacularly after it lunged at political editor Nicholas Watt's face and tried to peel it.

Honestly! You couldn't make it up!! It's an increasingly difficult time to be a comedian!!! (And before I forget, message to Bernard 'Jenkin': Jenkin is a French name. No one is called 'Jenkin' here. Your British name is Jenkins. Bernard Fucking Jenkins. So start using it.)

But Corbyn's Own Brexit Fudge™® is as impossible a proposition for the EU in its own way as Boris Johnson's pre-referendum fantasy of the magic cake that grows again, no matter how much of it you eat, an idea the massive liar surely gleaned from a visit to one of the cloud lands at the top of the Faraway Tree, before sliding back down the Slippery Slip with his friends Darius, Marina,† Petronella‡ and the Saucepan Man.§

* Lunn is in fact the world's leading expert on novelty bicycles.

† Wheeler, second wife.

‡ Wyatt, *Spectator* columnist. Boris Johnson lied about his affair with her, and so was sacked as shadow arts minister in 2005. Toby Young, *Spectator* critic, who was later appointed to the board of the Office for Students by Boris Johnson's brother Jo, co-wrote a play about the scandal called *Whose the Daddy?* Sometimes it seems that, for the tight-knit circle of the Tory Brexiteers, the world is just a playground in which everything is a wizard wheeze and nothing matters.

§ I had been reading Enid Blyton's badly written fantasy *The Magic Faraway*

Whether you are a kamikaze hard Brexiteer or a diehard traitor Remoaner, the precision-applied works spanner of Corbyn's Own Brexit Fudge™® means hard Brexit is far less likely. *Banzai!* Boris Johnson's dream of bendy bananas for ever withers on the banana vine, a cowed people cowering for eternity beneath the blow of the straight banana, a straight banana squished on a human face – for ever. But the culture war continues.

Last Monday, on the Twitter, the *Mad Max* writer and Milo Yiannopoulos cheerleader Brendan McCarthy called me a 'decaying Morrissey impersonator and leftwing donut-eater', and declared: 'It's end times for the Oxbridge comedy establishment as their own Roy "Chubby" Brown lashes out at an indifferent public.'

While I never knowingly eat doughnuts, I am admittedly too heavy to be allowed to use some waterslides, and 'lashing out at an indifferent public' is a reasonable description of the impression I strive to create live. In fact, detractors often inadvertently illuminate exactly the effect I aim for, their harshest criticisms helping me to sculpt the on-stage character of Stewart Lee.

But as I stood, on the 194th date of my current 220-date tour, on stage in Dartford last Sunday, my hyper-acoustic ears still ringing from a catastrophic sound-operator error at Hereford Courtyard on Thursday,* the room somehow just would not quite catch fire. I wondered if *Mad Max* McCarthy was right.

Tree to my daughter, as my mother in turn read it to me when I could not sleep for fear of monsters in the dark. I was twenty-eight years old.

* I was knocked to the floor by a feedback blast during the soundcheck, caused by an inexperienced technician. I couldn't stand or see. All I could hear for hours was shrieking. I did the show blind, on autopilot, and threw up at half-time. My dormant tinnitus was triggered and is still humming two years later. I suppose it's an occupational hazard. I wonder if you can perform your set from behind a Perspex screen, like the drummer from Mission of Burma?

Was it indeed 'end times for the Roy "Chubby" Brown of the Oxbridge comedy establishment'?

In April last year, the *Daily Telegraph*, the *Daily Mail*, the *Daily Express*, Breitbart, the *Spectator*, *ShortList* and *Spiked* all ran the same demonstrably false story saying I was experiencing mass walkouts because of doing anti-Brexit jokes. This wasn't the case, even in archly Eurosceptic Lincoln, although, to be fair, the people there may have struggled to find the exits without hard-working eastern Europeans to show them the way and carry their cauliflowers around. The only walkout of the tour was a very funny man in Canterbury, who shouted 'I'll wait for the DVD' as he left, but I don't think his departure, unlike David Cameron's, was Brexit-related.

Last year, it was fun doing anti-Brexit material on tour. The Brexiteers in the room had won the referendum, after all, so as a Remoaner I was in a position of weakness punching up at them, as the comedian is required to. Laughing Brexiteers would come up afterwards and magnanimously get me to sign their books and DVDs 'to a Leave-voting c*nt', an amusing transaction that genuinely renewed my faith in humanity nightly. We could all be friends after all.*

But on Monday, after Corbyn proposed his hard Brexit-sinking 'bespoke customs union', it seemed like no one was going to get exactly what they wanted out of Brexit now.† There probably weren't going to be any winners, certainly not the Leave voters of

---

* How long ago those halcyon days of agreeing to differ seem now.

† Sadly for die-hard Remoaners like me, this Corbyn strategy failed, and his subsequent interventions in the Brexit process were to become increasingly equivocal and ineffectual, as he tried to keep Brexit-voting Labour voters onside, gradually alienating Labour's Remain-voting membership.

Leave-voting Dartford, now condemned, even their figureheads agree, to an even less prosperous future.[*]

So on stage in Dartford, I didn't feel I quite understood how to pitch the Brexit stuff any more. In a situation where no one will win, there were no winners to aim at. It was not clear any more which way was up, and I no longer knew which direction to punch upwards in.

Since the referendum was called I've had to listen to complete idiots argue the same points and rehashed quips over and over, both Leave and Remain. It's like watching two neanderthals repeatedly head butt each another, showing increasing signs of brain injury as the debates go on. To know that both neanderthals are going to be absolutely fucking miserable, whatever happens, is the only solace I can find. Vanmyp

The earliest art in Europe was created by Neanderthals. Wardpj

'So on stage in Dartford, I didn't feel I quite understood how to pitch the Brexit stuff any more.' Brexit as comedy hinged on

---

[*] Before my evening performance there was an afternoon show at the Dartford venue by the '60s Irish singing group The Bachelors, which I missed. In 1971, at the age of three, I saw them sing Paul Simon's 'Sound of Silence' while being held prisoner by the giant in *Jack and the Beanstalk*, at the Birmingham Hippodrome. It was a formative experience, and one which I was subsequently to try to recreate via the lighting state for one of the numbers in *Jerry Springer: The Opera*. The Bachelors were fumbling about by the stage door in Dartford as I arrived, and I wanted to explain all this to them, but I thought it would be weird. Peter Glaze and Don Maclean, from *Crackerjack*, and Frank Carson also appeared in the pantomime, but I have no memory of them at all.

a kind of Schadenfreude that those voting for it could be such idiots. Laughter was of the smug, group-think type, taking joy in being in the company of like minded people. It always was polemicism, and now it's polemics with old, hackneyed jokes, or maybe no jokes at all. You're going to have to find some new material. Or just give up, and leave the stage for others. Tongariro1

'. . . but how do I pitch my Brexit gags now?' Maybe stop desperately trying to pander to what you think is popular public opinion and tell some decent jokes, maybe? Dan York

Brendan McCarthy called me a 'decaying Morrissey impersonator and leftwing donut-eater'. You have to admit Stew, that is funny. Although I thought Jerry Sadowitz's observation about your 'comedy' were far more accurate: 'takes 3 hours to tell a barely adequate anecdote' Can't you just make people laugh instead? 'As s Remoaner I was in a position of weakness punching up at them, as the comedian is required to be.' Comedians aren't required to be anything other than funny. There is only one rule – making other people laugh (not just your friends) and that's it. There is no other. NoLivesMatter

I am in a foul mood this morning. And a comedian who used to be funny witerring on about Brexit (again) felt like the tin lid. Can you shut up about Brexit now? Many of us on this septic isle no longer care how it pans out, or even how it will be implemented – hard, soft, banana-shaped, bareback or droopy brewer. There comes a point when you just want the thing over. Unbritannia

pathetic virtue signalling. Taadaa

™ is used to indicate an unregistered trade mark and ® is used to signify a registered trade mark. It is nonsensical to use both of them together. I'm all ears if you can come up with any more hilarious material on intellectual property management. Caressofsteel

'Honestly! You couldn't make it up!! It's an increasingly difficult time to be a comedian!!!' This article makes that very clear. Leon Sphinx

Except of course that the EU did have regulations about bendy bananas as Annex 1 Subsection II point 10 highlights about there being no abnormal curvature allowed. They did of course later amend this due to all the ridicule they got – but why pretend that a regulation on bendy bananas never existed when it clearly did? The Ducks

Let's be fair Stewart Lee, the Brexit vote was on 23 June 2016, and yet you seem to think that the actual vote is still enough material to be riffing on, 20 months later. You've made the mistake of attempting to be a topical comedian, like on that *Mock The Week*, and it patently hasn't suited you. I realise that it is causing one of the biggest skidmarks in political and social history for many a decade, but it is a long, brown, ever thinning path, down which, you should not have gone, or at least, when the path became too thin for your overlapping waistband, you should have had the good sense to turn back . . . Hesalrightmydad

American Cornish pasties?
Did King Arthur die for this?

11 March 2018

Say 'Cornwall' to an uncontacted pygmy brave deep in a New Zealand forest and his bamboo flute will swiftly carve the shape of the Cornish pasty into the Shotover riverbank sands. 'Oggy, oggy, oggy,' he will cry, as he mimes pushing a too-hot Cornish pasty into his unambiguously delighted face. 'Oggy, oggy, oggy!'

But last Monday, the feast day of Cornwall's proud St Piran, American food industry lobbyists revealed plans to exploit the end of our protection by the EU's regional foods scheme. American 'Cornish' pasties could be on their way into Britain. And yet Arthur, who swore to return if his land was imperilled, sleeps soundly still in his Tintagel cave.*

---

* I chose to do my O-level history project on the difference between the King Arthur of history and the King Arthurs of literature and myth (you could do whatever you wanted, and most of the boys chose to study either Football, the Electric Guitar or the Holocaust). Thus, at fifteen, I had a working knowledge of the works of the Dark Ages chroniclers Nennius and Gildas, and of the medieval romances of Chrétien de Troyes and Godefroi de Leigni. My life since has been a gradual backsliding into ignorance, it seems. The summer after O-levels, in 1984, I remember discoursing fluently on the subject of Nennius with an antiques dealer at the Cornwall hippy/crusty rock festival the Elephant Fayre, which my mum reluctantly allowed me to attend alone as I was desperate to view The Fall for the first time, who played by the light of flaming brands in their mighty double-drum-kit incarnation. It was the greatest night of my life to date. My Nennius lecture seemed to last all night, as did the version of 'The Fool on the Hill' played by the covers band in the

American Cornish pasties? Say the horrible words and savour their bitter taste. Was this desecration what Leave-voting Cornwall voted for? Did proud Cornwall want the crusty food-stuff that has made Kernow beloved worldwide replaced by a foul foreign fake? Did Arthur die on adulterous Mordred's lance to see the sacred pasty cuckolded so? Did Henry Jenner, bard of Boscawen-Un, strive to revive Cornwall's lost language just so his cultural inheritors could ask the man in Pengenna Pasties for a King-Size American? Did the noble Cornish folk want nothing more than to be Donald Trump's Brexit pasty whores? Because that is all they are! Especially the people from London who own cottages there!! And Rick Stein!!!

The Leave-voting Cornish comedian Jethro Tull has appeared twice on the Leave-voting comedian Jim Davidson's *Generation Game* show, demonstrating how to make Cornish pasties.*

---

little tent where a nice lady had given me an unusual-tasting cup of tea. I mean, they must have played it for hours, round and round and round, with that crazy fairground-organ break. It was only years later that I worked out I had had my first psychedelic experience without even realising. The morning after seeing The Fall, and being spiked with psilocybin tea, I woke up in a field feeling ill. In the afternoon, I crapped rivers of blood in Gordano services, on the M4. And by the evening, I had been hospitalised in Birmingham with ulcerative colitis, my father having swiftly despatched me back to my mother's care at the first sign of trouble. Though this condition was to plague me for years, at least it kept me reasonably slim until my mid-thirties, and the worse I felt, and the more I bled, the better I looked. I wonder if the vision of medieval monks I saw at Fountains Abbey thirty years later was connected to my unwitting adolescent ingestion of hallucinogens, or did they, like my mother, have a message for me?

* I don't know the transmission date of either of the Jethro/Davidson pasty collaborations, and it has been impossible to check, but the footage is on YouTube.

During one sequence, Tull mocked the interfering EU for insisting pasty preparers wear gloves. Now, he and Davidson will be able to fly to America and see Cornish pasties being made by Hispanic slave labour from factory-farmed, hormone-ridden cattle, which are doused in petroleum, reduced to pulp and squeezed from automatic tubes into pre-moulded pasty pastry Hot Cornwall Pockets™®. Doubtless they are delighted.

If he could see the meat and potato atrocities about to be enacted in the name of his beloved Cornish pasties, Cornwall's holy St Piran would turn in his grave, had his remains not been split up and sent all around the country in the fourteenth century. As it is, one of St Piran's arms revolves in Exeter Cathedral, the other in Waltham Abbey, while his missing head spins somewhere undisclosed in St Piran's Old Church, Perranzabuloe.

In the *Mad Max* dystopia of our post-Brexit nation, it is unlikely hungry Britannia will have the luxury of rejecting Donald Trump's food regulation-relaxing advances, no matter how many times she slaps his tiny hands away from her cool thigh. Scotch whiskies, Melton Mowbray pork pies, Jersey Royal potatoes, Solihull stickleback slices* and Cumberland sausages,

---

* In 1970s Solihull, there were always sticklebacks in any freshwater between my home and the city centre, in the little streams and brooks that I played in as I crossed the fields of Tudor Grange school, Alderbrook school and the Technical College on my way to the park, unafraid of knife-wielding teens and predatory paedophiles, though in retrospect that latter were all around us, grabbing our pre-pubescent testicles in the showers or the bunk beds to see if our voices were due to break soon. Now, like the invertebrates, the sticklebacks are all gone and the world is visibly dying around us. It is strange to be able to have the thought, 'I took sticklebacks for granted,' but I did. We all did. In 1973, I watched from the passenger seat, thrilled, as a wild hare charged along Arnold Road, Shirley, in front of my grandfather's car, having

all sourced from the finest American processing plants, will soon foul our patriotic British palates. First they came for the West Cornwall Pasty Company. And then they came for me.

I will miss the West Cornwall Pasty Company's cheery wayside retail outlets, a Greggs for road-worn wayfarers who fear not the harsh crust nor the hot steak steam. Doubtless they are soon to close when cheap American imports undercut the business, sending hundreds of gainfully employed Cornish pasty-makers back to their old ancestral ways of piracy, smuggling and wrecking. The West Cornwall Pasty Company's honest fayre is one of the comforts of the road for an endlessly touring comedian,* and last week I needed my Cornish culinary compensation.

During these final weeks of my eighteen-month stand-up comedy tour around broken Brexit Britain, I have been reading the 1967 novel *Ice*, by the science-fiction pioneer and heroin enthusiast Anna Kavan, newly rescued from oblivion by Peter Owen Publishers. *Ice* eerily depicts a man travelling through a Kafkaesque collapsing society, beset by an encroaching ice age, against the backdrop of some imminent but unspecified political catastrophe. What ghostly forces of guidance compelled me to read this prophetic novel at this exact moment in time? Mother? Are you there? Is that you?

---

bolted from an ancient scrap of bluebell wood that had somehow survived between Ralph Road and Jacey Road, finally cut off from the Warwickshire wilderness by the outward expansion of Birmingham. I have only seen hares twice more in my life: once in the fields near Chedworth Roman Villa, in Gloucestershire; and again in Orkney, on the week of my fiftieth. Nearly half a century later, that urban-hare story seems unimaginable, like I'm saying I saw an ostrich in the back garden or a seal in an open sewer.

* I am currently too heavy, remember, to use some waterslides. Life on the road comes with collateral damage.

On Thursday night, I and my tour manager were trapped in Bristol by the Beast from the East* and I was denied two days back with my resentful family in London, as we remained there until Sunday and a date in Plymouth. An audience member's ice-skidding car had crashed into the loading doors of the Bristol theatre, where it remained for days, blocking our exit, closing the Overton window of our departure and tripling our hotel bill. I missed the kids and sat in reading *Ice*, worrying about their futures until my heart ached.

On Sunday we set off towards Plymouth.† Though the sudden snow was thawing, all along the A386 abandoned cars lay shipwrecked in laybys, ditched during Thursday's snowstorm and now stripped clean of parts and fabrics, the Devonshire locals reverting to type at the first sign of social breakdown.

At the Fox Tor café in Princetown, high on Dartmoor, above the prehistoric stone rows of Merrivale, I suspended my diet to stand and scoff a Cornish pasty, looking out across the ancient, frost-flecked landscape of the nation that made me. The pasty was good eating, and authentically Cornish too, but there was a bitter aftertaste not of its own making. As I ate into the pasty, I felt the very notion of Britain itself being eaten away, like some kind of enormous metaphor.

* The Beast from the East is the name of a now-annual cold wave of weather. It was this that trapped me in Bristol, and not Dokken's 1988 live album of the same name, recorded, predictably, in Japan.

† It occurs to me as I read this that I have spent most of my adult life on the move between gigs, like I was afraid of stasis. I've just booked another trip to Orkney. I want to get to the outlying islands this time, the ones you need to either charter a boat or take a weekly light aircraft flight to reach. I want to look at the crumbled funereal structures of dead civilisations on a blue-sky day at the very end of our islands, and to be beyond reach of mobile phones, staring into the northern horizon.

On his Cornish deathbed in 1934, the last Cornish words of the Cornish-language revivalist Henry Jenner were: 'Here in Cornwall, we do not need other meat and pastry products. The whole object of my life has been to inculcate into the Cornish people, and the Cornish pasties, a sense of their Cornishness. Either that chicken and mushroom slice goes or I do. Aaaagh!'*

How sad that Brexit befouls Jenner's legacy and turns his Cornish pasty to cows' dungs in our mouths. Wake, proud Arthur! Wake and bake!!

It's just 'Jethro' for the Cornish comedian. Jethro Tull is a '70s rock band, named after the 17th/18th century English agricultural pioneer. Jonoisalive

'. . . reduced to pulp and squeezed from automatic tubes into pre-moulded pasty pastry . . .' Too late – at least one major 'pasty' producer has been doing this for years and its products bear the description 'Cornish pasty' on their packaging. Fortunately there has been a revival of proper Cornish pasty baking by a number of small and even medium-sized pasty shops over the last few years and I've bought pasties that even my gran would have been proud to serve – and she was practically supernatural in the pasty-baking stakes! I've

---

* Supposedly, on his deathbed, Oscar Wilde said, 'This wallpaper will be the death of me. One of us will have to go,' which is remembered in the popular imagination as 'Either this wallpaper goes or I will.' (The Australian comedian Greg Fleet has a classic routine about this idea.) On *his* deathbed, Henry Jenner said, 'The whole object of my life has been to inculcate into Cornish people a sense of their Cornishness.' Not as funny as Wilde's quip, admittedly, but not without merit.

always done my best, since the early 1960s, to keep myself aware of where the nearest good pasty shop was. However, there seem to be many more decent to good pasty shops now than there were 20 or 30 years ago. This was the point I was trying, albeit not too clearly, to make. One of the salient points about pasties is that they are designed to be carried away – to work, on a walk, on a boat-fishing trip, whatever. They are a complete meal in a handy and completely recyclable wrapping. And a good pasty is food that's too good for any mere god. Bergisman

Disappointing that Stewart Lee should include a reference to *Mad Max* but not use the opportunity to have a third dig in a row at frenemy Brendan McCarthy this week. Feralprole

It's great comedy when remoaners attempt faux outraged patriotism. Structuralengineer79

Lies. All lies from Big Pasty. The pasty industry want you to believe they're all made by quaint Cornish villagers but they're all made by monstrous machines. Where are the machines made? Not by hand by Cornish people! That's a fact! Now go away! Loopdiggs

Anna Kavan had heroin recommended by her tennis coach, to improve her serve. This is where i have been going wrong. Polish French

As soon as I read 'Oggy . . .' used in relation to an apparently isolated community referred to in derogatory terms, I changed my reading style for this article from Detail to Gist. And I have felt the need to comment. This article is not worthy of the esteemed newspaper it has been included in. Please refer the author of this article to the *Daily Mail* when they wish to publish their thoughts in future. Chris D Horner

As a Cornishman I have to say what an imbecilic article. The name of the Cornish comedian is just Jethro, real name Geoffrey J Rowe, Jethro Tull was a rock band! And thirdly the Cornish have huge connections with the United States, the Cornish emigrated there in large numbers for mining, whaling and farming. I myself have family there. Americans pilgrimage to Cornwall daily seeking out their heritage. I believe most Cornish would be less offended by a pasty manufactured by Cornish Americans than someone from London. And you wonder why Cornwall voted leave? JB1968

No, his name is Geoffrey J Rowe Tull, hence Jethro Tull. The rock band Jethro Tull is named after him, and he also invented the seed drill during an episode of the *Generation Game*, by accident. Mick Conley

No it's not, there's no Tull in his name! JB1968

I think you're mistaken. His last name is actually Tull. And the J stands for Jethro, that's why he's called Jethro. He just drops the Tull bit for his stage name. Mick Conley

'Say "Cornwall" to an uncontacted pygmy brave deep in a New Zealand'? I find it hard to believe that I have just read this. I thought it was common knowledge that the use of the word 'pygmy' is considered by many people to be racist. Stewart Lee once said: 'the kind of people that say "political correctness gone mad" are usually using that phrase as a kind of cover action to attack minorities'. 'Uncontacted pygmy'? Over to you, Stewart Lee. Luftwaffe

Who is Jethro Tull the comedian? Jethro be his name and nothing added. Roger Hyde

That's where you're wrong: his name is Geoffrey J(ethro) Rowe

Tull. He drops the Tull from his stage name to make things easier for his audience. Mick Conley

The name of the comedian is Jethro. I know because I saw a snide DVD in a bootsale with 'Best of Jethro' hand-written on it. I didn't buy it, though. I think Cornish yokel comedians is a bit like minstrelsy. Jethro Tull is bearded prancing flute player. Alexito

Stay focused, Brexiteers.
Russia is not the enemy

18 March 2018

Last Sunday, diners at the Salisbury Zizzi were belatedly advised to burn all their clothes as a precautionary measure;* as was anyone who had ever visited a Jamie's Italian, but for different reasons. Enemies of Putin expire and nuclear threats are proliferating across the Earth. Perhaps the trademark robust diplomacy of the foreign secretary, Boris Johnson, deployed via scatological limericks in his chicken-feed *Telegraph* column, might defuse the tension?†

Needless to say, shameless Remoaners are already exploiting the Salisbury poisoning to sabotage Brexit. Is there no pig trough low enough into which they will not now stoop themselves?‡ Even given Russia's nuclear threats, we must not be so weak as to go, dunce's cap in hand, to the Brussels fat cats who gerrymandered us into building wheelchair access ramps in libraries and planting wild-flower meadows. Brexit means Brexit.

---

* The Russian double agent Sergei Skripal and his daughter Yulia had been poisoned with the nerve agent Novichok in Salisbury. A blameless British woman, Dawn Sturgess, subsequently died from exposure to the same batch. Colonel Anatoliy Vladimirovich Chepiga and Dr Alexander Mishkin were thought to be responsible. Putin's trained killers' flimsy alibis openly mocked the international community's anxieties, and the deceased, all part of his brilliant strategy of organised chaos and confusion. How he must love Brexit.

† Boris Johnson had a limerick about the president of Turkey having sex with a goat published in the *Spectator*.

‡ I am very lucky that the *Observer* allows me to write such deliberately poorly constructed sentences.

Unfortunately for diehard traitors, when Mrs May described 'an indiscriminate and reckless act against the UK, putting innocent civilians at risk', she was talking of the Salisbury poisoning, not hard Brexit.

Brexiteers must remember that Britain's real enemy is not our anti-EU ally Russia and her toxic Novichok. Britain's real enemies are Michel Barnier, Donald Tusk, Jean-Claude Juncker, Peter Stringfellow, Lily Allen, Marcus Brigstocke, all High Court judges and endless bloody red tape! Better to live free for a day in a Britain full of rogue killers roaming Italian restaurants with nerve agents than to live a thousand years as the straight-banana slaves of Brussels!

We have all seen the famous film of an un-trousered Putin riding wild boar piglets bareback in the snow. Is it time to be talking of freezing our Front National-funding Russian allies' assets, especially when Putin's own assets seem resistant to cold?

Christ, I can't keep this forced nonsensical tone going any more, even to provoke the usual online Kremlin gremlin comments. I'm on tour, and it's Tuesday in a Dundee hotel. I have to file this tomorrow from Perth by close of business, and the story unravels as quickly as I can rewrite it. Since I started scribbling, Rex Tillerson's* disappeared, the *Sun* says a Russian's been strangled in New Malden† and even Stephen Hawking's and Ken Dodd's deaths look like Putin might have had a hand in them. Did anyone toxicity-test the telescope and the tattyfilarious tickling stick? Thought not.

The Brexit British are a joke now. Putin knows no one will stick their neck out for those wankers. I don't know anything

---

* Oil-money loyalist, sacked that week as Secretary of State by Trump for criticising him.

† Nikolai Glushkov, former deputy director of Aeroflot, critic of Putin.

about Russia anyway. Someone online in Russia has a tattoo based on one of my stand-up routines. And I have a Russian relative who is nice.

My only other Russian experience was a fever dream, frozen in the few winter weeks between the death of my mother and the birth of my daughter.* In the dying days of December 2010, I was with my three-year-old son on a train travelling through the falling snow from London to Worcester. I had to visit my bereaved stepfather, my wife at home in the painful throes of a problematic pregnancy.

Coincidentally, my friend the poet John Hegley was in the same carriage, I remember, and we said goodbye and good luck at Oxford, where the train surrendered to rapidly worsening weather, and the railway company bundled us into optimistic black cabs to take us towards our respective onward destinations.

My son and I found ourselves sharing our cab ride through the suddenly Siberian Cotswolds with a groomed Russian businessman and his younger English companion, a glamorous, cut-glass woman who said she worked 'in fashion'. They were on their way to a party at a country house in Worcestershire, swaddled in designer coats that mocked our cagoules, their eyes darkly ringed, their demeanours distracted. The pair seemed to have nothing in common with one another and no shared frame of reference. They were not delighted by the sudden beautiful world beyond the window. They did not hold each other's cold hands in hot wonder.

* This story is entirely true as written. The strangeness of the experience has haunted me since, and it was years before I even twigged what was actually going on. I could piss out these meaningful, moving vignettes in my sleep – and you'd love that, wouldn't you? – but I prefer instead to continue a personal vendetta against the very idea of a newspaper column.

I tried to make small talk. The fashion woman could not elaborate on her fashion-job criteria, and they both looked away from us, out of the windows in different directions, as the snow fell hard and thick upon the darkening wolds. It came out that I was a comedian, but they did not find this especially interesting; nor were they engaged by my eloquent and delightful infant, whose cherubic curls and indefatigable innocence created an angelic counterpoint to the black mood of the taxi's interior.

I asked the Russian what he thought of gay rights at home, and of Putin, whom I found newly comical, as he had recently been photographed wrestling a bear naked while shooting an assault rifle. Or something. The Russian explained forcefully that I needed to understand that there was a vodka-fuelled crisis of manhood in Russia, and that Putin was selflessly providing a role model to inspire the men of the nation. The discussion was closed.*

To me the pair seemed shrouded in shame, as if they had committed a crime, the presence of a chirruping child magnifying their corruption. I think the kid saved me from going under that evening – a psychic lifebuoy. They were my own devils, come for me, I think. That black cab was my blues crossroads.

At Worcester Shrub Hill, the taxi's elastic limit, our farewells were not fond. I left the silent couple awaiting collection, halogen-lit in the falling flakes, and my little boy and I struggled onward through the drifts into the shadow of the Malvern Hills.

I will never forget our odd quartet's awkward three-hour black-cab journey in that snow-shrouded English twilight, an iconic British brand traversing the worsening terrain, a global

* I now understand why a Russian wouldn't do anything other than praise Putin when quizzed by a stranger with whom he found himself on a long-distance cab journey. He must have wondered who the hell I was.

183

darkness drawing in behind it. But the Russian was just passing through. The land and its people were a playground for him.

And I often think of the quiet woman, Komarovsky's Lara reimagined. I hope that fashion thing worked out for her.

You are another of Putin's useful idiots. Borderguard

What a load of old twaddle – Putin would love this article! Enfield Chappie

Well done Stewart, bit better writing in this article than recently; Keep it up. Tom Woody

You actually write very well when you stop dicking around. You should drop the comedy thing – it's not really working out, is it – and write ful time instead. I believe the *Guardian* are looking for a jazz columnist. BuyDogHasDohDose

Stay focused? This article is a series of words drunkenly walking out off a bar late at night, in ever more danger of tipping off the pavement onto the road whilst waiting for the taxi he forces us to read about. JerMacDon

I got as far as the word remoaner. that was enough. the world is full of assholes. European Observer

Lee is a fool, our enemies are Johnson, May, Fox, Davies etc the Brexit Faragists in the Tory party. They are the real enemies of the people, together with their press barons who report more fake news than 'Pravda' ever did. The Tory Faragists are leading us to economic and social disaster unless this Brexit stupidity is stopped in its tracks. Putin knows the we are led by a bunch of dim-wits and has been exploiting the situation. 47Andrew

What a load of tosh. If cooperation, Richer nations helping the poorer members, interdependence, peace, prosperity, a larger political and trade bargaining voice and freedom of movement make people an enemy of Stewart Lee, then may I suggest that he buys a bigger notebook for the names, for he can add mine right away. As a Comedian his jokes aimed at the remain side will fall on deaf ears in Dundee where the pragmatic Scottish people are polling at 68% remain about now and will have the last say on Brexit soon. May I suggest when he does his last gig at the Royal Festival Hall in London he stays down there with all the other Brexit Bampots intent on breaking up the Union of Great Britain. InternationalMusic

I'm sure apologists for Stalin wrote in much the same jocular vein as they commended the latest tractor production figures, or dismissed reports of gulags and mass murder. Putin's killers still stalk our streets armed with state developed poisons, the threats and military overflight's continue, weapons development continues apace. Is it all just for a bit of a laugh? Liberclown

Europa. Every second third word. Europa. *Also Sprach Zarathustra*, Proliferating across the earth. ManUpTree

This site was absolutely swamped with badly spelt, anti-EU comments for weeks before the referendum. It was completely impossible to have a normal conversation on here, and it felt exactly like an organised propaganda effort. As soon as the result was announced, they all disappeared, and it went back to normal. The difference was huge and totally obvious. It's very clear to me that some group with significant means was manipulating the online conversation to insert coordinated pro-Leave messages and drown out pro-Remain messages. Someone has the data trail for all this, and sooner or later it's all going to come out. What we've heard so far is only the tip of the iceberg. TruthSay3R

The Russian and his partner in the taxi just wanted to be left alone I think. Telling that they weren't aware you were a comedian. Lansing

Ah yes, I am remembering black taxi ride with Lara on way to party when all I want do is touch her and there is English comedy man with smirk asking me questions instead of talking with his boy. Often I am wondering what is happening to this poor Stuart Little boy and if father still making clever joke about Russia. Edwina666

Poor English call girl. Stuck with a tedious Russian client and an impertinent stranger who wished to discuss 'what the Russian what he thought of gay rights at home', a topic which many, even here, find similarly tedious. Mind you, she doesn't seem to have had much of a sense of humour to enjoy this comedy to culture clash. Fakecharitybuster

Not only buying up our houses but these Russians are also buying up our women. Where are these Brexiteers when we need them? Chashurley

They were bored by you. Fancy that. Many comics can be amusing for an hour or two, but it takes months to write the material. Without that material they can be as dull as the rest of us. MarcAdams

Someone trying to make small talk with complete strangers on a journey can be really annoying. Then you want these strangers to be amazed by your career. Did you tell them how much money you had too! No wonder they looked out of the window hoping you would shut up. Pinball1170

No wonder that Russian man acted like that if you offered such stupid topics of the small talk. IvaNotTerrible

I do like the image of the strange and slightly disturbing Russians forced to share a small space with the strange and slightly disturbing Stewart Lee, whilst travelling through a frozen landscape. However, I suspect the rest of the piece, tedious and convoluted as it is, has been banged out at speed on a laptop in a depressing hotel room. Alastai

I asked the Russian what he thought of gay rights at home – Yet another reason I would hate to be stuck in a train with Stewart Lee. Facing an interrogation about ones political correct potentials. Wonder how many people have had to pay a £50 fine to break that alarm so they can avoid him? SAuszy

'It came out that I was a comedian but they did not find this especially interesting;', having read to the end I would concur. Initalyperora

A Stewart Lee piece about Brexit. I haven't read one of those since last week. Phewwords

I don't know what purpose this story has. Nor do I understand why comments remain open on this but not on Andrew Rawnsley. DrSHWilson

Putin is cold. He is sensible. He is safe. He will not start a nuclear war. Putin is the safe bet. So let us hope the polls are right and Putin wins today's election. This election is special. 7th (the perfect number, religious) Presidential election. On the 18th March 2014 the treaty allowing for Russian takeover of Crimea was signed. 2018 is a special year for Russia, FIFA 2018 WC. Best Regards,/Per. Per in Sweden

I don't think there's any need to worry about the polls, comrade. :) Robofish

This is an 'opinion article' based on fancy words and expressions, little substance, a lot of blaming and characterising others and splitting . . . i am unclea why the *Guardian* chose to publish it. Asteri11

What garbage article I hope the *Guardian* didn't pay for it. Bluesinbrussels

Probably the most stupid and ridiculous piece of writing since the universe began. DrChris

The racists won. So are
they happy now?

29 April 2018

I feel sorry for Theresa May. And that Rudd one, who looks like she is wearing a rubber Halloween mask based on her own face. What if, because you were all going on about how great UKIP were, and how Nigel Farage was only saying what people had been thinking all along, and all these people coming over here, May and Rudd thought you wanted them to be racist too, like you are? And so back in 2013, to please you, they did some racism, and wrote racist stuff on racist vans and drove them around, laughing.*

And in so doing, May furthered the creation of the Hostile Environment, which sounds like an irradiated wasteland where teenage Amazons get sent to die in *The Hunger Games*. May probably wasn't really all that racist herself, and only did the racism because she thought you wanted it, you racists.†

---

* In 2013, the Home Office authorised vans with intimidating slogans on them to drive around areas populated by immigrants. The use of the phrase 'Go Home' resonated depressingly with the sort of racist abuse experienced by immigrants, both legal and illegal, and prefigured the public-relations disaster of the *Windrush* scandal five years later, when it turned out loads of Jamaicans who had been told to 'go home' by Theresa May and Amber Rudd were already at home, here, legally, anyway.

† In a survey undertaken by Ipsos MORI in 2011, 64 per cent of the country thought immigration was bad for Britain. In March 2019, after nearly three years of hearing immigration discussed in a post-referendum context, 16 per cent fewer people thought that, with 48 per cent of the country feeling immigration had had a negative impact.

And now look what's happened. Last week, Mrs May spilt a massive silver tureen of hot sticky racism right into the laps of diners at the Commonwealth Heads of Government slap-up supper, leaving the poor old Queen to get down on her knees between Andrew Holness's* Jamaican knees and sponge up all the racist mess herself: 'Never mind, Theresa, it's probably best if I do it. You've done enough.'†

When the royal family, their 1930s Nazi sympathies now walled up in a sealed room at Windsor Castle, are your secret weapon for papering over the racist cracks, you know you're in trouble. But Prince Philip's embarrassing colonialist gaffes of old now seem like the charming handmade racist woodcuts of a delightful artisanal bigot, compared with the mechanised Model T Ford production-line racism of the current government. May's industrialised prejudice, a vast Amazon.com of nastiness, aimed to put the corner-shop, snug-bar UKIP supporter out of business. And suddenly, small-time racists everywhere are nostalgic for the days before racism went mainstream.

Franz Kafka's novels of bureaucracy gone mad have given us the adjective 'Kafkaesque', without which it would be impossible to describe the experience of being billed as two slightly different addressees at essentially the same address by British Gas; and then, when threatened with the bailiffs for not paying the bill of an addressee who didn't exist, finding the best way out

---

Perhaps the threat of seeing friends, co-workers and family members deported made people realise the mysterious 'other' that was ruining everything was actually people they knew and loved.

* Prime minister of Jamaica.

† The same week as the *Windrush* scandal broke, Theresa May had to attend a dinner for the Commonwealth Heads of Government. Awkward! (as the young people of today say).

of the situation was to pretend on the phone to be an old, confused pensioner who had forgotten his own name, while your
wife pretends to be his carer, who doesn't speak English as a first
language. There was no 12b Shanley Road. It was 'Basement flat,
12 Shanley Road'. And I am not eighty-four and senile. My wife
is not Latvian.*

But this was not my most Kafkaesque situation. In Prague last
summer, having booked four tickets online to visit the Kafka
Museum, and then finding they had been issued with the name
Kafka on them instead of Lee, the guide advised us to pretend to
be the Kafka family named on the ticket, to save time, and to satirise administrative incompetence as a celebration of dead Kafka
himself.† How we laughed. The children, three and six, could
not have enjoyed their tour of the dimly lit literary tomb, with
its morbidly fading handwritten letters and projected images of
death, more.

An American family called Kafka arrived soon after us, visiting their distant relatives' home town, and were denied entry
as their tickets bore our name, until the guide came out and
advised them to pretend to be us.‡ This was undoubtedly the
most Kafkaesque situation any of us had ever been in, and we all
had a good laugh about it in the café afterwards, before becoming fixated on the absurdity of existence and crawling away on
our bellies to die. To die like dogs.§

* This is all true.

† This isn't.

‡ Nor is this.

§ While we were in Prague with the kids in 2017, I was able to bargain
my way into a night out on my own. My plan was to sit in the Old Town
Square, next to the bar where Kafka used to drink and Einstein used to
play the violin, and drink Czech beer, while reading Kafka's *The Hunger*

In Franz Kafka's Kafkaesque novel *The Trial*, which no one has ever read, the protagonist, Danny K, makes a complaint about two arresting officers, whose treatment of him – eating his breakfast and trying to steal his clothes – he felt was unfair. The next day, Danny opens a store cupboard at work, to find the officers being flogged for his benefit, but far more violently than he would have hoped. Danny protests, but the flogger explains that K had set wheels in motion.

Artist in its entirety, opposite the windows of the very flat where it was written. Just as I was about to finish the novella, a young Englishman, who proclaimed himself a fan of my work, sat down to join me, amazed that it was really me drinking and reading alone in Prague. He was a nice enough bloke, in town for a stag night and separated from his friends, and being recognised is a small price to pay for my privileges, but all the same, it punctured a perfect experience. It is as nothing, however, compared to the Jewish comedian David Baddiel's contemplative visit to Auschwitz, during which a young man came up to him to ask if there was another series of *Fantasy Football* in the pipeline.

The first time I ever met my half-sister, we went to try and find a quiet pub in the afternoon. I hadn't ordered, and had barely spoken to her, before a man drinking alone started pestering me for a photo. I asked him, very politely, if on this occasion it would be OK if I didn't do that. I didn't want my social interaction with my newly discovered sister to be characterised from the outset by me having to pose for photos with a stranger, while she waited, patient and embarrassed, and he fumbled with camera-phone functions he didn't know how to use, or worse still, asked the barman if he'd take it. I assume it was the same man, 'Harry', who tweeted, a few hours later, 'Don't meet your heroes they say. If that hero happens to be Stewart Lee it's excellent advice. What a cunt. A chance conversation in a pub in Norwich suggests he's a dislikable individual. Also fatter, greyer and drinking more than you'd imagine.' The weird thing is, we left without ordering because of him, so I don't know how he knew how much I was drinking. He was the one who was in a pub on his own in the afternoon too.

Likewise, it now appears you didn't want May and Rudd to be too racist after all, and now there's all this unpleasantness – old guys homeless and living in storage units, and old ladies told to pack their bags, and no medical treatment for pensioners who paid in for decades. But that wasn't what you wanted at all, was it, you racists?

Deporting and depriving those nice old black people who have been here for ever was wrong. And when they came for that Canadian dinner lady in Wolverhampton, who was actually white, and told her to go home, as life in Britain was about to become 'increasingly difficult' for her, that was definitely too much.

How could someone who had lived in Wolverhampton for forty-seven years, breathing toxic smog, dancing to Slade and eating only faggots and peas,* be expected to readjust to the land of clean mountain air, the thoughtful roots rock of the Tragically Hip† and light and fluffy blueberry muffins? It is inhumane.

---

* I love faggots and peas. My mother's Black Country-born father fed them to me as a child, when no one was looking. When the kids were young, I convinced them a dish of faggots and peas was a rare delicacy, and got them to eat it enthusiastically by telling them it was an important part of their cultural inheritance, a notion my wife has otherwise monopolised in favour of Irishness. Finally, this same wife, who is working class but has accidentally become middle class by appearing on Radio 4, told me I wasn't to feed the children faggots any more, and any that were still in the freezer were ostentatiously thrown away before my eyes. My new favourite Black Country dish is grey peas, as served at the Great Western Pub, Corn Hill, Wolverhampton, and as soon as I have finished these footnotes I am going out to buy the ingredients – peas, onion, barley and bacon – so I can make a massive bowl of the stuff. Remember, though, before you eat loads of grey peas, I am currently too heavy to use certain waterslides.

† Being a record-collector nerd has been a useful device in all sorts of social situations all over the world, and I escaped being beaten up in an

No, it wasn't the dinner lady and the nice black family from the electrical shop who had to go. It was the other foreigners. The bad ones, who scrounge and steal and are lazy. Not the ones that were like people you knew, harmless tropical fish caught in a dragnet sweeping for sharks. It's the anonymous parade of frightening brown faces on that Vote Leave poster. They're the bad ones.

Tough British cheddar. You stoked this hate volcano, racists. And now it has exploded all over your front garden and melted your Ford Focus.* Is this what you wanted?

How come as hominem attacks on women's appearances are just fine if they come out of the mouth of a lefty darling? You've got all of UKIP, Brexit and *Windrush* to play with Stewart, and one of your openers is to criticise Rudd's face? Try harder. Girlstuff

Oxford pub in 1989 by knowing all the different line-ups of Hawkwind. Having a working knowledge of the intermittently impressive Canadian national band The Tragically Hip was enormously helpful in avoiding violence in a potentially problematic sports bar in Prince George, British Columbia, in the summer of 1994, during the screening of an ice-hockey final. But now my office is full of records and CDs, more than I can ever process or love. I imagined someone would want them, or that they formed some valuable archive, but no one will, and they don't. Everything is worthless now, and music just streams out of our devices like slurry. Now, I am just trying to throw away the plastic CD boxes and file everything away, so that there isn't an awful job there for some poor child when I die. What a waste of a life.

* I have a Ford Focus. It's the most practical motor I've owned since we had kids and is a very reliable family car with good all-round visibility. I wish I'd got one years ago, to be quite honest.

Besides this article being utter bullcrap conflating bureaucratic incompetence with racism I'm disgusted that a fully paid up Social Justice Warrior would be so misogynistic to shame Amber Rudd by mocking her for her looks. You should be ashamed of yourself. Hardboiledchicken

May I quote Hardboiledchicken back at yourself from an April 11th comment? 'Hopefully', you wrote, 'in a few more years there will be a backlash against this culture of taking offense at everything. The outliers are these entitled snowflakes who see racism and sexism everywhere, if they had there way comedy wouldn't be funny anymore.' So are you an entitled snowflake or just a hypocrite? HarryHardy

'Franz Kafka's Kafkaesque novel *The Trial*, which no one has ever read.' Excuse me? I have read it. I read it on an unheated train journey back from Morecambe, where the employer I had been prosecuting for underpaying his staff had just got off by proving that they were illegal workers, a situation he had himself ensured by lying on the form he had filled in for their entry to the UK about them all being recruited as chefs then employing them as waiters. Somehow, Kafka's much vaunted surrealism didn't quite work for me that day. IMSpardagus

'And so back in 2013, to please you, they did some racism', 'lived in Wolverhampton for forty-seven years, breathing toxic smog, dancing to Slade and eating only faggots and peas', 'exploded all over your front garden and melted your Ford Focus'. Smug, condescending, middle-class, public schoolboy much? QuietRich

Parroting the views of the privileged and entitled. Poor effort. Pleasetryalternative

Full plans for the porn president's visit to the UK revealed

14 May 2018

Desperate for American co-operation with post-Brexit trade, Britain is hamstrung in her reaction to Donald Trump's withdrawal from the Iran nuclear deal. A man in Southend-on-Sea, who just wanted bendy bananas, eats takeaway butterfly wings, and a nuclear missile hits Tel Aviv.*

In July, *Guardian* and *Observer* readers, their furious tofu-smeared faces red with righteous rage, will doubtless wish to greet visiting American president Donald Trump with well-punctuated placards, laced with Pythonesque whimsy.†

Realpolitik appeasers like Boris Piccaninny Johnson assure us, with one eye on transatlantic trade deals in the dystopian post-EU wasteland he has engineered, that we must respect the office of the president of the United States. But Boris Watermelon Smiles himself previously described the current president, in 2015, as 'unfit to lead the United States', 'clearly out of his mind' and 'stupefyingly ignorant'. Less impressive U-turns have given Richard Hammond whiplash.

But life goes on, and the really important cultural questions blare from the Sunday supplement headlines. 'Wham! Bam!! Pow!!! Have Superhero Movies Finally Grown Up?' 'Gnngh! Squish!! Yuk!!! Is Our Love Affair with the Smoothie Maker Finally Over?' 'Squelch! Squish!! Ker-ching!!! Has Porn Finally Entered the Mainstream?'

---

* I'm not entirely sure what I meant by this now.

† Trump's postponed visit was finally happening.

At least one of these great debates is at last resolved. Porn has finally and undeniably entered the mainstream, like a massively mammaried Milk Tray man, slopping his pendulous udders one at a time through the unlocked hotel bedroom window of one Donald J. Trump, the forty-fifth president of the United States of America.

Franklin D. Roosevelt bequeathed the New Deal, Theodore Roosevelt the teddy bear. Donald J. Trump means even Sister Wendy Beckett may now have read about the president's paid-off lover's 2004 video vehicle, *Toxxxic Cumloads 6*.

Obama was the first black president. And Donald J. Trump is the first porn president. He has pornified not the high street, not the world of fashion, but the whole world itself. What unregulated Internet access began, Donald Trump has finished, his porn-star affair inadvertently dissolving the last vestiges of modesty displayed by the world of monetised desire. And the phrase 'porn star' now sits comfortably in the mouths of *Today* programme presenters, TV newsreaders and year 4 schoolkids.*

This presents a dilemma for Theresa May, who looks increasingly like something that lurches up at you on a ghost train. And so, in the interests of gender equality, does her husband, Mr Theresa May. How does the vicar's daughter from Eastbourne court and entertain the president of porn, upon whom our post-Brexit future depends? My Whitehall mole has leaked Theresa May's plans to welcome Trump in an appropriately pornographic way.

---

* The main driving force behind the loss of my children's innocence has been them overhearing news coverage of Donald Trump. Because of Trump I have had to define the words 'pussy' and 'porn star', and explain the idea of being urinated on by prostitutes. This is Trump's gift to the world.

On Friday 13 July, at 11.08 a.m., President Trump and Melania Trump will be met on the tarmac at Heathrow airport by the prince and princess of British pornography, Ben Dover and his ex-wife Linzi Drew, who have been persuaded to partner up again in the interest of post-customs-union trade opportunities.*

Having explained to the Trumps how the joke in Ben Dover's name works, and that Ben Dover is not his real name (it is Simon Dover), the Drew-Dovers will then whisk the Trumps away in a Routemaster bus with a bouncy suspension, driven by the late Reg Varney.

On the way, the Drew-Dovers will explain to the Trumps the fascinating differences between saucy home-grown British pornography and the more airbrushed fantasies of the American version, and what this tells us about our two historically close nations and their unbreakable special relationship.

While the president will doubtless have a lot to contribute to this discussion, his wife is expected to sit in silent, smouldering resentment, like a big pile of disappointed hate, brushing away any attempts at physical contact, as Ben Dover tries to smooth over the situation with seaside-postcard humour and amusing anecdotes about lube-based mishaps on the set of *Ben Dover's English Muffins*.

At 1.17 p.m., the Trumps will arrive in newly gentrified Soho, where they will be met by the billionaire pornographer and former Birmingham City chairman David Gold and his daughter, the sex-toy retailer Jacqueline Gold (CBE). The Golds will show the Trumps around the historic pornographic district, temporarily restored to its '70s glory, with swathes of hairy suede-denim

* The Drew-Honeys' son, Tyger, was the child star of the sitcom *Outnumbered*. I sometimes worried that our kids were treated weirdly by people because of what we do. I think I should get a sense of perspective.

filth flung over the contemporary ciabatta outlets, bringing innocent joy to Donald Trump's orange face.

Now hopefully suitably buttered up, and in a brief respite from pornography, the first family will proceed to the otter enclosure at London Zoo, where the foreign secretary, Boris Johnson, dressed as a glistening wet otter,* will cavort and frolic to the Trumps' delight with real otters in their pond and toss a stone from hand to hand, hopefully disorienting Donald Trump to the point where he will accidentally agree some kind of trade deal.

Melania will be invited to choose which otter she would like made into a hat, and the doomed mammal will then be slaughtered and skinned in front of her by a vengeful Terry Nutkins, to the obvious distress of schoolchildren, before the bloodied pelt is presented to Mrs Trump on a silver tray.†

That evening, at Buckingham Palace, alongside the royal family and armed forces veterans, the Trumps will enjoy a late-night charity gala screening of the Stormy Daniels Gulf War-themed 2007 sex comedy *Operation: Desert Stormy*, with a Kentucky Fried Chicken finger buffet.

Oh, for God's sake, it's going to be awful for everyone, much worse than all the rubbish I've written above. And someone's bound to get killed.‡

---

* Writing in the *Telegraph* about the Olympics in 2012, Boris Johnson, then mayor of the host city, said, 'There are semi-naked women playing beach volleyball in the middle of the Horse Guards Parade immortalised by Canaletto. They are glistening like wet otters.'

† I didn't realise Terry Nutkins was dead when I wrote this, unforgivably, and would have written it differently if I had known the otter-loving naturalist had passed. Sorry.

‡ I was wrong. Nobody died. But kids at my daughter's school, walking in crocodile formation on a trip, saw Trump's cortège drive along Camden Parkway and were quietly horrified.

I find that leftie humour relaxes the face muscles. Isleoflucy

I regret to inform Mr. Lee that Terence Nutkins 'passed' (i.e. departed the mortal realm) in 2012. I sincerely hope this doesn't come as too much of a shock; I am aware of Mr. Lee's age and physical condition, but there's really no way to break this gently. Dee Emsey

Shame on you. Terrys family lawyers might already be writing the letter . . . LeftOfCentre

Frankie Boyle is far better at focusing and channelling his scorn, which is just what a piece like this needed (and lacked). Haemodroid

Kentucky Fried Chicken finger buffet. He was in the Magic Band. Clark Gwent

Erdogan's visit would have been a good subject for this article but simpler to go for the easy target. I guess this is populist satire. Voyageresque

Is this the famous British sense of humour? It must be an acquired taste. Because this smug snide style of writing, with no content or wit, does nothing for me. I am Swiss but educated at Oxford. Kusomak

Ben Dover's real name is Simon Honey not Simon Dover. Drumboy

As a species we will likely kill ourselves. It won't be the end of the world. Just the end of the human one. It will be a shame and a wasted opportunity, as we could have created something close to a paradise on this blue gem of a planet. Perhaps it is just not in our nature to live peacefully. Perhaps we couldn't stand paradise anyway and would destroy it as soon as we had it in our reach. Unbritannia

the man has built two of the best golf courses in the world up in scotland ,turnberries and aberdeen, with his own money. i will be there with a few friends to welcome to these shores. skintman

A vile piece written by, I imagine, a vile man. DrBill

How daring for a mainstream newspaper to publish a piece bashing Trump! Its about as brave as coming out as heterosexual. Yawn. Luka69

I'm impressed with your knowledge of porn stars. This must have required extensive 'research'. StuartBaker

Stormy Daniels is not a porn star. She is a person. How she earns her living is up to her. I detest the dehumanisation of her in this piece and throughout the press. Trump has reportedly been unfaithful with other women, but that doesn't tickle readers' fantasies in the way that this one does. Lee is exploiting her as much as he is mocking Trump. BeckyThatcher

There is no point in public school educated, neoliberal class warriors laughing at Donald Trump. It's over. Morrisseysmiff

'it's going to be awful for everyone, much worse than all the rubbish I've written above.' Well, Mr Lee, I very much doubt that. Rest assured that whilst your increasingly incomprehensible columns will no doubt continue to be a testimony to your superior (public school) intellect, us humble proles will manage. There are many places where life is a miserable and dangerous attempt to survive; and where Trump is an irrelevance. Maybe you should travel more . . . Quietrich

'Stewart Lee appears in benefit shows for Action on Hearing Loss'. They should be so lucky. MsSnoopier

Is not tofu-smeared a racist idea – I happily read the *guardian* and live in a country whose population eats tofu many times a week or daily. Why turn it into a insult as it directly insults those people, my kids included, who enjoy eating tofu. MattyJ101

So that's Trump's game!
The Second Coming

20 May 2018

Bear-baiting is officially banned by the bear-loving, politically correct, snowflake brigade. Go and marry a bear and live in a wood eating worms if you love bears so much! And I think you'll find it was Adam and Eve!! Not Adam and Rupert!!! But after bear-baiting, Thomas Markle teasing is the next best thing.*

The least I expect for my tax contribution to the royal coffers is to see a future princess's confused elderly father thrown to the dogs by Buckingham Palace, and hounded and manipulated by newspapers whose tenacity and cynicism he could never have predicted. That's entertainment!

Thank heavens our politicians are seeing some sense, as they peep out from the pockets of the press barons, by attempting to kick the Leveson report into the long grass, where it belongs, along with some Fanta cans and an old, torn-up *Razzle.*

This week, I wanted to write about the beautiful synchronicity of the Leveson recommendations being declared as unnecessary at the same time as Thomas Markle gets pulverised by the press, the paparazzi's piss-tears over Princess Diana's death a distant memory. But I have to file these columns on Thursday, and you, reading this, now know more about what actually happened after Thomas Markle's heart scare than I do. Perhaps things have already ended tragically and a beatified Thomas Markle is being declared the

---

* Nobody seemed to have warned Meghan's dad that having a royal daughter meant he had to know how to conduct himself in front of the press, and wedding- and journalism-related stress gave him a heart scare.

King of Hearts, the People's Award-Winning Seventy-Three-Year-Old Television Lighting Cameraman, by the same tabloids that ran apparently staged photos of him buying a toilet at a DIY centre last week. I can't write this. I'm not Psychic Sally. But Doris says, 'Look after your feet.' And Betty's ring is in the budgie's cloaca.

So, in other world news, an unpopular politician has made an alliance with dangerous religious fundamentalists and inflamed passions on both sides of a contentious border in a desperate bid to maintain power. No! I don't mean Mr Trump in Israel!! I mean Mrs May in Northern Ireland!!!

There! That's how satire works! But satire isn't as easy as I make it look, week after week, especially when the actual real news reads increasingly like a poorly plotted dystopian science-fiction novel written as badly as possible by a disillusioned Dan Brown in an attempt to sabotage his own career.

The opening of Trump's new Israel embassy, for example, suggests he is courting the support of millions of American Christian fundamentalists, who believe that when the Jews reclaim Jerusalem, the Apocalypse will begin, and with it Christ's Second Coming, which American Christian fundamentalists want even more than an end to abortion rights.

To suggest that the Jerusalem embassy isn't opening for the benefit of the Israelis isn't to legitimise or delegitimise the notion of a Jewish homeland, but to ask if it has been opened instead for the benefit of the American Christian fundamentalist hate preachers Robert Jeffress and John Hagee. The Christian Chuckle Brothers led prayers at the ceremony and have said, respectively, that all Jews were going to hell and that Hurricane Katrina was an overzealous divine attempt to squash a gay parade.

To Palestinians, Trump's Jerusalem embassy is a provocation. To American Christian fundamentalists, it is a kind of giant mousetrap for a giant mouse Christ, designed to lure him back to Earth a little earlier than he was perhaps planning. But thou shalt not tempt the Lord thy God, not even with cheese.

Mrs May's latest plan for the Northern Irish border is similarly fraught. Work has already begun on a series of giant watchtowers, named the Pillars of Democracy, each several hundred feet high and electronically equipped to read the details of people and products crossing the border.

But in an error of judgement as catastrophic as Trump's Christ-baiting embassy, each tower will be made to look like a massive Oliver Cromwell, who, while honoured here in mainland Britain as the founder of the democratic process that delivered the electorate's beloved Brexit, is viewed by Catholics on both sides of the Irish border as a genocidal war criminal.

Similarly, the folly of Trump's Jerusalem Christ trap is obvious. We don't need to shoot protesters to bring Jesus back to Earth for the benefit of American Christian fundamentalists. If I were a religious person, here in London, I would see Christ every day.*

Last year, he meandered, in shawl and slippers and female form, along my tube carriage, singing polyphonic clicks and buzzes, and holding out an empty cup. I put in some coins, and the woman opposite me, who was wearing a silver crucifix, made a disapproving face. I leaned forward, gestured towards her jewellery and the departing beggar, and whispered, 'That was Christ. Just there. And you missed him.'†

---

* I remain an atheist, but my Catholic wife has inculcated in me the value of Christ as a metaphor, and now I keep seeing that metaphor, schlepping about the city of London at all hours of the day and night. Only this morning she was weeping uncontrollably on the pavement outside Tesco's in Finsbury Park, and I gave her all the change I had from buying the *Observer*, a finger in the dam of the world's misery, and virtue-signalling to boot no doubt.

† I actually did this. I hope the woman was suitably chilled.

Sometimes I see him in Kentish Town, a man I vaguely knew in south London a quarter of a century ago, now street-sleeping, and I buy a bag of toiletries from Boots and leave them at his feet. He is Christ. And so am I, I suppose, for buying those toiletries. Greater love hath no man than to lay down his Lynx.*

If I were faithful, I would see Christ everywhere, on buses and at borders, both pulling the trigger and taking the bullet, and I would not be able to bear the sorrow of it. But I don't think I would have seen him in the triumphal, hate-filled benedictions of Trump's surrogate Jerusalem speakers.

Christ was at the bus stop outside the house this morning, where I waited with the kids; Christ manifest as two street prostitutes, crazy and angry from a long night of low earnings, their curses the blood of Christ, their kicks the body of Christ; and Christ was in the newspaper just now, contemplating his toilet purchase and the loss of his privacy, preparing for surgery.†

* The man in question used to be a male model, on the fringes of my mid-'90s circle. He loves to ridicule me in front of my kids about how different I look now I am fat, and how handsome I was when I was young, and I take the hit. He looks pretty different too, to be honest, but it would be churlish to go on about it. I am glad the kids understand that a homeless person could be anyone, could be someone your dad once knew, but when my daughter asked why the former Cool Britannia face couldn't come and live with us, I realised the limits of the extent of my concern. Virtue signaller.

† I was in a church choir for five years as a kid, though I personally was neither sexually abused nor converted to Christianity. I listened to the service three times every Sunday from the stalls. The liturgy never leaves you, however monotonously it was recited, and it was, in retrospect, a formative influence.

How to treat Morrissey?
Stop listening to him

8 July 2018

Morrissey fans have for years equated his more unpalatable pronouncements with the babblings of a beloved but out-of-touch relative. Some of the things Uncle Steven says seem a bit racist, but he has seen a lot of changes in the area he lives in, he got food poisoning from a bad curry on the Bristol Road in 1978 and he says he couldn't get on *Top of the Pops* in the '80s because he wasn't black.

But are Morrissey fans justified, in the light of Morrissey's unambiguous support for both the violent tanning salon entrepreneur Tommy Robinson* and the far-right For Britain party, in finally losing faith? Either way, it looks like I picked the wrong year to take an eighteen-month break from stand-up to work incognito as a Morrissey impersonator, fronting a Smiths and Morrissey covers band.† I know it's over. My Boz Boorer

---

* Tommy Robinson enters our tale, a far-right football hooligan, mortgage fraudster and founder of the English Defence League, who, under normal circumstances, would have made little impact, but has become a freedom-of-speech cause célèbre for right-leaning libertarians, and was briefly seen by Steve Bannon as a flagpole around which to rally various aggrieved racists. After Robinson was appointed to the position of advisor by UKIP, the party's former leader Nigel Farage described him as a 'thug'. Farage prefers fascists in suits. Robinson is a little too authentic.

† I am now too fat to be a Morrissey impersonator anyway. Despite the ravages, I doubt there are any waterslides that are off-limits to the former Smiths singer, who doubtless delights in whooshing down massive tubes in his trunks and splashing into a big pool.

lookalike has been put to work in the garden, trapping jackdaws and building a gazebo.

Until last week, I had four Mexican musicians holed up in the spare room, working on a mash-up of 'This Charming Man' and a Paul Simon song, entitled 'Here's to You, Tommy Robinson'. 'Why ponder the law's complexities, when Robinson's done for a breach of the peace?'

My deliberate Morrissey-style weight gain was all for nothing, it appears, and now I am just a fat fifty-year-old man, of whom passers-by remark, 'Morrissey has let himself go. What with the weight gain and the Tommy Robinson stuff.'

The late Sean Hughes, a fellow stand-up comedian to whom Morrissey meant a lot, had insisted on being cremated last year to the sound of The Smiths' 'Heaven Knows I'm Miserable Now', and Morrissey's calculated black-comic misery made even Sean's actual immolation momentarily funny. Sean also had the perfect Morrissey joke: 'Everyone grows out of their Morrissey phase. Except Morrissey.'*

But Morrissey's controversial song lyrics should not be taken as evidence of their writer's true feelings, any more than this column, by the *Observer*-reading columnist character of Stewart Lee, represents what the real Stewart Lee actually thinks.

Thus, in 1988, when Morrissey told the titular hero of 'Bengali in Platforms' to abandon his 'western plans' and understand that life in England was difficult enough even if you 'belong here', the bewildered immigrant was perhaps merely an ill-judged metaphor for loneliness; in 1992's 'The National Front Disco', when Morrissey sang 'England for the English!' from the point of view of a disenchanted young man seduced by the far right, we accepted that exploring that point of view was not the same as endorsing it.

* A lot of fifty-something comedians died in 2018.

Just as, in 1967, when John Lennon said he was the walrus, goo goo g'joob, goo goo goo g'joob, goo goo g'joob, goo goo goo g'joob, we knew John Lennon was not the walrus goo goo g'joob, goo goo goo g'joob, goo goo g'joob, goo goo goo g'joob at all. John Lennon was in fact the eggman. The walrus was Paul.

The credibility problem would arise if John Lennon, having said he was a walrus in a song, had then gone around actually being a walrus, choosing to live as a walrus and do all walrus stuff, like eating benthic bivalve molluscs and engaging in competitive courtship displays. Then we would have had no option but to believe that John Lennon actually was a walrus after all. Which is sort of what Morrissey has done.

This isn't the time for ambiguity, or irony, or publicity-seeking controversy. Those days are gone, and I miss them, as I am part of a generation that profiteered from the assumption that political correctness was a done deal, and now we could have fun jumping in and out of its boundaries, like street kids round a spurting water main. But the Nazi-saluting pug bloke has just joined UKIP, so his racist dog doesn't seem remotely funny any more.*

---

* Markus Meechan, aka Count Dankula, is a 'shitposter' from Coatbridge. A shitposter is a man who tries to annoy people on the Internet. In 2018, he was arrested for posting film of his girlfriend's cute pug dog, which he had trained to do Nazi salutes whenever he said, 'Gas the Jews.' The joke was that the girlfriend loved the dog, so he made it to do the worst thing possible. I get this, but it was an excuse the judge didn't buy. I was among the self-loathing comedy liberals who signed a petition in defence of Meechan, a threadworm broken on a wheel, and of free speech generally, though I read online somewhere that I had called for him to be banned. Meechan subsequently spoke alongside Tommy Robinson at his Day for Freedom rally, and then joined UKIP. I don't know what I think of the whole thing any more. I suppose if you aren't in

If Breitbart or *Spiked* can roll out your comments approvingly online, you have fucked up. Nowadays, your true intentions have to be written through every inch of your content, like the word 'Blackpool' through a stick of rock, so if at any point the useful idiots of the hipster alt-right and their fellow travellers in the opinion industry choose to snap it, it still can't be repurposed.* The trouble is, there's no longer any way to make the case that Morrissey ever means anything other than what he says.

But what to do when our idols disappoint us? Like a lot of the centrist dads who constitute his audience, I suddenly found I finally had to decide what to do with my Morrissey records.

I've got vintage and modern psychedelic vinyl by actual murderers, and books of poetry by anti-Semites and paedophiles, who are hard to write out of literary history. And the increasingly reactionary comments made by Mark E. Smith in his latter

---

a racist organisation, or aren't friends with racists, and you teach a pug to *Sieg Heil*, maybe it is funny, but if you are in a racist organisation and you're friends with racists, and you teach a pug to *Sieg Heil*, it isn't. I don't know if there is a name for this nuanced position. Whatever, I blame the Internet. I wouldn't sign a petition like that again, and I don't know what I think of that.

* Writing in the *London Review of Books* in February 2019, Patricia Lockwood described the current situation, in relation to its online manifestation, thus: 'In contrast with [my] generation, which had spent most of its time online learning to code so that it could add crude butterfly animations to the backgrounds of its weblogs, the generation immediately following had spent most of its time online making incredibly bigoted jokes in order to laugh at the idiots who were stupid enough to think that they meant it. Except that after a while they did mean it, and then somehow at the end of it they were white supremacists. Was this always how it happened?' I read this and it made me feel less alone, which is what the best writing does, I suppose.

years will not tempt me to part with even the most unnecessary Fall compilation. But somehow, illogically and sentimentally, I held Morrissey to different standards.

As it happened, the break came easily. The last few weeks, I've been smashing the plastic cases of my CDs and filing the discs in folders, to save my children a tedious purge of obsolete physical media when I die. Oddly, when I got to 'S' (I file Morrissey's solo stuff alongside The Smiths), I found myself putting Morrissey's entire works, without really giving it any thought, into the box I was taking to the charity shop. I kept the vinyl of The Smiths' debut and the *Hatful of Hollow* compilation, totemic physical objects that link me to a certain mindscape, but the rest just suddenly seemed irrelevant.

There was no great fanfare. I didn't ceremonially smash Morrissey's works or burn them in the street like *Entartete Kunst*. It all happened with a whimper, not with a bang, and with sadness for the sorry state of things, not erectile pride in my own virtuousness. Suddenly, I just didn't want Morrissey in my home any more. And I couldn't imagine any circumstances under which I would ever listen to him again.

Morrissey has developed some pretty outrageous views but he's never been predictable, unlike Stewart Lee, a great peddler of dull but worthy opinions. Mike Spilligan, Twitter

After 25years of such stories still not sure Morrissey is bona fide racist. But on the basis of two ghastly evenings am certain Stewart Lee's stand-up shows are sanctimonious, self-indulgent & tedious. Oliver Horton, Twitter

Stewart Lee is a virtue-signaling dolt. Johnnydodo, Twitter

Morrissey is as irrelevant and dated as *Guardian* anointed public school class warrior, Stewart Lee. PollyTicker, Twitter

Lee throws Morrissey stuff but keeps books by pedos and anti-semites. Typical leftist. Dee Dangus, Twitter

Trump's struggle not to
tie himself in nots

22 July 2018

I spent the weekend at the Latitude festival in Suffolk with my children, Nelson and Mandela. Like a good metropolitan liberal elitist, I had all my tastes and prejudices confirmed, and all in a safe family-friendly environment. But when I left the site on Monday, it seemed that, while I was eating sushi in recyclable rice coatings and cheering the snowflake oi of Idles, the post-Second World War power balance had shifted beyond all recognition. I can't turn my back for a second.

Donald Trump, having spent the previous week calling the European Union his 'foe', like a mad medieval king, was now taking the dictator Vladimpaler Putin's side against evidence-based investigations into the kind of Russian meddling that helped swing an American election, destabilise the EU, fan the global far right, popularise *Fortnite*, drive swarms of hornets into Dorset, kill our English newts and deliver Brexit.

'I don't see any reason why it would be Russia,' Trump proclaimed at the press conference, having already fondled a football presented to him by master puppeteer Putin, which made the president look like a disturbed zoo monkey given toys to stop him flinging his excrement at visitors.* I expected the tanks

---

* An orangutan threw its excrement into my gran's hair from its moated island in Dudley Zoo in 1972. I think this had a big impact on me as a child. I mean, this is the third time I have mentioned it in this book alone. I have no memory of falling down drunk while talking to Sonic Youth in Boston in 2002, which I apparently did, according to others

to roll west into the Baltic states unchallenged within hours, showered with Stars and Stripes confetti in a New York-style ticker-tape parade.

Luckily, overnight, Trump realised that what he had meant to say was not 'I don't see any reason why it would be Russia,' but 'I don't see any reason why it *wouldn't* be Russia.' This is fortunate, as otherwise he could have been executed for treason, an event that would doubtless have drawn even larger crowds than his famously full inauguration, especially if it saw a repeat performance from the TwirlTasTix baton-twirling group.

Overnight, the Republicans had constructed a paper-thin plausible denial, hoping that no news agencies, in our micro-attention-span world, would run Trump's explanation of his misspeak alongside the press-conference footage, where context and his repeated use of the preposition 'but' would show he had clearly meant to say exactly what he said in the first place, without a shadow of a doubt. Which is exactly what happened.*

Nonetheless, even in a period of unprecedented stupidity and cynicism, Trump's 'would'/'wouldn't' gambit represents a new low in contempt for human intelligence, and a rejection of language itself, words and their actual meanings now a kind of obsolete tool in the battle for the hearts and minds of the very worst people on Earth.

How easy it appears to be to unravel and reverse the great statements of the past with a simple negative insertion. Neville

---

who were present, but this orangutan shit thing seems to be indelibly lodged in my consciousness. How come I have forgotten so much, and yet remain fixated on this?

* Why are news agencies so cowardly and weak and non-forensic? Brexit and Trump could have been stopped in their tracks if people had just asked the right questions.

Chamberlain returns from seeing Hitler in 1938 and utters the reputation-saving denial, 'I do *not* have in my hand a piece of paper.' Martin Luther King's 1963 address is re-remembered, to satisfy the racist vote, as: 'I do *not* have a dream, and anyone who says I did must have misheard me.' Descartes is reverse-engineered to proclaim the perfect philosophy for the Trump–Brexit era: 'I do *not* think, therefore I am.' And his philosophical forebear Shakespeare is retooled to offer the timeless truism 'To not be, or to be, that is *not* the question.'

Meanwhile, our cowardly, self-interested MPs were given many opportunities in Parliament earlier this week to sabotage Brexit in the national interest, but the traitors put pride and party loyalties before the future of the country, choosing instead to stoke the petrol engine of the out-of-control Brexit Flymo™ with even more incendiary lies as it hurtles towards the land-scaped no-deal ha-ha.*

Instead of voting against Brexit, the Liberal Democrat Tim Farron was actually in Dorset, charging milkmaids £5 to watch him struggle to accommodate his feelings about the homosexuals and his feelings about an all-knowing God whom he imagines has very strong views on the specifics of marriage legislation.

God would have wanted Tim to vote. Anyone can tell that snowflake God would obviously be a Remainer, but if the result of the corrupt referendum must be honoured, the Lord would at least favour a soft Brexit. Like Jeremy Corbyn, Jesus Christ would be a hard Brexiteer, but only because he imagined a fairer society could be built from the ruins of the old one. Drive your plough over the bones of the dead.

Nonetheless, if Tim and Vince Cable had turned up, Monday's

* An attempt by pro-EU MPs to force us to remain in a customs union-style arrangement was defeated by 307 votes to 301.

Brexit trade vote would almost have been a dead heat, and the nation would be a little bit closer to avoiding the need to stockpile tins of alphabetti spaghetti in its cellars.*

As an ardent Remoaner, I was at least looking forward to enjoying a degree of post-Brexit *Schadenfreude*, as Leavers were forced to own their bullshit. But Trump's 'would'/'wouldn't' strategy must be a great comfort to our bold buccaneering Brexiteers, many of whom have recently quit their jobs in order to avoid being held accountable for statements they made two years ago, now demonstrably revealed as dishonest and undeliverable.

Now the brave Brexiteers can merely rewrite what they said in retrospect. What's that squeaking noise? It's Brexiteer privateer Daniel Hannanananan, peering out from behind an effigy of Elgar, to declare: 'Absolutely nobody is *not* talking about threatening our place in the single market.'

And there, towelling himself down in the sauna on a Union Jack Jolly Roger, Liam Fox announces that the Brexit deal 'will *not* be one of the easiest in human history', before hopping onto a bus emblazoned with the legend 'Let's *not* give our NHS the £350m the EU *doesn't* take every week', driven by a doleful Boris Johnson, looking at a cake he has on the dashboard, but which he is, on this occasion, unable to also eat. Once you were post-fact. Now you are post-post-fact. That's going to work out well. Not.†

* As I write this, it is February 2019, and I am genuinely stockpiling tinned foods and toilet rolls in the utility room where the cats' bowls are. I am also stockpiling the cats' Science Plan biscuits, as they are made in the EU and are unlikely to be prioritised in the increasingly likely event of a no-deal Brexit. The vet told me to.

† In January 2019, a pro-Remain guerrilla group called Led by Donkeys took to posting the Brexiteers' historic and now proven lies on massive

'I spent the weekend at the Latitude festival in Suffolk with my children, Nelson and Mandela.' Sheesh. The left is far, far beyond parody at this point. Baconbutty

'Meanwhile, our cowardly, self-interested . . . traitors'. Oh dear Stewie, Is Dacre writing your material now? TonyDZ

About as funny as root canal treatment. Notmytype

---

billboards around the country, holding them to account in a way the mainstream media had utterly failed to do. But by then it was probably too late.

Bannon's crush on Britain's old bootboys

12 August 2018

'The skinhead smashed the still steaming grill plate of the state-of-the-art Breville sandwich toaster into his red face, to stem the violent impulses rising within him. His skin fizzed, like cold piss on a hot Guy Fawkes bonfire. Ancient burned pieces of cheese and tomato, remnants of his well-heeled host's cocaine-fuelled midnight snacks, buried themselves in the tight fuzz of his No. 1 crop. Through the open window of the politician's luxury million-pound west London flat Robbie could smell the stench of the Notting Hill night wafting into the exclusive mews of former stable buildings, where some famous film actors and racing car drivers also lived. Goat curry. Chicken jerky. And sweet sweet waccy waccy tobaccy. "Those spades got one thing right," conceded the skinhead, closing the lid of the sandwich toaster and putting it back on the Formica surface of the expensive designer kitchen' (*The Right Honourable Skinhead* by Richard Allen, 1981).*

It's well known that the racist news-website wizard and former Trump confidant Steve Bannon, currently planning a pan-global

---

* There is no such novel as *The Right Honourable Skinhead*. James Moffat (1922–93), a Canadian alcoholic hack paperback writer, churned out novels about Britain's violent '70s skinhead subculture under the name of Richard Allen, and lived long enough to see his work critically rehabilitated for its undeniable vitality, if not for its protagonists' distasteful politics. The extract from *The Right Honourable Skinhead* has been created by cut-and-pasting different bits of Allen's work, keeping the dialogue more or less intact and changing some of the nouns, and this falls within the law of 'fair usage'.

far-right resurgence called The Motion, was inspired by Jean Raspail's controversial 1973 French science-fiction novel *The Camp of the Saints*, which uses an invasion of western Europe by disenchanted brown people from below the equator as a satire of white European privilege and colonial guilt.* But is it possible that Bannon's current championing of the sunbed magnate and mortgage fraudster Tommy Robinson as 'the backbone' of the UK has been inspired by his acquaintance with a less well-known piece of fascist-flavoured fiction?

The Canadian alcoholic Richard Allen is thought to have written 290 novels in his lifetime, and between 1970 and 1980 he penned eighteen violent books set in the milieu of Britain's fractious youth culture, such as *Skinhead*, *Skinhead Escapes*, *Skinhead Returns* and the martial arts-themed *Taekwondo Skinhead*.†

Principally chronicling the adventures of a racist skinhead thug called Robbie Tomlinson, the books were top sellers for the cheap and nasty New English Library imprint, also home to Alex R. Stuart's disreputable Hells Angels series *Angel*, *Angel Escapes*, *Angel Returns* and the martial arts-themed *Taekwondo Angel*.‡

Allen was rediscovered in his twilight years by the experimental author Stewart Home, who was inspired by the novels' repetitive formula, and it is possible to view Allen's skinhead as a Nietzschean anti-hero akin to Henry Williamson's instinct-driven, eponymous

---

* It is true that Bannon loves *The Camp of the Saints*. Normally alt-right readers rave about Ayn Rand's *The Fountainhead*, like it's the only book they've ever read, so Bannon's choice is a little bit left-field.

† Allen's martial-arts skinhead book is actually called *Dragon Skins*. There is no *Taekwondo Skinhead*.

‡ I don't really like Allen's skinhead books, but I love Alex R. Stuart's biker series, which has a weird folk-horror feel to it. Peter Cave's Hells Angels series, for the same publisher, is more reactionary and not as imaginative.

animal protagonists Tarka the Otter, Salar the Salmon, Valkyrie the Vole, Mitford the Moth, Hitler the Hamster and the martial arts-influenced Taekwondo Hitler Hamster.*

But Allen's last skinhead outing, which was due to be published in 1981, proved too controversial even for the ambulance-chasing New English Library outlet, and saw the character retired. Allen's final job for the publisher, under his real name, James Moffat, was an ignominious novelisation of a suppressed erotic film entitled *Queen Kong*.†

---

* I devoured Williamson's 1927 novel *Tarka the Otter* when I was about nine, as Puffin had repackaged it as a children's book rather than as a piece of experimental adult fiction, and it made me a lifelong lover of otters, though it does read a little differently when you know Williamson was a Nazi sympathiser.

† When I was a kid, my dad would often take me to stay with his parents in Budleigh Salterton, in South Devon, in the school holidays, and in retrospect I realise how good it was of him to give my mother, from whom he was divorced, regular breaks from her precocious child. Most days, Dad would sit on the beach all day, spying on sunbathing women through a pair of binoculars he called his 'bird-watchers', and I would be given a small allowance to spend in the beach shop, its spinning racks full of American horror-comic anthologies and pulp paperbacks, which weren't so easy to source in the Solihull suburbs. It was here that I first discovered my later literary hero Arthur Machen, in an uncredited adaptation of his story 'The Bowmen' in DC's *Weird War Tales* 29, from September 1974; it was here I realised Robert E. Howard, whom I knew only from his Conan books, had written swathes of blood-soaked semi-historical fiction, re-pressed by the cheap-looking Orbit imprint; and it was here that I read *Queen Kong*, a novelisation of the 1976 Robin Askwith movie of the same name, whose satirical feminist subtext escaped me. I did not know that its author, James Moffat, was *Skinhead* author Richard Allen writing, unusually, under his own name. I was into Moffat about fifteen years before he was critically rehabilitated. Even as an eight-year-old I was a cultural influencer.

Queen Kong was the first in a doomed series of giant-monster sex comedies, in which the genders of famous horror-movie creatures were reversed, all due to feature the dream team of Robin Askwith, Rula Lenska and Carol Drinkwater from *All Creatures Great and Small*. However, legal action ended the project before filming on the follow-up, *Queen Kong Versus God-Sheila*, had been completed, let alone the series' third, martial arts-themed instalment *Taekwondo Queen Kong Versus Gwonbeop God-Sheila.**

Allen's sad monkey book appeared in a cover very different to the iconic street-style imagery of the *Skinhead* series, depicting as it did a man dressed as a giant female ape, with permed hair and exposed furry genitalia, looming over the London skyline in a frenzy of animal lust for Robin Askwith. And yet it is from the author of this ape-sex work that Breitbart's Steve Bannon appears to be drawing his current political thinking.

The unpublished manuscript of Allen's nineteenth New English Library youth-violence novel, from 1981, is somehow available for download on the dark web, and is entitled *The Right Honourable Skinhead*. The overlap between the plot points of Allen's final skinhead outing and Bannon's apparent plans for the far-right activist Tommy Robinson is too great to be coincidental.

Having failed to capture the hearts of the nation's disenchanted voters via the scripted racist gaffes of a posh clown-puppet politician called Horace Thompson, a secret cabal of fascists sets about trying to position the street-brawling racist football thug

---

* *Queen Kong* was in fact prevented from being released by the film producer Dino De Laurentiis, in order to protect his investment in the 1976 remake of *King Kong*. I recently found it on a dodgy DVD and thought it a better film than, for example, the acclaimed *Three Billboards Outside Ebbing, Missouri*.

Robbie Tomlinson as a serious political player, and the character gives voice to the same voter discontent Bannon clearly hopes to weaponise through the conduit of Tommy Robinson.

'Bloody MPs, he thought. They got elected to do what their constituents wanted done and the bastards thought they were little tin-gods better than the voters! If he had his way every politician would be slung in prison and given a taste of what they deserved' (*The Right Honourable Skinhead*, Richard Allen, 1981).*

Indeed, Steve Bannon seems to be carrying vast sections of dialogue from *The Right Honourable Skinhead* around in his head, which spill unbidden from his careless face. Bannon said, off air, to the LBC presenter Theo Usherwood, who had queried his support for Tommy Robinson, 'Fuck you. Don't you fucking say you're calling me out. You fucking liberal elite. Tommy Robinson is the backbone of this country.'†

And on page 103 of *The Right Honourable Skinhead*, the news magnate Steve Mannon, Robbie Tomlinson's chief cheerleader, who differs only from Steve Bannon in that he is a Welsh born-again Christian, addresses radio presenter Leo Isherwood thus: 'Flip you, boyo! Don't you flipping say you're calling me out. You flipping liberal elite. Robbie Tomlinson is the backbone of this country, by which I mean the whole UK, not just Wales.'

Worryingly for Britain's embattled liberals, while the unscrupulous New English Library considered Allen's dystopian fascist fantasy *The Right Honourable Skinhead* too hideous to publish, Steve Bannon seems intent on belatedly making its bleak fiction a chilling reality.

---

* This is a more or less verbatim quote by Allen's skinhead character, Joe Hawkins, but I forget which book it appears in.

† Verbatim quote, from an off-air incident at LBC, 15 July 2018.

It's all true. arghbee

No it isn't. Stewart Lee rewrites the wiki pages and links so that you think it is all real to play with your mind and make himself out to be a intellectual obscurantist. And then he goes back in time to recreate the past to make the web true in for the geeks that try and delve further into his twisted world. And every time he does that the world gets crazier as lies chase truth along the Moebius strip of reality. Have you ever noticed that his name is an anagram of Wattle Seer? He's a practitioner of the medieval art of divining the future from bumps in the wall. Franklyn Howe

Lets just stay nice and safely within the parameters of liberal establishment orthodoxy. Meanwhile populist movements grow ever stronger though the champagne socialists find it far beneath them to ever wonder why. The Debunker

The writer really should have studied the difference between Skinheads/Hard Mods and Oi Punk inspired Boneheads. lazy journalism. Gate13

Who makes the Nazi's? Bad television. ManUpTree

'Principally chronicling the adventures of a racist skinhead thug called Robbie Tomlinson,' Wasn't it Joe Hawkins? SpencerCGB

Yeah. but in this newly discovered masterpiece which has only ever been rumoured to exist, the name is changed to something suspiciously like Tommy Robinson's current name. Either the manuscript is a fake or maybe it doesn't really exist. The other half, who has read some of these, has pointed out that the

protagonist is Joe Hawkins, not Robbie Tomlinson. So either this was a shift from the original series, or, it has been changed or fabricated to suit Bannon's weird Tommy obsession by giving the protagonist a similar name. Simpletheory

Those small New English Library paperbacks were aimed at working class teenagers, so it is to be expected that they would be regarded with disdain around here. I must have read hundreds, you could trade them in on Preston Market and get more for 10p each. They were meant to be outrageous, with lots of random sex and violence, not to represent any sort of reality, and the readership were plenty sophisticated enough to know that. Very interesting to know that having read the 'Skinhead' series now qualifies me as some sort of neo-nazi. BrainDrain

Honestly can't remember the last time I saw a skinhead. Maybe, instead of tedious hand wringing, *Guardian* columnists should reflect on why Europe and America have lurched significantly to the right. Brotherlead

The jester performs his old routine and the courtesans chuckle at his tribute to their wisdom and grace. Outside the palace walls, the streets are restless. Edmundberk

Stewart Lee (AKA Stewart Home) stole my name in the 80's to promote his metropolitan liberal Elite art strike agenda, before letting himself go and becoming a left wing self parody of johnny vegas. Karen Eliot*

---

* According to Wikipedia, 'Karen Eliot is a multiple identity, a shared nom de plume that anyone is welcome to use for activist and artistic endeavours. It is a manifestation of the "open pop star" idea within the Neoist movement. The name was developed in order to counter the male domination of that movement, the most predominant multiple-use names previously being Monty Cantsin and Luther Blissett.'

So, to summarise, despite all the 'is it possibles' and 'too great to be coincidentals' you haven't got a clue whether Bannon has even heard of Allen. Bluefinch

Tommy Robinson and Robbie Tomlinson (the protagonist of the book) are such similar sounding names that it's almost a stretch to believe they are coincidental. Hades59

A floppy-haired beast of
Brexit walks among us

19 August 2018

The Herefordshire legend of Black Vaughan tells the story of an evil fifteenth-century nobleman who returns in various spectral forms – a black fly, a black dog, a black bull, some gerbils – to molest farm girls, spill milk and upset apple carts.*

But the dead aristocratic pest is eventually subdued by twelve priests and a pregnant woman in the Welsh border town of Kington, in a priest/pregnancy-based variant on Kurosawa's *Seven Samurai*.† Folklore tells us that we too could defeat our current existential crisis, or Boris Piccaninny Watermelon Letterbox Johnson, as it is commonly known.

Despite initially supporting people's right to wear the burqa this week, cake-and-eat-it style, Boris Piccaninny Watermelon

---

* I first came across this story in Frederick Grice's 1952 *Folk Tales of the West Midlands*, which I read aloud to my cold and hungry children by candlelight while staying in an old hunting lodge on Offa's Dyke in Monmouthshire, with no electricity or heating. It always seems odd to me that our national folk tales and myths are not part of the school reading curriculum, especially as loads of them are fucking fantastic, and certainly better than *Horrid Henry* or David Baddiel's children's book, *Captain Farty Smell Pants and the Poo Poo Monsters of Wee Wee Island*. Perhaps we could have bound our country together and avoided Brexit if all children were taught the tale of, for example, the magic milking cow of Mitchell's Fold?

† I also took the kids, when they were four and seven respectively, to see a screening of *Seven Samurai* in Japanese, with English subtitles. Don't you, again, wish I was your dad?

Letterbox Johnson ridiculed the ancient holy face window, simply to court the support of shy racists in his Gollum-like quest for the ring of power.*

Boris Piccaninny Watermelon Letterbox Johnson was doing the same thing when he embraced the Brexit he never believed in, a lie built on bendy bananas, non-existent NHS funding promises and millions of imaginary migrating Turks coming over here, with their massages, their baths and their Delight.

While there is a need for a robust debate on the role of religious symbolism in a pluralistic society, it is not clear if Boris Piccaninny Watermelon Letterbox Johnson is the most sensitive thinker we can throw at the issue. Especially when Boris Piccaninny Watermelon Letterbox Johnson appears to be colluding with the white supremacist news-fabricator and former Trumpeteer Steve Bannon, who hopes to initiate a far-right rising across Europe, while simultaneously wearing as many shirts as possible.†

Boris Piccaninny Watermelon Letterbox Johnson is a fat naughty dog, running away from the butcher's with a string of racist sausages, made of all the least nourishing parts of already discredited arguments, chased by betrayed Leave voters in straw hats and blood-stained aprons, shaking their fists and waving their cleavers.

As my wife will happily tell you, barely a day goes by without my referencing the mythology of our isles to decode current

---

* Earlier that week, Boris Johnson had said that Muslim women looked like letterboxes. Boris Johnson doesn't say anything by accident. Eight months later, when Muslims were massacred by a neo-Nazi in New Zealand, he delivered the customary message of condemnation.

† In July, it was revealed that Boris Johnson and Steve Bannon were in regular contact.

events, and indeed I file this column from a campsite on the cliffs of Tintagel, deep in King Arthur's Cornwall. My wife claims to be working all summer, and I have taken the children, Gina (seven) and Miller (eleven), away in a two-man pop-up tent, now strewn with filthy pasty wrappers, empty clotted-cream cartons and unspooled Jethro tapes, pilfered from garage forecourt bins.

Sadly, the ease of modern communication means it has been impossible to escape from current affairs, even here, where news of Cornwall's forthcoming post-Brexit collapse is finally making its way across the Tamar two years too late, borne by stumbling pack horses along EU-subsidised tracks.

Legend tells us that Arthur and his Knights of the Round Table will rise from their Tintagel cave in a time of national need. But when Arthur wakes, it will be too late, and he will emerge blinking into a swastika night of burning burqas and adequate food, cursing his cockerel and blaming a bad pint.*

Look instead for a solution to the Boris Piccaninny Watermelon Letterbox Johnson problem in the tale of Black Vaughan. According to Frederick Grice's 1952 study, *Folk Tales of the West Midlands*, it was a wise man from the Welsh Marches who told the people of Kington to fill St Mary's Church with twelve stout clerics and a pregnant woman, the latter to tempt Black Vaughan, in a strange half-echo of Boris Piccaninny Watermelon Letterbox Johnson's own reckless proclivities.

Sure enough, the chaotic spirit, a slippery devil that evaded capture by conventional means, soon entered the midnight church. But each time one of the clerics actually stood up to Black Vaughan's verbal provocations, the demon shrank a little in size, until he was finally trapped in a snuff box and thrown into the deep lake at nearby Hergest Court, where he remains to this day.

---

* King Arthur again! He is the new golem.

Stand up similarly to Boris Piccaninny Watermelon Letterbox Johnson's bullshit, and he too will shrink to snuff-box size. But who will defy him? The collaborators of the *Today* programme genuflect giggling before him; the *Daily Telegraph*, Britain's worst newspaper, funds his blatant falsehoods and algorithmically generated controversies to drive web traffic through its collapsing gates; the *Have I Got News for You* team, who taught Boris Piccaninny Watermelon Letterbox Johnson the skills he now uses to court the very worst people on Earth, hand their single tooth along their panel-show desk powerlessly; Theresa May cowers in impotence like King Théoden, as Jacob Rees-Mogg's hard Brexit Uruk-hai approach the citadel; and news folk are wafted away with a tea tray.[*]

Those in positions of power – journalists, fellow Conservative Party members wondering how things will pan out, people biding their time on the divided opposition benches, trembling television presenters in search of 'balanced arguments' in the face of blatant lies and transparent manipulation – know what this incubus is and what it is doing, and how it is prepared to put our futures at risk to achieve it. And yet they do not hold Boris Piccaninny Watermelon Letterbox Johnson to account. They will not shrink Boris Piccaninny Watermelon Letterbox Johnson to snuff-box size and sink him into the black lake of legend where he belongs. They will have to live with their failure. And, sadly, so will we.

Twelve wise priests and a pregnant woman cast Black Vaughan out of Kington church and into the deep water. But, to be fair,

---

[*] Boris Johnson defused the letterbox row by offering a tray of tea to journalists camped at the gates of his country house, which they, as usual, found to be a delightful example of his charming eccentricity. Good old Boris! Such a wag!!

what if the devil man Black Vaughan had his own funny weekly newspaper column? What if, instead of looking like a giant fly or a bull, he had amusing floppy hair, messed up to order? And what if, instead of swooping about like a frightening spectre, he had a tray of tea at the ready to catch his opponents off guard?

No one could realistically be expected to stand up to such powerful strategies.

Denmark sows the seeds of
discontent over Brexit

3 September 2018

It was Andrew Rawnsley's column in last week's *Observer* that first made me aware of the danger a no-deal Brexit would pose to British sperm supplies. Up to 50 per cent of our sperm is imported into the United Kingdom from Denmark alone, its cross-border movement currently micro-managed by EU organ and tissue directives, but now red tape may leave fresh sperm rotting at customs.*

The sperm shortage sounds, initially, like a rather silly story, an example of 'Project Fear' at its most desperate, and it has been covered in a typically smutty way by the tabloids, who say we must stiffen our resolve, and harden our intentions, to produce more sperm, exactly as one would expect them to.

But the breakdown in supplies of European, and specifically Danish, sperm will have genuine detrimental consequences for British couples trying to conceive artificially, and for scientific research, an area already set to be severely damaged by the withdrawal of EU funding and data sharing. With a national fertility crisis mushrooming, and our status as a global leader in scientific breakthroughs threatened, there has never been a worse time for Britain to be shut out of the sperm loop.

As a diehard Remoaner, the troubling statistics piqued my interest. Perhaps I could exploit them to criticise Brexit? After a little late-night googling at my laptop, I realised that, typically of overworked journalists who can no longer afford to cover

---

* This horrifying scenario is entirely possible.

anything in real depth, the *Observer*'s Andrew Rawnsley had only scratched the surface of the Danish semen story. The sperm crisis ran far deeper than even Rawnsley imagined, and over the last week I have become the Carole Cadwalladr of sperm.

It's not a coincidence that in 1969, liberal Denmark became the first country to legalise pornography, including with animals (NB: it's banned now). The vast proliferation of sexually stimulating material available, from everyday vanilla through to the strongest chocolate and/or strawberry flavoured imagery, soon made the cake and Lego loving land the international capital of onanism.

Indeed, throughout Scandinavia, the act of solo sexual gratification is still euphemistically known as 'going for a Danish' (in Swedish, '*går till en Danska*'; in Norwegian '*går til en Dansk*'; and in Finnish '*menee tanskaksi*').

To give you some idea of how deeply the notion of the Danes as lonely self-pleasers is embedded in Scandinavian culture, the popular 1970s Swedish satire show *Pappa Olaf's Karneval Av Idioter* included a famous sketch, voted the funniest joke of all time in a recent Swedish poll, where a foolish Norwegian visitor to London becomes angry when he is offered a Danish pastry by an effeminate cockney baker.

At first, commercial Danish sperm production was a small-scale affair. In the '70s and '80s, Danish sperm, packed in heavy, thick glass test tubes, was most commonly used as a mildly profitable ballast in the hold of their cargo ships. These Danish '*semen-både*', as they were known in the shipping industry, mainly carried more profitable Danish products, such as bacon and fish bits, to Europe, the semen subsequently sold on to collectors and enthusiasts for minimal return once the more commercial products had been disposed of.

But it was inevitable, as even the socialist Scandinavian states fell under the spell of the capitalist doctrines of Reaganomics and Thatcherism, that sooner or later the great national Danish pastime would be monetised. By the end of the '80s, Denmark was the unchallenged world leader in the business of commercial human sperm production. The Danish '*sperm-salg*' industry became a major concern, swiftly nationalised under the Dansk Sperm-Salg I Hele Verden banner, and employing tens of thousands of men in the manufacturing process.

But joining the dots of the supply chain of Danish sperm to modern Britain throws up a remarkable discovery: not only is nearly 50 per cent of our sperm sourced from Denmark, but nearly 85 per cent of that sperm is actually sourced from one Dane.

Hans Thrigger Andersen is a wiry fifty-year-old who enjoys the life of a comfortable *flâneur*, and he FaceTimed me from the jazzy counter-cultural enclave of Aarhus, on the Jutland peninsula. It was easy to understand why Hans's sperm-donor-directory profile pictures have, over the years, seen millions of British couples clamour for his sperm above that of most other Danish donors.

As a younger man, Hans, who is one of a small handful of full-time sperm-donating Danes, had the hard-rock angel good looks of Chris Hemsworth's Thor, and he's aged to sport the same rugged Viking charisma evidenced by the Canadian stand-up comedian and woodcutter Tony Law. It's a ludicrous coincidence that Hans's parents met in 1968, at an early Aarhus performance by Pekka Airaksinen's experimental Finnish band Sperm, and conceived him that very night, but he dismisses any idea of environmental determinism as deftly as he evades my attempts to inculcate him into the second referendum narrative.[*]

---

[*] Pekka Airaksinen's experimental Finnish band Sperm, whose work I had previously only owned as a bootleg CD-R, recently saw their entire

Despite the damage it will do to his livelihood and lifestyle, Hans is an unlikely champion of Brexit. 'Listen, I have spent my life lying on my back like a lazy hog. Brexit will force me to make something of myself. Same as maybe it will for Britain. The kitten is out of its sack, man. You make nothing and you can't feed yourselves and all your fruit is picked by Latvians. Sure, in the short term we are both taking a heavy cash hit, but maybe Brexit will make us get our shit together.'

I tried to press Hans further on exactly what he meant, but he had a daily quota to meet. In the short time we spoke, the tired Dane had already given me food for thought. If a man whose precarious lifestyle, predicated as it is on an endless cycle of continual self-abuse, can rationalise the destruction Brexit will wreak on his career as an opportunity for self-improvement, maybe it's time for all of us here in Britain to move on too and embrace the no-deal uncertainty as a chance for a new beginning.

The bit about 'going for a Danish' is news to me. I am Finnish, and the proposed Finnish translation is not even idiomatic Finnish, grammatically speaking. I think the author has been had. It is possible that a variety of this works in the other Nordic languages; Finnish is not a Nordic language, not even an European one, and Finland is not a part of Scandinavia either . . . and the proposed Swedish and Norwegian phrases look phoney to me too. Aaaargh

Are you sure you are a stand-up comedian? I would love to have seen you perform in a Sunderland working men's club

catalogue reissued as a luxury box set by Svart Records, under the title *50th Erection*.

in the days when stand-up was actually populated by talented observational comedians, before talentless people people thought they could be a comedian and a journalist, when in reality they are neither. Radsatser

Mastrubation in Swedish, '*går till en Danska*'. Never heard that expression. *Runka* is the most common bad word in Swedish for this form of self satisfaction. From *Runkesten* – the 'rocking stone'. The stone is resting on a very little surface that makes rock back and forth. Swedish '*Fika*' with a nice newly baked danish is also a wonderful type of self satisfaction. Best enjoyed in god company. I live in Sweden just to kilometers across from Denmark and I love Denmark as much as they evidently love them selves. I'm sure that mastrubation is more healthy than brexiting. Why not provide your own sperm instead of making things difficult? Scandia

Geez the EU even control our wanks. FFS!! Catonaboat

It seems genetically risky. If Hans is a long time serial sperm donor, he could have fathered many thousands of children. This could result in some half-siblings forming relationships and having children. Plus it's probably time Hans retired from the sperm donor business if he's in his 50's. Janaka77

Well as a Finn, I was slightly embarrassed that I had never heard the expression '*menee tanskaksi*': have I lived such a sheltered life? If you google '*menee tanskaksi*' or even the Swedish '*går till en Danska*' the only hit you get is to this very article. I was wondering whether someone had played a trick on the author. Eearweego

It's probably just simple invention to try to validate yet more remain propaganda. Nicetimes

As a Swede, let me tell any foreigners that there seems to be a lot a questionable claims in this piece . . . 'the act of solo sexual gratification is still euphemistically known as 'going for a Danish'. No, it's not. Some people may possibly use that phrase, but as a 40+ y.o Swede I can safely say I've NEVER heard it before. Certainly not even in the top 20 of euphemisms for that act. '1970s Swedish satire show *Pappa Olaf's Karneval Av Idioter*' is completely unheard of – and dosen't even produce a result when googled. And Regarding Danish pastries, they're actually famous for using chocolate more then frosting. So I wouldn't trust any of this, frankly. Rattenkrieg

If you can't be bothered to do some research and write proper articles, then choose a different career. Trevor Portman

I've heard it all now, i fell down the stairs yesterday but it was not my fault, it was because of Brexit, how pathetic this article is. Brightdaysahead

Cancel brexit because of a shortage of sperm? You really are scraping the bottom of the barrel now. Notfedupanymore

As a Finn, I have never ever heard the phrase '*mennä tanskaksi*' and in our language it does not really make any sense. Neither me or anyone in my family had ever heard of the idea of self pleasuring as something particularly danish. This is a very minor detail in the article, I know, but still I'm left wondering where the journalist has gotten the idea or found the odd phrase. Iturpein

I have come across the expression 'going for a Danish' when talking to a Swedish friend, who the had to explain as I did not understand why he couldn't eat it while he was playing (World of Warcraft). Hoppier

236

It shows the desperation of some remainers that Danish sperm becomes one of their last 'scares'. Springinamsterdam1

Hans wont get his act together. He will simply fall back on the Danish welfare state to fund him. ID1834560

Another example of Fake News from Project Fear. Bryanyali

'going for a Danish' Really? Never heard the term, which of course may merely demonstrate my own ignorance, but the fact that a Google search for the phrase turns up nothing but a reference to Mr Lee's article above and a reference to a four-year-old programme on Swedish Radio which deals with the natural sciences and discusses «*Spekulation om dagens nobelpris i fysik kanske går till en danska*» (speculation that today's Nobel Prize in physics might go to a Danish woman – it didn't) perhaps says a bit more on just how frequent this purported meme is in Swedish. Besides, anyone one with an elementary knowledge of Swedish orthography would realise that nationalities are not capitalised; i e, danska rather than Danska . . . Once upon a time, perhaps, the *Guardian* employed journalist who cared for the accuracy of their stories, rather than making it out of whole cloth. Mhenri

The author is a comedian, not a journalist, Henri. I know, most people don't realise either. Including those who have seen his stand up set or his tv shows. Thomas James

'In the '70s and '80s, Danish sperm, packed in heavy, thick glass test tubes, was most commonly used as a mildly profitable ballast in the hold of their cargo ships.' Ships normally take on ballast to replace the weight of offloaded cargo. Sailing with both aboard, let alone with neither, is very unwise. Unreliable research! Havin_it

There is no such thing as 'Dansk Sperm-Salg I Hele Verden' (we don't usually talk of 'sperm' but use the term '*sæd*'), and most certainly 'swiftly nationalised under the Dansk Sperm-Salg I Hele Verden banner' is just utter nonsense. Also, 'Indeed, throughout Scandinavia, the act of solo sexual gratification is still euphemistically known as 'going for a Danish' (in Swedish, '*går till en Danska*'; in Norwegian '*går til en Dansk*'; and in Finnish '*menee tanskaksi*')' – although amusing – simply isn't true, and as has been pointed out, not even idiomatic. Lj1909

Take back control! Buy water!!
Bin the *Daily Telegraph*!!!

9 September 2018

It is very easy to sneer and criticise without offering any viable solutions yourself. And I should know. I have been doing it for the best part of three decades now myself, across a variety of media, to deadlines, for money, like a snowflake Clarkson.

But I am a shallow and cynical entertainer, not a politician who is supposed to believe in anything. And so, I suspect, when all is said and done, is Boris Piccaninny Watermelon Letterbox Johnson. And why not? It worked for Donald Trump.

Each morning in the small hours, Donald Trump's bladder slowly fills with urine. The president wakes and looks at his phone in the bathroom, while fumbling in his silken sleeping pants for the flesh pyracantha of his genital. He sees something true online and instantly sends off a combative tweet. Sad! Bleary journalists panic and the fairy tinkling of Donald Trump's cold night penis dominates the daily American news cycle once more.

Boris Piccaninny Watermelon Letterbox Johnson obviously aims to surf the British news wave in a similar fashion to the orange goblin. But unlike the instantaneous nocturnal pee-pee spatterings of Trump, the massive faecal log of Watermelon's weekly column in the *Daily Telegraph* takes a full seven days to bake. Straining his handbag-pug face into a purple Eton mess each Monday morning, Watermelon temporarily blocks the U-bend of the British news bog with his latest stinking offering, before standing next to the bowl, and gesturing at his produce, like a delighted toddler expecting parental praise for his mastery of basic bowel functions.

The *Daily Telegraph* clickbait trap is set. Watermelon is its mouse-murdering cheese. The paper's front-page news headlines duly re-trumpet the controversy. And this controversy was fuelled by the falsehoods of the Boris Piccaninny Watermelon Letterbox Johnson column that the *Daily Telegraph*'s own editor chose to run inside. It is an endless loop of lies.

In the 1997 James Bond film *Tomorrow Never Dies*, the state-sponsored assassin–rapist 007 thwarts an evil, global, multi-platform news agency that uses covert actions to generate newsworthy crises, which it then profits from by covering them. Twenty-one years ago, this plotline seemed as implausible as Roger Moore's third nipple. But it now appears to be the actual modus operandi of the *Daily Telegraph*.

And who can blame the paper for paying Watermelon £275,000 a year to disseminate lies, to drive the sewage of its readership through the sluice gates of both its print and online editions? These are tough times for newspapers, and before the *Daily Telegraph* re-employed Watermelon as a lifeline, it was pinning all its sales hopes on our humble friend . . . water.

For years, it seemed, whenever I tried to buy a bottle of water in a railway station WHSmith's, the cashier would suggest I bought a copy of the *Daily Telegraph* instead, which cost less than the water and came with free water. But taking the free water while buying a copy of the *Daily Telegraph* increases the apparent circulation figures of the *Daily Telegraph*, and by association its financial clout and its power to influence and manipulate the vermin that read it.

As someone who has suffered personally as a result of the *Daily Telegraph*'s half-truths,* I would like to pay for the water and not

---

* In November 2013, the *Daily Telegraph* ran a review of my live show, under the heading 'Why I Walked Out of a Stewart Lee Gig', which

take the *Daily Telegraph* with the free-water gift instead. Even though, as the confused WHSmith's assistant always insists, as if reciting a script she was forced to learn at gunpoint by Charles Moore, buying the *Daily Telegraph* and getting the water free is less costly than buying the water alone and not having the *Daily Telegraph* with it.

When I finally cracked and demanded, at Paddington's WHSmith's in October 2016, to take only the water and not the *Daily Telegraph* also, the poor assistant – an innocent victim here too, let's not forget – had to call her manager over. She explained to him that she had tried to sell me the *Daily Telegraph*, as instructed, but that I would only take the water, as he looked on disapprovingly, an unwanted copy of the *Daily Telegraph* flapping on the counter, like a dying and poisonous fish.

It was a Kafkaesque situation. Much of what I write in these columns is exaggerated for comic effect (I am not, for example, a confidant of a Danish man who supplies 85 per cent of

---

chose, presumably deliberately, to misrepresent my acted act as the work of a vindictive man genuinely undergoing a temperamental mental breakdown, a conceit the rest of the crowd understood and laughed heartily at. Despite having left at half-time, the critic filed the review: 'If Lee had a shred of interest or insight into the working lives of other people, he'd realise that those who give up an evening at the end of a week to see him deserve his thanks not his toxic scorn.' It has taken me three decades of painstaking practice to manufacture that level of convincing toxic scorn, and I offer it to the audiences with the greatest of love and respect, and at cheaper rates than any comparably acclaimed act. And the punters were eating that scorn out of my hand! Nonetheless, this shit hung around in the top ten Google hits of my name for years, portraying me as some kind of unhinged psychopath, and I suspect it cost the kids a few playdates. The following week, after facing mass ridicule online from people who were at the show, and who all got the idea, the critic returned and filed a more balanced report.

the semen imported into Britain, as I claimed last week), but this went down just as described. The frightened young girl was eventually absolved by the manager, and I was allowed to refuse my compulsory *Daily Telegraph* purchase.

But surely a world where innocent children are forced to buy the *Daily Telegraph*, when all they wanted was water, is exactly the kind of authoritarian, anti-individual society the libertarian think-monkeys of the *Daily Telegraph* don't want? Take back control!

Tragically, the unsustainable mania for marketing bottled water that the *Daily Telegraph* exploited to peddle its lies is one factor driving the planet towards being a lifeless, arid wasteland. One day, the only way you will be able to get water will be by buying a copy of the *Daily Telegraph*, which, after the cockroach and the comparably resilient Boris Piccaninny Watermelon Letterbox Johnson, may be the last recognisable traces of the world we knew. It's typical of the strange contradictions of Brexit Britain that the *Daily Mail*'s anti-plastic-straw campaign makes it a definable defender of the very world the *Daily Telegraph* seems determined to destroy.

But the tide may yet be turning against the planet-murdering, lying *Daily Telegraph* and its lying public face, as the Overton window[*] of Boris Piccaninny Watermelon Letterbox Johnson's accession to the throne of broken Brexit Britain narrows. Last Monday, Watermelon's latest empty, anti-EU *Daily Telegraph* missive barely even provoked outrage, just looks of tired despair

[*] This is the second mention of the Overton window in this book. And yet, as I sit here writing these footnotes, I can't even remember what the fucking Overton window is. You look it up. I've got early-onset Alzheimer's, I reckon. It's thirty years of gigs and never sleeping. I don't even know what the me from a year ago was talking about. Fuck! Fuck! I'm fucking . . . Fuck!

in the faces of those charged with delivering the impossible Brexit Watermelon himself once promised.

Boris and Trump are a lot funnier than most of today's comedians. Humour is often offensive, even cruel, unfortunately today's professional comedy isn't very funny. Morrisseysmiff

Wasn't it Scaramanga who had 3 nipples? This is just another example of the left wing misinformation that the *Telegraph* protects us from. Geomann9336

Not entirely fake, in the movie bond has a fake third nipple to assume scaramanga's identity. Coppered

Silly article really, especially the bit belittling 007. Stopped reading when you started that. Neosio

I had a similar problem when I tried to buy *The Guardian* without the Remain half-truths. I wanted to remove those and buy the rest but I couldn't. CufCo1

It would be interesting to know how old you are. I would hazard a guess that you are 11. Brotherlead

'When I demanded, at WH Smiths in October 2016, to take only the water the poor assistant had to call her manager' – could you not have just taken he paper and binned it? Do you really have to virtue signal at every opportunity? We will be leaving the EU. We had a debate and a referendum and yiurside lost. MrDW1968

Laugh? I nearly started. Idopas

Don't drag Abba into Theresa May's Dead-Cat Dance

5 October 2018

The only available room in Birmingham last Tuesday night was an Airbnb on Edward Street. Usually, the Birmingham tourist board is giving them away free, with incentivising jars of Bovril* and vouchers for the legendary Hurst Street café Mr Egg. 'Eat like a king for under a pound!'†

But tonight, Birmingham was buzzing. There was a heavy police presence, and Ladypool Road had run out of balti, which I assumed was because I was the opening comedian for local blue-collar Beefheartian post-punk survivors The Nightingales at the Hare and Hounds in King's Heath.‡

However, when I got into the room, I found I was overlooking the International Convention Centre, the home of the room-gobbling

---

* Hmmm. I am going to drink some Bovril right now, I think, and then carry on with these footnotes.

† Mr Egg is still there, but has reopened as a Chinese street food café, and doesn't only serve eggs. What's the point of that? It's political correctness gone mad.

‡ I went on tour opening for The Nightingales. Michael Cumming (*Brass Eye*, *Toast*) and I are trying to make a film about them. I had first played the Hare and Hounds in February 1990, on a stand-up bill with Frank Skinner, Steve Coogan and Henry Normal. This meant that when opening for The Nightingales, I was able to use, and attribute, Ian Macpherson's famous and much-copied opening line, which has been theorised about at length by the writer Robert Wringham: 'They say you play [the Hare and Hounds] twice in your career. Once on the way up. Once on the way down. It's good to be back.'

2018 Conservative Party conference, which was in progress beneath my window. After last year's stand-up stage-invasion debacle,* I was surprised security checks had allowed a comedian like me within sight of the conference, and would like those responsible for this oversight to be spanked senseless in Josef K's broom cupboard.†

Perhaps I avoided being on the radar of security staff looking out for comedians because I am 'about as funny as a bonfire in a burning orphanage. I thought comedy was sposed 2 b funny', as you will doubtless say in the below-the-article comments online, Mr TrueBritExitEuropeKremlinbot19.

On Wednesday morning, staring over my laptop at the Conservative Party conference venue, I assumed it would be easy to shit out Sunday's thousand-word screed of liberal elite humour, but I was sick of laughing at the Tories, so I trawled the papers for other stories. Tuesday's *Independent* newspaper headline 'Planning Glitch Delays Sex Robot Brothel', a sentence in which almost every word suggests a story in its own right, seemed promising. But then I saw a photo of a sad-faced blonde sex robot staring blankly out of the page, and I felt she had suffered enough ignominy without me adding to her woes.

I had the same feeling of mercy when I witnessed a mouse-faced Michael Gove eating wasabi peas alone in a Costa Coffee at Knutsford services last week, and quietly binned my latest Gove-mocking tract.‡

---

* The comedian Simon Brodkin had managed to get near enough to the conference stage to hand Theresa May a P45.

† I keep mentioning Kafka as well, don't I? Kafka, the golem, '60s/'70s Marvel comics and King Arthur's Knights of the Round Table. As I read back over all these pieces in one go, it's as if I've hardly ever read anything. I'm a fraud with an English degree and an Honorary University Fellowship.

‡ A few weeks previously, early on a Saturday morning, I was queueing

up alone in an empty Costa Coffee at Heston services on the M4, where I had previously been smirked at by Toby Young. Suddenly, someone joined the line behind me. It was Michael Gove, unaccompanied and vulnerable. I suspected he might remember me from when I wrote on *Stab in the Dark*, nearly three decades ago, and I knew from her *Daily Mail* column that his wife Sarah Vine was aware that I had written in the *Observer*, and subsequently said in my live show, that Gove having sex with her was worse than David Cameron supposedly having had sex with a dead pig. I assumed Gove would know this too. I realised I had to seize the initiative. 'Hello, Michael, how are you?' I said, taking him by surprise. 'Stewart Lee!' he said, immediately. 'Where are you off to this early, Michael?' 'I am going to an agricultural show,' he said, plausibly. There was a pause. 'What was that show I wrote for that you were on?' I asked in a mild suppressed panic, genuinely unable to recall its name. 'It was *Stab in the Dark*, a long time ago now,' Gove answered, before adding, 'I see your *Content Provider* show is on the BBC.' 'Yes, it's still hanging around.' Then there was another big pause, during which I realised I would probably never get the chance to speak to Michael Gove ever again, so I asked him, 'What are you going to do about the mess you have got everyone into?' 'I don't know,' said Gove, looking genuinely bewildered, and against my better judgement, I felt sorry for him. Gove hadn't intended to win the referendum. It was a public-school debating club exercise writ impossibly large, meant to give the rugger buggers he had hated since his teenage poetry days in *Independent Voices III* a scare that went rather too well. And having won it, Gove hadn't realised the disastrous chain of events it would set in motion. 'Well,' I said, 'you don't want Brexit to be your legacy.' 'Everyone seems to want it to be,' Gove answered, meaninglessly. I took my coffee, shook his hand, said 'Good luck', shrugged at him and left. My wife and kids were hiding in the WHSmith's, suppressing themselves. In the car, I said to my wife that as I had met the sorry-looking Michael Gove unexpectedly on neutral territory, where he had acted as dignifiedly as possible, it wouldn't be fair to write up the encounter anywhere, funny as it was, as what happens in Heston services stays in Heston services. But since that strange encounter, Gove has continued to be a grade-A bell-end and a lying, self-serving div, whose theatrically manipulative speech about Corbyn after

Then, that afternoon, in the van from Birmingham to Hackney's fashionable Moth Club, Nightingales guitarist James Smith showed me a clip on his phone of Theresa May prancing uneasily to an Abba record, like a mantis with an inner ear infection.

Dead-cat strategies attempt to distract the public from some impending political disaster, but this was off the scale. Theresa May hadn't so much thrown the dead cat on the table as slit it open, scooped out its guts, swallowed them whole and worn its eviscerated feline body as some kind of hideous hat of gore.

Nonetheless, her idiotic Dead-Cat Dance was received with loyal approval by the usual snap-on tools of democracy.* James

---

the Labour Party's no-confidence motion on 16 January 2019 was, I think, a new low in the dishonesty and vindictiveness of parliamentary politics. So fuck him, the stupid Heston services, Brexit-causing twat.

* When I was a kid, my mother let out our box room to students at Solihull Technical College and cooked them two square meals a day, as well as teaching medical shorthand at night school and doing a full-time job in the doctor's. One of the girls used to be picked up by her boyfriend in his company van, which had 'Snap-On Tools' written on the side, which my mother found very funny. I never understood why, until, when I was about seventeen, I managed to get really drunk in a pub in Solihull on Christmas Eve and went home in a state of disarray, unequalled until the night before my wedding, when I tried to shit in a drawer. My mother said, on Christmas morn, 'Were you drunk last night?' And I said, 'No.' She said, 'Oh, it's just that you came into my room, got your tool out and pointed it at the teasmade, and I said, "Do you want to go to the toilet?" and directed you to the bathroom.' In my mother's mind, 'tool' was post-war '50s slang for a penis, and so the van with 'Snap-On Tools' written on it had amused her, because it suggested a penis which could be clipped on to the owner's groin.

It was brilliant having student lodgers, who were like older brothers and sisters I never had, but who would go after a year or so and drift

247

Cleverly, Conservative MP for Braintree, who despite having the word 'clever' in his own name and the word 'brain' in that of his constituency, found time to tweet, stupidly, 'Great to see Theresa May dance on to the stage to Dancing Queen by ABBA. Classy.' This was something no one else anywhere in the world was thinking, as they watched, cringing with embarrassment, through their splayed fingers.

Meanwhile, the *Telegraph*, a monochromatic shit-sheet which is given away free with water in WHSmith's, opined: 'Journalists gasped. Politicians burst into applause and laughter. Abba's Dancing Queen played loud, and Theresa May shimmied her way to the podium.' Presumably, I have spent my entire life misunderstanding the idea of shimmying. If I am ever hit by a car and have to crawl towards the edge of the road to die, trailing my guts behind me, I will be sure to think of myself as 'shimmying' into the gutter.

And while her colleagues continue to nail Corbyn hard to the floor for his shortcomings, the BBC's Laura Kuenssberg remains a friendly face that Theresa May visibly looks for in a difficult

---

slowly away: Welsh Jocelyn, who read to me; Gordon from Manchester, who taught me karate moves and bought me contraband Conan magazines from Nostalgia Comics in Smallbrook Queensway; Rachel, whose uncle in America was the Marvel Comics writer John Byrne and who got me some signed Spider-Man art; and Emma, who liked The Velvet Underground, back when no one else did, and who let me and my sixth-form girlfriend sleep secretly and uneventfully overnight in a countryside hotel, where she worked after she absconded from Solihull Tech. I had a fantastic childhood, with my mother, in that little house, with all those groovy teens who thought I was a cool weirdo and were kind to me. Last week, Welsh Jocelyn texted me to check my current address, over forty years on. Maybe she remembered my birthday is coming up. No one in my immediate family did.

press conference, knowing she will throw her an easy question bone. Kuenssberg tweeted, 'PM massive sense of humour alert – comes on to Dancing Queen, jigs about – hall loves it.' But I thought humor woz sposed 2 b funny.

If May's ill-advised advisers were hoping to use her Dead-Cat Dance as a distraction from the impossibility of reaching a satisfactory Brexit solution, they may have misjudged the situation. Mung bean-munching musicians hate it when Conservatives appropriate their work. Johnny Marr commanded David Cameron not to like The Smiths, and presumably must now have extended that embargo to For Britain poster-boy Morrissey too.

ABBA have already expressed concern about the abuse of their work for political ends, and threatened to sue the far-right, anti-immigration Danish People's Party for appropriating 'Mamma Mia'. Former Hep Star Björn Ulvaeus himself has described Brexit as 'a disaster', and as the Eurovision Song Contest's most famous winners, Abba embody the spirit of pan-European cooperation that anti-immigration, anti-European Tories on the far right of the party seek to undermine.

Avatars of the '70s Keep Britain Tidy campaign, Abba were early adopters of the sort of environmental concerns that the Tories' drive towards a deregulated post-Brexit Britain will abandon. And in featuring such historical arch-rivals as a yellow-haired woman and a brown-haired woman, and a fat bearded man and a thin clean-shaven man, working in perfect harmony, Abba showed that different people could cooperate for the common good, rather than fight their fellows like horrid Brexit rats.*

It's highly likely that Theresa May's Dead-Cat Dance will end

---

* Abba are an essential element of my childhood, and so many of their songs are seared into my memory, irrespective of the fluctuating value of

in Swedish pop anger, and the spin-wazzocks who talked her into it will soon distance themselves from their suggestion. There is no solution to the Conservatives' impasse. Theresa's Dead-Cat Dance aimed to ensure that people talked about her moves, however humiliating, rather than her speech. And you fell for it. 'The Winner Takes It All' would have been better walk-on music. All the cards are played and there is nothing left to say.

On a point of infomation, Bjorn was not a member of the Hep Stars it was Bennie, Bjorn was in The Hootenanny Singers a sort of folkish group based on the early 1960s US style folk bands including their characteristic liberal/leftish earnestness. Who can forget their first hit Jag väntar vid min mila (translated as 'I'm Waiting at the Charcoal Kiln')? Poppa Alcohol

---

their cultural currency. My dad had their tapes in the car, and my mum had their analogue synth-driven masterpiece *Arrival* on vinyl, which occupies a similar sonic territory to Pulp's 1995 breakthrough, *Different Class*. We took the kids to the Abba Museum, in a snow-smothered Stockholm, at Christmas 2018, which my Swedish brother-in-law thought ridiculous. I found it very moving, especially the stuff about how the (often superb) Swedish psychedelic and progressive bands ostracised Abba for their perceived crimes against music, but I bailed before I reached the room dedicated to that *Mamma Mia* musical, and the subsequent film, which I think are cheesy and trivialise Abba's legacy. I didn't want to see that music-theatre filth. That's not the Abba I remember.

Is it ethical to raise a royal baby in captivity?

21 October 2018

Royal babies are baked to order, like lucky pies, to provide gurgling distractions in times of crisis. Last week, the world's scientists agreed we have twelve years to limit the worst climate-change damage or else face mass extinction. Within days, as floods washed away the villages of the Aude valley and their delicious French wines, we began fracking in Lancashire in the face of heroic protest, and a dismissive Donald Trump accused scientists of having a 'political agenda'. Nothing changed. But look! A baby!! A baby!!! A bouncing royal baby!!!!

Like many former *Class War* subscribers now approaching late middle age, I belatedly find myself quite a fan of the Queen, largely due to Dame Helen Mirren's amazing acting in the film *The Queen*, in which she invested the eponymous heroine with imaginary depths and assumed feelings.

Michael Parkinson is such a fan of Dame Helen Mirren's talents that he keeps a stuffed toy of Nyra, the magic owl Mirren played in *The Owls of Ga'Hoole*, under his pillow. Sometimes, in the restless night, Michael Parkinson sneers at the felt owl for its voluptuousness and accuses the woodland creature of trying to bewitch him. But the Yorkshireman is from a different time and must not be judged by the owl-respecting standards of today.*

Monarchists' last line of defence of the royal family boils down to the fact that they, and specifically their newborns, are good for

---

* Michael Parkinson's creepy 1975 interview with Helen Mirren is an object lesson in how the world has changed over the last forty years.

tourism. But if this is the case, then surely we as a nation are guilty of failing to fully monetise the royal babies' tourist appeal. Can we afford to be so profligate with our assets in the forthcoming era of Brexit-driven financial uncertainty?

For the last four and a half years, I have worked on my laptop most days in the café of London Zoo, where I am unknown to the tourists. The zoo's marketing people persuaded me, over an enchilada one lunchtime, to provide the recorded voice of an ennui-stricken black widow spider in the Bug House, but other than that I am virtually invisible in my café corner. And so I am able to eavesdrop on the staff.*

Plans are afoot, so it would appear from the brown-coated huddle I overheard last week, to repurpose Berthold Lubetkin's iconic 1934 penguin pool. While recognised as a twentieth-century design classic, in 2004 the enclosure was emptied of penguins, who didn't like swimming in it as, like Boris Johnson, it was too shallow to be of any use to anyone.

Having frustrated generations of sea birds for more than eighty years, Lubetkin's white elephant now languishes drained and dry, too famous to demolish and too impractical to function, the Millennium Dome of marine aviaries. Now, it is to be inhabited again, but only, it would appear, during usual zoo opening hours. Would the normal keepers be doing the feeding or would the zoo's latest addition have its own handlers? the hushed staff asked one another. Would they be allowed to look it in the eye? Would there be special protocols? And above all, how was the zoo going to cope with the tourist numbers when the next royal baby was put on permanent public display in Lubetkin's empty penguin pool?

---

* This zoo spider voice-over job is the only thing I have ever done that gives me any credibility with my daughter's friends.

Everything had been thought through in meticulous detail, the possibility of public objections overruled in deference to our desperate need for tourist dollars. Tickets will be auctioned to the highest bidder and income projections are already off the scale, knocking pregnant pandas into a cocked hat. Royal chefs will prepare the child's food on site, but the normal zookeepers will be required to hurl the luxury dinners from buckets towards the royal baby, encouraging it to leap and caper for the paying public's delight.

When the royal baby reaches school age, a tutor will sit in the enclosure with it all day, to make sure it is properly educated, though he or she will bring their own packed lunch, which must not contain nuts. The royal child will be permitted to do its main toilet on tabloid newspapers in the private penguin nesting area, but everything else will happen in public view, thus preparing it, perhaps more successfully than with any previous royal, for a lifetime of spotlit scrutiny.

And should the royal baby, heaven forbid, suddenly choose to dress as a Nazi stormtrooper and parade around the penguin pool saluting, or to show its bottom to partygoers, the child will learn the hard way what it means to live a life in full public view, as the camera-phones of those surrounding the enclosure flash into social media-integrated life.

And at the end of each working day, the royal child will be air-lifted by helicopter to Kensington Palace, where it will then live a completely normal existence as a member of the royal family, waited on hand and foot, opening hospices and being stalked by photographers.

But once I saw a gang of young men leaning over the Asian short-clawed otter enclosure wall to feed Starbursts™ to the animals. I told them that the sweets would surely be very bad for the otters, and to their credit the boys went off, horrified, to find a keeper to confess to.* And everyone knows the implausible, but not necessarily untrue, urban myth of the amorous Florida zoo employee who died due to his overfamiliarity with an alligator.

Can we expose a member of the royal family to these kinds of risks in the name of national solvency? We need to take a long, hard look at ourselves, as a society, if we are prepared to prioritise the generation of money over the mental and physical well-being of a child, even if that child is a member of the royal family. Call me unpatriotic, or a snowflake, call me what you like, but I for one will not be queuing up to see the newborn royal baby leaping around for food flung from buckets into a disused penguin enclosure. I think it is wrong.

Well they already live in a zoo, don't they, albeit a series of luxury ones? Tepapa

* I spent about four years writing most days in the café of London Zoo, and I would go and see the otters, which I have loved since reading Henry Williamson's *Tarka the Otter* as a child, whenever I wanted a wander. The stupid way members of the public behaved with them, feeding them crisps and sweets, made me think the world would be better off if all humanity were exterminated and otters were left to inherit the Earth, tossing tiny pebbles from paw to paw.

A no-column Brexit is the
only way forward

18 November 2018

Dear readers, it has been an honour to try to write this week's supposedly funny column about Brexit for you. But I regret to say that after a long and painful struggle through Wednesday 14 November and the morning of Thursday 15 November, attempting to write a funny column on this week's proposed Brexit deal, I have found that, for my part, I cannot complete it.*

Throughout my attempts to deliver this week's funny column, I have been hampered by the fact that Brexit moves either at impossible speed or remains in a state of terminal inertia. I am like a photographer, commissioned to document the offspring of the hideous forced mating of a slug and a hummingbird, still wondering what shutter speed I should use. It has proved impossible to reconcile the need to provide a column that will still make sense on Sunday with the demand that it is delivered to my editor on Thursday morning.

I hadn't quite understood the full extent of this, but if you look at the *Observer* and you look at how it works, it is particularly reliant on content being delivered in advance of the paper being printed. I think probably the average reader might not be aware of the full

---

* This piece is basically former Brexit secretary Dominic Raab's resignation letter, and his speech about the Dover–Calais crossing, with some of the words changed. The writing was on the wall for Raab anyway, after he had said, the week previously, that he 'hadn't quite understood' how reliant the UK's trade in goods is on stuff coming in on boats.

extent to which the choice of content in the finished newspaper is dependent on stuff being written in advance of publication.

Who caused the Brexit disaster? I wondered aloud on Wednesday morning, as I looked for a peg to hang this flimsy piece on. Was it Disaster Capitalists, like Arron Banks, planning to profiteer from the chaos? Was it Disaster Socialists, like Jeremy Corbyn, hoping to home-bake a better Britain from the wreckage in his Islington patisserie? Was it Disaster Racists, like my relative who voted Leave to 'get rid of the Pakistanis and Indians', and whose existence will now be questioned in below-the-line comments on the online version of this piece, accusing me of inventing a straw man to demonise stupid Leave voters, as if there were any need to fabricate one. Or was it the Disaster Johnsons, like Boris Piccaninny Watermelon Letterbox Cake Disaster Johnson, hoping to drop an Etonian biscuit into his reflection in the melted molten-metal puddle of post-Brexit Britain and let lustful nature take its course?

Whoever is to blame, as Wednesday afternoon turned into Wednesday evening, and my 10 a.m. Thursday morning deadline loomed, the full impossibility of delivering the mildly satirical column expected of me by both my readers and my editor began to dawn on me. I emailed my editor to ask if this week's piece could be absent from Sunday's printed edition of the *Observer* and then belatedly inserted into the online edition, by unilateral agreement, perhaps in as much as two years' time, as a kind of satirical column backstop, when the meaning of the week's events finally becomes clear. But, like the EU, she is inflexible and cruel, and rejects my unilateral backstop arrangement, and instead demands that I continue to provide the levels of content I had been contracted for at the time stipulated.

During Wednesday afternoon, on talk radio, the phrase 'vassal state' started to emerge as a mantra, chanted by angry people who didn't understand it, and I wondered if this was the sort of thing that might fill up a paragraph or two. Indeed, the same furious Leavers now fixated on the 'vassal state' previously offered up the words 'WTO rules', as if they were a protection against Euro-serpents. And what did 'vassal state' mean exactly? Perhaps I could have pretended that it meant we wouldn't be able to import or export our own Vaseline, or decide ourselves what was an appropriate use for it, and then make a column out of that idea? Perhaps not?

I waited for two and a half hours, from 5 until 7.30 p.m., for Theresa May to come out of No. 10 and solve the riddle of the Brexit sphinx, hoping I could make a column out of her statement. I started drinking cider and began to find the word 'backstop' funny in and of itself, as if it were some kind of innuendo. I wondered how, as a vassal state without its own supply of Vaseline, we would cope with our backstop arrangements. My friend Kevin Eldon, who plays an old wizard in *Game of Thrones*, suggested the vassal/Vaseline/backstop idea could perhaps be linked to the notion of 'frictionless trade'.

For a while I thought maybe I could make a whole column out of this trivial and smutty conceit, but I realised it would leave everyone dissatisfied, diminish my standing in the columnist community, and discredit the *Observer* newspaper, and that a bad column was perhaps worse than no column at all.

In short, I cannot reconcile the content of the proposed column with the standards expected from me by both my readers and my editor. This is, at its heart, a matter of public trust. I appreciate that you may disagree with my judgement on this issue. I have weighed very carefully the alternative courses of action which I could take. Ultimately, you deserve a column which can satirise the week's Brexit events with conviction and understanding. I am only sorry, in good conscience, that this column is not that column, and so I hereby announce that I am abandoning this week's column forthwith, shrugging my shoulders with a 'will this do?' insouciance, pressing 'send' and leaving someone else to deal with the mess I have made.

My respect for you and the fortitude you have shown while reading this difficult column remains undimmed.

How about using your column to explore the idea of CANCELLING BREXIT? Or perhaps you are another media ostrich with your head in the sand . . . ignoring the fact that unless we CANCEL BREXIT we are committing to years of the same mess since June 2016. Kalumba

Man up! Hairy Scrotum

Nobody voted for this column. Moose Tickler

Ha, like I give a fuck, I qualify for an Irish column on my father's side. Not In A Million

In this case, no column would have been far preferable. Brodie Jigsaw

You just can't help taking a potshot at Corbyn, can you? Socialism – sharing resources – is simply too radical for mainstream press mouthpieces. Shame on you. Eegarcia

Why Jacob Rees-Mogg is still voting with his feet

2 December 2018

As the lies that drove Brexit unravel under the spotlight of actual fact, so the reasons bewildered Leave voters gave for supporting it seem increasingly tragic. My relative who wanted to get rid of Pakistanis and Indians and other people from the far south-eastern region of the EU, finds they are still here, curing him, presenting the news and cooking delicious baltis.

Those wooed, understandably, by the bus-borne '£350m a week for the NHS' bullshit now know it was just one of Boris Piccaninny Watermelon Letterbox Cake Disaster Johnson's many self-serving falsehoods. But even now it is being regurgitated by Theresa May, a horrible vomiting cormorant sicking up lies into the squawking beaks of the terminally and furiously disappointed, hoping that if their gullets are at least full of something, anything, however baseless, they will at last shut up.

Those who voted Leave as a protest, hoping to give the elite a scare, reluctantly admit they overplayed their hands somewhat. Even Michael Gove, who, in the words of his *Daily Mail* wife, was 'only supposed to blow the bloody doors off', now chooses to attach himself, the limpet of regret, to the hulls of various blameless environmental causes, in an attempt to disassociate himself from the national catastrophe his pitiful vanity has initiated. Michael Gove hopes to be remembered, instead, as the Dian Fossey of Surrey's hedgehogs. But Brexit is Michael Gove's only legacy. And the shame of it will outlive all of his hedgehogs.

Only Jacob Rees-Mogg, one of our few conviction politicians, can still hold his head up high and say that he had a reason to leave the EU that remains not demonstrably untrue. For, in the early days of the Leave campaign, Rees-Mogg nailed his colours to the same mast of hope that he was again saluting last Monday morning, when he made the case for hard Brexit once more to his familiar, Nick Ferrari, on LBC: the benefits of free trade focused through the lens of Cheaper Footwear.

It is true that in 2006, the shoe-producing EU nations slapped blocks on Asian shoe imports that drove up high-street prices. But only a genius like Rees-Mogg could realise how emotive this footwear issue was for the UKIP/Brexit axis. Brexit supporters, it appears, get through a lot of shoes, after hurling them at the television whenever Gina Miller comes on *Question Time*.

And now, long since all other supposed good reasons for exiting the EU have been invalidated by facts, Rees-Mogg's 'cheaper footwear' gambit remains undiscredited. But this is largely, it must be said, because no one from the corrupt pro-EU elite thought it important enough to try and discredit, which just shows how out of touch they are with what ordinary people care about.

For many Brexit voters, the financial benefits of EU membership – investment in rural infrastructure, sharing of scientific research, work and education opportunities – remain tantalisingly abstract, and seem geared to the needs of the metropolitan liberal elite. But the cost of footwear is a tangible concrete concept, and it is this notion that Rees-Mogg harnessed to arouse the Europhobia of the British people. After all, everyone has feet, or knows someone who has, whereas not everyone knows someone who has benefited from the work of the European Space Agency. And if it is trying to contact queue-jumping aliens, that is hardly likely to endear it to the Brexit voter.

But even Brexit supporters with no feet might want to buy a shoe, if only to hurl at the television in case Gina Miller comes on *Question Time*. And they would probably want that shoe to cost as little as possible. And they wouldn't care if it was an Asian shoe, as long as it wasn't jumping the shoe queue.

Rees-Mogg's own two feet continue to fascinate all of us, and one can see why footwear would be of such importance to him. Rees-Mogg has always looked younger than forty-nine, especially when he was a child, though he is finally beginning to decay. However, a swift Internet image search will show that Rees-Mogg's shoes have remained unchanged throughout Rees-Mogg's life. Either Rees-Mogg is wearing a new pair of shoes every day, in which case one could understand his obsession with footwear prices and their relationship with EU membership, or some more sinister factor is at play. Rees-Mogg's shoes, always shiny, always bright, never scuff or age. I looked at 570 consecutive photographs of Jacob Rees-Mogg's unchanged shoes online and then gave up, the horror seeming to tear at my throat.

In *The Picture of Dorian Gray*, by Oscar Wilde, a man sells his soul to the devil or something, I expect, and there's a drawing of him and it gets old and he stays the same. Brexit rots in front of our eyes, wilting on the vine. But Rees-Mogg's shoes remain unchanged. And who is this 'nanny' who has accompanied him since birth, guiding his political progress, steering us towards our doom? Whatever diabolical deal the footwear-obsessed free-trade evangelist struck, I just hope it was worth it.

What a smug, unpleasant article. Another column poking fun at BJ, JRM and leave voters? It's hardly work, I would have

thought they could have an algorithm to churn them out by now. This is lazy writing. Karl Gibson

The hedgehog lifespan is 2–5 years, so yes it seems likely that Gove's infamy will outlive his proteges. Izzy The Dram

Just the sort of sardonic sneering that underscores why Lee and supporters of the Remain cause are so despised by the majority of the country. And why they lost. Vivrant Thing

Humourless drivel as per usual. As a self acclaimed 'comedian' he should be prosecuted under the Trades Description Act. Four Cough

Prepare yourselves for a
no-Christmas Brexit in 2019

23 December 2018

Merry Christmas, Brexit Britain! And a crap EU year!! It's me, guest Christmas *Observer* columnist Father Christmas!!! Or Gender-Fluid Parent/Carer Winterval, as Boris Piccaninny Watermelon Letterbox Cake Disaster Weight Loss Haircut Bullshit Johnson probably pretended the EU insisted on calling me, in his lying column in the *Daily Telegraph*, Britain's worst newspaper. But whatever name you know me by, I ho ho ho hate Brexit!*

---

* I wanted this column to look as if it had been written by, and be attributed to, Father Christmas, but there was some legal or technical reason why the *Observer* couldn't do this, although I think it finally appeared with a Father Christmas hat Photoshopped onto my head in my byline photo. Ironically, if they had used an actual photo of me taken at the time, I would have looked exactly like Father Christmas. Firstly, I was really fat; and secondly, after I finished touring the last show, which contained lots of Brexit material, I decided to grow a massive beard so no one would recognise me and I wouldn't be murdered in the street by a Leave voter (you know what they're like). I now looked so like Father Christmas that I was able to make a great Santa at my daughter's school that year, and I played the part using the plummy voice and abrasive personality of the former Island Records A&R man Nick Stewart, who discovered U2, and whom I had recently interviewed for an article about The Long Ryders for *Shindig* magazine. One of the girls' mums told me her daughter said that usually Santa was just a man dressed up, but this year it was amazing as the real Santa had actually come to their school. I am keeping the beard to see how the next stand-up tour, *Snowflake/ Tornado*, plays with a hairy face, and in case there is more Santa work next Christmas.

While Christmas is expected to progress as usual this year, unless you manage to extricate yourselves from exiting the European Union pronto, Britain had better start making plans for a no-Christmas Brexit in 2019. Stop up your chimneys, deep-freeze your figgy pudding and stockpile your stockings! And it doesn't matter who has been naughty and who has been nice!! Because Santa Claus ain't comin' to Brexit-town!!!

Like a lot of business people whose work involves moving large numbers of goods over a succession of borders and/or the transportation of hoofed livestock across different national boundaries, the possibility of a no-deal Brexit leaves me pretty much up the creek of shite *mit keine* paddle. The existence of the European Common Aviation Area, for example, has avoided some of the awkwardness that accompanied my circuits of the Earth in the '50s, when I was regularly pursued across Europe by hostile Cold War fighter jets, Rudolph's tedious nose making us an easy target for state-of-the-art missile systems.

And although I do appreciate that many unscrupulous employers exploit this, the fact that the short-term seasonal staffing needs of my Finland workshop can be fulfilled each festive season without friction has meant I have still been able to meet all my toy manufacture and delivery targets, each and every year. And that's despite needing to service a global Santa-believing customer base that has expanded significantly, year on year, since I first transitioned myself from a folkloric Yuletide nature spirit into a Christianised personification of the winter season sometime in the early seventeenth century.

Take the Irish border question, for example, and it's a shame you never did. I have no desire to go back to the bad old days of the '70s, when I was shot down between Armagh and Dundalk, kneecapped and then had all my presents stolen and resold to fund the revolutionary struggle. Little Tommy in Cork was crying because he didn't have a Stretch Armstrong; meanwhile, a post office north of the border was on fire.

And furthermore, at the moment I can save an enormous amount of time, on what is already a very busy night, if you don't mind me saying so, by traversing the island of Ireland east to west and back again, as the crow flies, from Belfast in Northern Ireland to Donegal in the Republic of Ireland, without the necessity of customs checks on my gifts (are they up to EU standards?) every time I cross the border, or on my livestock (do they carry foot-and-mouth disease?), or on my small green-clad seasonal staff (do they have the relevant legal paperwork?).

Even assuming that this was all smoothed over by some frictionless arrangement involving yet to be invented technology, which it won't be in the event of a no-deal Brexit, then there is a further problem. I take off from Lapland, which, as part of Finland, is an EU member state, so it is not even certain whether I will be able to land in Britain at all, unless its future relationship with the European Common Aviation Area is maintained.

I wrote to the Department for Exiting the EU, asking, in the event of me not being allowed to fly over the UK after Brexit, if I could do my British deliveries on land? They invited me to enter a lottery for one of only 2,000 European Conference of Ministers of Transport permits, allowing me to complete my cross-Channel deliveries by road. Do they know who I am? Clearly not. Do they know it's Christmas time at all?

Put it this way. If you leave the EU with no deal, then I can promise you, people of Britain, that irrespective of whether you have been naughty, i.e. you voted to leave, or nice, i.e. you voted to remain, Christmas 2018 will be the United Kingdom's last Christmas. And there is no room for further negotiation.

If you want to make all that extra work for me, then as far as I am concerned, some other mug can be Britain's own personal

Santa in 2019, 'cos I ain't doin' it! Perhaps next Christmas the job of Father Christmas could be done, in quick succession, by David Davis, Dominic Raab and then some anonymous fall guy no one's ever heard of, the Lee Harvey Oswald patsy of Brexit.

Clad in a red, white and blue Brexit Santa suit, Raab could fly over the land in his sleigh, scattering valuable medicines and tinned foods to the bedraggled people traversing the ruined *Mad Max* wasteland of post-Brexit Britain.

Or perhaps Boris Johnson could be Santa. He has the physique, and the international aspect of the job would give him a chance to display his well-loved facility for diplomacy in a variety of different nations.

Now, in closing, a lot of people ask me: do you exist? To which the simple answer is: no, obviously not. But there is a more complex answer. I do exist, but only if you really, really, really believe in me. And in that respect, I am very similar to Brexit.

What garbage. Seriously. Zico44

'Prepare yourselves for a no-Christmas Brexit in 2019' That would be about the only good thing from Brexit – ending this shopping spree madness. Waterlilli

That was an excellent satire! Can you do one for us Brexiteeers too. We could start off with Scrooge in his factories with his poor EU workers that he sources through freedom of immigration! Or what about the EU banning you from flying Rudolph on grounds of it now being animal cruelty to expect animals to work on Christmas Eve! I enjoyed your Brexit Satire, but would still love to see a Remainer Satire too. Fair's fair. Libertyisnotgiven

The single worst article ever written. Mapatasy

Oh dear, Project Fear mongers scraping the bottom of the barrel now. After a Clean Break Brexit, not only will we all starve next year, there will be lorry queues at our ports stretching to the moon, you won't be able to buy so much as an aspirin from the pharmacy, and now . . . now, Christmas will be fucked as well. Hilarious. Go and hawk your Project Fear drivel to the moron Remoaners who will listen to your drivel. Hector Bloodbath

With Brexit gifts, it's the thought that counts

6 January 2019

The new year slips in, tailgating quietly through the closing crack of the old, and the elderly Brexit-voting racist relatives you tolerated through gritted skull over the festive season, their presence turning Christmas into a three-dimensional LBC phone-in, to be survived only with the anaesthetic of alcohol, have departed.

But blood is thicker than water. And so are your elderly Brexit-voting racist relatives. They are also thicker than egg-nog, thicker than Harvey's Bristol Cream, thicker even than Sainsbury's Turkey Gravy mixed with the actual fatty juices of the bird and then left congealed in a Pyrex™ pint jug for five days, until finally scraped away by a hungover uncle into a squirrel-gnawed council food-recycling bin. And now it is time to write these saboteurs their thank-you letters.

'Dear Auntie Gladys. Thank you very much for the Chinese air pollution masks you gave us for Christmas this year. Toxic nitrogen dioxide levels are 50 per cent more than EU legal limits outside our kids' schools here in London, so the masks are sure to come in handy in order to help us respire. I agree. It is lucky we will be leaving the EU in March so we can stop wearing them, as the stupid red tape from Brussels will no longer apply. As you say, Auntie, "Up yours, Delors!"'

'Dear Auntie Caddis. Thank you very much for the four-pack of baked beans and the toilet roll you gave us for Christmas this year. I will put these in the Anderson shelter in the cellar with the cheese crackers, to stockpile in the event of no-deal Brexit food shortages. I understand that you remember the war and what fun it was, especially jiving with the GIs in exchange for nylons, and so you are doubtless looking forward to the camaraderie the coming hard times will generate in dancehall toilets and picture-house cloakrooms. I think you will find, however, that "our coloured friends" will still be here, as they are from Africa and Pakistan, not Poland. You're right, though, the man in the corner shop is "lovely" and is "not like the others".'

'Dear Auntie Gladioli. Thank you for the book vouchers you gave us for Christmas this year. I will put them in the Anderson shelter in the cellar to use as hard currency in the event of a no-deal Brexit. And yes, Barbie from *Love Thy Neighbour* was a lovely girl. It made fun of both sides! I'll have a half!! Brexit means Brexit!!!'*

---

* I have a vivid memory of watching an episode of the now understandably unbroadcastable race-relations sitcom *Love Thy Neighbour* on TV in a caravan site in Tenby, South Wales. I was on holiday with my mum's parents, who looked after me a lot when I was young and she was working. I assume it was 1978, when I was nine or ten, as I remember that Queen's nauseating single 'Fat Bottomed Girls' was on heavy rotation on the jukebox in the club room. At the end of the episode, white working-class socialist racist Eddie (Jack Smethurst) ends up dancing naked around a tree at night to remove a voodoo curse he believes his black Tory co-worker Bill (Rudolph Walker) has put on him, and you see his bum and everything. I was quite traumatised by it. Maybe that is why I hate Queen so much. My gran loved the trade-union bloke, Jacko Robinson (Keith Marsh), in *Love Thy Neighbour*, who only drank halves of bitter and always said, 'I'll have a half.' 'There he is,' she would laugh, 'old "I'll have a half"!' Some would argue that suppressing material like *Love Thy Neighbour* created the blocked back passage that exploded into Brexit. Certainly, Smethurst's white working-class Labour supporter, who is also deeply racist and profoundly opposed to immigration, is a trope that the metropolitan Left forgot existed until

'Dear Auntie Gadfly. Thank you very much for the leftover high-blood-pressure tablets, flatus filters and spare suppositories you gave us for Christmas this year. I will put them in the Anderson shelter in the cellar with the inhalers and the rabies vaccine, to stockpile in the event of no-deal Brexit medicine shortages. It was kind of the woman in the chemist's to let you have them. And yes, you are right, she is "not like the others" and is "quite westernised, really". Take back control!!'

'Dear Auntie Caddisfly. Thank you very much for the autobiography of Michael Caine that you gave us for Christmas this year. It is interesting how things in the '60s were different to things in the '40s, and things now are different to things in both those times, though some other things have stayed the same, or gone back to what they were like in the first place, having been different for a period of time in the middle, which was bad. As Mrs Gove said to Michael Gove on Brexit day, "You were only supposed to blow the bloody doors off!" You're right, though, Lady Caine seems very elegant and "westernised" and is not like the other Muslims. Not a lot of people know that!'

'Dear Auntie Savage. Thank you very much for the set of illegal zombie knives you sent me for Christmas this year. They will, as you suggest, come in handy in fighting the civil war that is sure to engulf the country if "the will of the people is not respected". I agree that we should all practise with them by stabbing things, perhaps our own feet? And yes, you are right, hands are probably

---

Brexit reminded them. I don't know what I think any more, other than that it's probably good that you can't say 'nigger' on TV as a term of abuse over and over again. I watched the *Love Thy Neighbour* movie on the Amazon channel last year and found it fascinating and oddly stylish in a *cinéma-vérité* kind of way. While the men were depicted as confrontational racists, their wives, Joan and Barbie, were peacemakers, in a knowing echo of Aristophanes' fifth-century BC comedy *Lysistrata*.

better than feet, but some feet could pass for hands and have been quite "handified". I think you'll find we voted to leave!'

'Dear Auntie Zavvi. Thank you very much for the record tokens you sent me for Christmas this year. There is no need to worry, as HMV, despite being in administration due to the pincer movement of downloads, streaming, online sales and Amazon's tax avoidance, have agreed to honour the tokens. That said, I am going to put them in the Anderson shelter in the cellar, alongside the book tokens Auntie Gladioli sent, to use as hard currency in the event of a no-deal Brexit. You are right too, Nipper the HMV logo dog is not like the other dogs. He listens to an old Edison Bell cylinder phonograph like a Victorian Englishman and seems quite "humanised".'

And I am in the grey street, drunk and banging a dustbin lid with a bread sauce-smeared wooden spoon. You! You stole your grandchildren's dreams. Get out! Get out and get back to where you came from!! Inside, I pen my own below-the-line online critique. 'It's writing like this that caused Brexit!' And on it goes. And on and on. Happy New Year.

Why did the BBC let
Andrew Neil combust?

3 March 2019

This week, supposedly unprecedented spring wildfires raged across dry, bushy and exposed areas. On Monday, having dealt with serious incidents at Saddleworth Moor and Hundred Acre Wood, teams of specialised firefighters also attended the small piece of Shredded Wheat that lives on top of Andrew Neil's head.*

Dozens of grateful weevils were saved from certain death in the breakfast bisc inferno by the firefighters and rehoused in temporary accommodation in the nearby clumps of Andrew Neil's ear hair, while his nostrils became emergency treatment centres for scorched pests.

Andrew Neil's head wheat had begun smouldering when he heard that Penny Mordaunt MP had agreed to be filmed for *This Week*, making the case for hard Brexit while swimming around a giant floating model of the UK in Liverpool's Royal Albert Dock.

Neil's morning bisc crown had crumbled during the blaze, and so its remains were eaten as a *This Week* green-room snack by Michael Portillo, who lapped up the wheaten fragments with warmed milk from his dish, like a pleased cat.

Nonetheless, weatherwomen smiled cheerily on Tuesday as they announced the hottest British February on record. Their happiness perhaps tells you that the so-called 'climate change'

---

* It was the hottest February on record. Idiots thought it was brilliant, and dry stuff was catching fire. I thought, 'What else looks dry? Oh yeah, Andrew Neil's hair!'

situation isn't as serious as the doomsayers and gloom-mongers out there would have us believe. After all, if it really was too hot for the daffodils to survive, wouldn't they just stay in the ground and wait?

Last week, *The Times*' Quentin Letts and *Julia Hartley-Brewer*'s Julia Hartley-Brewer both tweeted, with delight, that they were able to ski across the Swiss border unhindered. This apparently showed that there was no need for a British border in Ireland, because of blah blah blah shit piss wank.* It also proved that it can't be that hot, as otherwise there wouldn't be any snow, which is all made out of coldness, like in *Frozen*.

Some misery-gongers and doom-dongers have even suggested that the late Professor Stephen Hawking's 2017 warning that Earth had only one hundred more years of habitability now looks optimistic. But Hawking was a liar, because if the world really was in trouble like how he said it was, then why wouldn't he of used his mind to invent a invention to mend it?

It has proved very convenient for the biased hard Remainiac BBC that this supposed climate emergency emerged this week. It distracts from any positive coverage of their hated Brexit. Indeed, the crisis of democracy in our parliament has barely been talked about since Andrew Neil's carbohydrate yarmulke combusted on Monday.

Instead, all we seemed to hear about all week was the

---

* The Brexiteers Letts and Hartley-Brewer had both tweeted during February 2019 that the fact that they could ski over the Swiss border meant the need for a post-Brexit British border in Ireland was exaggerated, their comments betraying such a lack of understanding of the Schengen Agreement, and the fact that goods aren't being transported by skiers through alpine passes, that it didn't seem worth even trying to explain. Hence 'blah blah blah shit piss wank', which was what most pro-Brexit arguments sounded like to me by February 2019.

imminence of the climate threat to all life on Earth, the inevitability of major environmental disasters, killing billions, and the need to change immediately to a zero-carbon global economy or face mass extinction by the middle of the century.*

What we should still have been talking about, of course, and at the expense of everything else, for years and years, today and every day, is our membership, or non-membership, of a European trading block, and how this affects the power bases of the principal political parties in the United Kingdom in the short term. Not the death of all life on Earth.

On Monday night, tiny Jeremy Corbyn shifted his two buttocks slightly on his north London fence, the kitten weight of his coddled egg-nourished frame pivoting slightly towards the possibility of maybe having a second referendum, if Tom Watson and Keir Starmer and the Labour Party membership absolutely insist, but not really, obviously.

Indeed, the British people's democratic right to ruin their own country for a generation at least, destroy the livelihoods of their most vulnerable communities and sabotage food and medicine security indefinitely, must be respected without question, like an old-fashioned village policeman or a violent Ape-God.

Those who tremble at the prospect of shortages of vital supplies just need to think of creative solutions. If each one of the veritable tide of migrants currently swamping British beaches were required to bring with them some plasters and a courgette, we could soon compensate for a ferry service optimistically

---

* There was very little coverage of this catastrophic news in the media. Only ten government MPs turned up to discuss it in Parliament on Wednesday 27 February, even after thousands of concerned children had staged a mass walkout from lessons in protest the previous week. Meanwhile the Brexit bus trundled on.

274

expected to operate at 8 per cent of the projected required capacity.

By Wednesday, the biased hard Remainiac BBC had begun looping mobile-phone footage of Andrew Neil's burning cereal hair, including shocking film of Michael Portillo rescuing the charred remnants from a filthy bin with his bare hands in order to make himself his milky treat, even as Alan Johnson tried to hold him back.

The scheduling of the controversial hair-inferno clip seemed designed to shunt Brexit down the news pipe, and to distract from the fact that the promise of finally leaving the hated EU seemed to be slipping from the betrayed British public's grasp. But there is so much more to be said about Brexit. We need to know the exact terms upon which, in the near future, our scorched nation will be exporting the deformed vegetables retched up from its charred soils to other ruined lands; and we need to know the exact levels of violence we are allowed to use to repel economic migrants attempting entry to the UK from soon-to-be-uninhabitable regions of France and Spain.

Can a hungry Spaniard be shot or merely punched as he makes landfall in Dover? What about a Frenchman, desperate for sparkling mineral water and the grapes that will now grow in newly temperate Scotland? Will it be acceptable, under the terms of our future trading arrangements, to force him back from the beach into the sea with a wooden club? Or to poke him with a poisoned spike?

Happy about this February summer? It's like hitting puberty at three years old and getting excited about being able to choose a bra ahead of schedule.

Nero fiddled while Rome burned. Now the world is burning while Britain fiddles about. What a waste of time!

Typical biased *Guardian* article and gery unfanrile and certainly not funny. Patrickrd

The article above by Andrew Lee tries too hard. It lacks clarity, purpose and it fails to inform. Layng1

I don't consider my self a member of the grammar police but this looks like it's been written by a twelve year old, with poor English. Cheznice

He's a comedian is he? Would never have guessed. Russ Clarke

'Shit piss wank'? Is that the best you can do? My six year old can employ more description than that without having to resort to that kind of puerile language. JeffNuttBee

We used to think the *Guardian* a serious newspaper. Now it publishes garbage like this. At least we never thought Stewart Lee (who he – ed) a comic. Andrew Neil, Twitter

I'll never forget seeing Stewart Lee do his routine about Jeremy Clarkson where he wound himself up so much he basically started crying. Yes, that's correct, a comedian was so angry about Jeremy Clarkson he basically cried on stage. Unintentionally hilarious. People were like . . . oh yeah it's like an act he does. No it isn't. It wasn't just acting/showing the fake anger. People started to laugh at him, not with him. Crying over Jeremy Clarkson though is the ultimate beta male SJW thing to cry about. Shall we cry about mass murder and rape . . . no . . . we need to cry about Clarkson. Lee's not an actor though and in later performances of the same routine he didn't cry. He realised that letting Clarkson get to him like that had us all laughing for the wrong reasons. It was tragic to watch.* Ben Roberts, Twitter

There's a reason why nobody's heard of Stewart Lee, and that load of tripe is probably it. And he uses 'of' instead of 'have'. Alberto, Twitter

UKIP have been lied about and called names by the MSM for years. Hang in there Andrew. Right is might. Alison Parr, Twitter

I've always thought Lee should be prosecuted under the Trade Descriptions Act for calling himself a 'comedian'; he's the unfunniest man alive. Neil Kirby, Twitter

As expected Lee is privately educated, on a permanent guilt trip ever since, and filled with self-loathing. Steve Walker, Twitter

At Oxford with Cameron I believe. Jamessir Bensonmum, Twitter

They laughed when Stuart Lee said he wanted to become a comedian . . . . Dennis Kearney, Twitter

---

* Beyond a certain point, applying proper performance skills to stand-up is pointless. People have such low expectations of a stand-up's ability to do anything that if you attempt to portray a feeling, the assumption is just that you have had some kind of mental breakdown. I tried to cry most nights in this bit if I could, during the section about Gordon Brown being blind in one eye, but I'm not a good enough actor to turn on the face-taps at will for every performance. When I was in Dublin, performing a routine about being haunted by the ghosts of dead comedians, a journalist from the *Sunday Times* ran out of the show to live-tweet to the world that she was watching Stewart Lee having an actual psychotic episode on stage. Idiot. And such tender journalistic concern for a man with mental-health problems. Poke the freak and laugh!

He's just another self-hating establishment Leftist who punctuates the dreary orthodoxy of his politically correct diatribes with swear words in a pitiful attempt to appear edgy. Remain-stream Media, Twitter

Does Stewart Lee have heart issues I wonder? He always looks like a bloated heart attack in a bag. I can just imagine him all sweaty, red faced, belt cutting him in two, getting his dander up and writing angry pieces like this. Can't be at all good for the lad. Ant Antonelli, Twitter

Stewart Lee: a sweaty paunch tottering around Waitrose in high-heeled cowboy boots & pre-worn Pixies t-shirt, mumbling ironic insults at the veg. Cavalcanti, Twitter

Is the *Guardian* having a meltdown? Lord Ashcroft, KCMG PC, former deputy chairman of the Conservative Party, International Businessman, philanthropist, author, pollster, Cameron-pig-sex fantasist, toilet-cubicle tax fugitive, Twitter

You're quite right, Tom.* I should not have let my anger at the *Guardian* get at your excellent Venezuela coverage. I've deleted. It's not a quid pro quo, but could you now get *Guardian* to delete some of the garbage it's recently published about me? Andrew Neil, Twitter

* Tom Phillips, the *Guardian*'s Latin American correspondent. God knows what is going on here.

Possessed by Brexit?
Time to call an exorcist

10 March 2019

A newly discovered birth relative of mine, a Catholic priest, is an exorcist, from County Cork.* The Exorcist came to stay on Wednesday. The next evening, he was doing what he called 'a fairly straightforward overnight identify, isolate, subdue and expel job' in Angel. He wasn't allowed to talk about it and knows I'm an atheist, so avoids putting us in situations where we'd argue. The Exorcist displays a natural diplomacy my Brexit-voting relatives could learn from.

But with his boisterous sense of humour, four-pints-a-night Guinness habit and lifelong addiction to *Viz* comic, my Exorcist cousin isn't anyone's idea of a spiritual warrior. I introduced him to Sandi Toksvig, whom he loves, at a radio-comedy recording, when he'd come straight from an especially distressing Solemn Exorcism. Toksvig took one look at the portly Irishman, assumed I was joking about his line of work and let loose that hysterical laugh she does on *Bake Off* when a poor old man ruins his pie.

Because he was still wound up from fighting what he believed had been a servant of Hell, the Exorcist and Toksvig nearly came to blows and had to be separated by Nicholas Parsons. I think that after thirty years in the game, this is still probably my best showbiz anecdote by some distance, and is the only reason I still get invited anywhere for Christmas dinner.

---

* My ancient Irish ancestors, the Hurleys, left County Cork – specifically, Clonakilty, Ireland's black-pudding capital – in the potato famine. Weirdly, I love black pudding.

I was glad of the Exorcist's company on Wednesday, as I myself had felt possessed, if only by a sense of confusion, all week. Last Sunday, I had written a deliberately silly article, comparing burning Yorkshire brushfires to the apparently combustible Shredded Wheat hair of Andrew Neil, which somehow went viral, Neil's own indignant tweet about the column driving a further 24,000 people through to it.

Googling 'This Week', 'Andrew Neil' and 'Stewart Lee' to try and find out what was going on only brought me further stress. I had enjoyed appearing on Neil's show in February 2014 with the Scottish nationalist, and former Kane Gang frontman, Pat Kane. And yet now I saw that afterwards Kane had tweeted his followers to say, 'Jolly end-of-term feel backstage. Got to meet (somewhat odiferous) hero Stewart Lee.'

To be fair, I had just come straight from doing three hours on stage at the Leicester Square Theatre, but it is a disturbing comment to read about yourself. One of the great things about Google, I think, is that years after a social interaction which you felt had been a success, you find that all the while the other people involved were fighting back their urge to vomit because you stank.

By the end of last Sunday, even the Cameron-pig-sex fantasist, tax toilet fugitive and former Conservative Party deputy chairman Lord Ashcroft had accused me of having a 'meltdown', while Neil was tweeting some guy called Tom, apologising for 'Venezuela', and pleading, 'Could you now get Guardian to delete some of the garbage it's recently published about me?'

Something I didn't understand was kicking off, and I was out of my depth. So you'll forgive me if today, instead of inadvertently bringing down the wrath of the online 'alt-right', I share with you a true story that has been bothering me that I can't quite make sense of. There'll be nothing so divisive as Andrew Neil's smouldering Shredded Wheat hair this week.

Ridiculously, the Exorcist is another person with an impossible job who, when the subject of stand-up comes up, says to me, 'I don't know how you do what you do. I'd go to pieces. You must have some balls.' He still won't accept that what he does for a living, even though I think it's all a delusion, is harder than talking about farts to strangers.

We watched a news report together saying that since the Brexit vote, British people's mental health has deteriorated rapidly compared to their European counterparts'. This came as no surprise to the Exorcist. 'People who think they are possessed are canaries in the mine,' he told me.

'I know there's a national mental crisis brewing when I have to order extra bottles of Holy,' the Exorcist continued, pouring himself another Guinness. 'I'm getting through gallons of the stuff! Brexit has brought people down and weakened their spiritual defences. There's folk thrashing about, foaming at the mouth, and some of them spouting Tourette's level 1970s racist bollocks on top of it all. The lads in my department are run off their feckin' feet.'

'Are you saying Brexit has let the Devil in?' I asked the Exorcist, smirking. 'You realise people will say that is the most extreme manifestation of "Project Fear" to date.'

'I'm not saying any more to you, Stewart Lee,' the Exorcist said, and suggested we agree on our usual compromise. And with that the Exorcist leant forward and did a fairly convincing impression of my own supercilious English tones. 'People who think they are possessed are just displaying symptoms of mental-health problems, and if Brexit is exacerbating them, then there's going to be more of these supposed "possessions".'

I agreed, laughing, that yes, that was exactly the sort of thing I would say. 'Well, you're wrong,' the Exorcist said, shaking now, 'and let me tell you, once Brexit kicks in, not being able to get fresh mozzarella is going to be the least of your feckin' worries. Don't you see? This is what He wants. The Lord of the Flies. The Lie Father. Division. Social breakdown. Brother against Brother. That Mrs May. Your man Neil with his hair. People like them. They could have stopped this. They're His servants, and they don't even know! And you just think it's funny, you smug bastard!'

I'm not surprised about Pat Kane's revelation. I was working as a cleaner at the local theatre when Stewart passed through a few years back and you could tell by the unholy whiff coming off the seat in his dressing room that he wears his trousers with no underwear underneath – that horrible sort of belly button on steroids/acid scent. When I finished my shift that night I went shopping and found myself in a lift with the man himself. For ninety seconds he stood there burping swear words, a real volley of them like a 12-year-old would do, with the scent of rider crisps. As he stepped off the lift before my floor he put his hand into his shirt and began doing armpit trumps at a rate of two a second. I suppose it's a kind of release. Anorobime

Stewart Lee proving that Nish Kumar isn't the only one who can be really unfunny about Brexit. Owlface

A much better article than the last one. Spotthelemon

PART II:
BREXIT IN PERFORMANCE
2016–2018

Introduction

After what was to be the final series of *Stewart Lee's Comedy Vehicle* was broadcast in January 2016, I had a number of meetings with various BBC types who clearly wanted to keep some kind of version of it on air. This suited me, as I was hoping to change the thirty-minute small-room format to hour-long shows, filmed in larger venues, anyway. The material developed on the last two tours was calibrated to reach the sort of hysteria tipping points found in audiences of one to three thousand, but once it was scaled down to one hundred people in a room, fifteen of whom were confused BBC executives, and a further twenty of whom were fans' resentful spouses, material that had caused collective madness on the road seemed deliberately obtuse instead.

But I think the head of comedy, Shane Allen, wanted to spend the money on something else and give other people a crack of the state-subsidised comedy whip, which was fair enough, really. I don't have any of the anger about these kinds of decisions that I had twenty years ago, when I took the cancellation of some half-baked project as a personal insult. I view the process by which broadcasters choose to favour certain projects over others as essentially meaningless, and ascribe no value to it, and am thus not mentally vulnerable to it. I would have preferred it, though, if I could have nominated a successor, like some kind of abdicating king, but this wasn't the case.

In the end, it was clear things were going to fizzle out just through sheer neglect and bureaucratic inertia, as they usually do in TV land, so I got on with getting a new live show together. I don't hang around waiting for TV people to make decisions. Years pass, and suddenly you've put your life on hold and have nothing to show for it. I wrote and toured *41st Best Stand-Up* and *Carpet Remnant World* in the gaps between series one and series two, and series two and series three, when no one at the BBC was able to commit to recommissioning *Comedy Vehicle*, despite its BAFTAs, British Comedy Awards and Chortle statuettes.

After four series of the show, I doubted that I would ever be this popular again. So, as a mid-life mortgage-clearing cash-in, I resolved to write a show that would hang together for eighteen months or so – twice as long as I usually toured – and which I could take back to everywhere that had sold out first time on a second pass. I would monetise the fuck out of a once-in-a-lifetime opportunity I doubted I'd ever be physically or mentally fit enough to exploit again. This was my hit-single tour, like when Fountains of Wayne went on the road with a rock'n'roll light show after 'Stacey's Mom', with its Rachel Hunter-in-swimwear video, peaked at number eleven in 2003.

And I'd try to write a show that instead of trying to reinvent the wheel of stand-up and then smash that new wheel into bits, like I had for *Comedy Vehicle* series four, was just a fun two hours to delight the punters, rather than confuse them and punish them for their imagined crimes. In the end, I did over 240 dates on the tour, playing to nearly a quarter of a million people, with two three-month runs at the lovely Leicester Square Theatre and a week of mopping up the remaining demand at the Royal Festival Hall.

I had decided to call the new show *Content Provider* – confusingly, the same title as a collection of columns I had coming out – as a catch-all phrase, as I wasn't exactly sure what its content was going to be. I had an idea about taking Caspar David Friedrich's 1818 *Wanderer Above the Sea of Fog* painting and sort of recreating it, but flipping it, so the subject was posing for a selfie against a backdrop of natural wonder, rather than facing

286

it to contemplate it. This seemed to sum up my attitude to the modern age. It was a start.

The Brexit referendum was brewing, but like most in the metropolitan liberal elite bubble, I assumed we would stay in the EU and had not predicted the deep divisions it was to create in British society, although I knew loads of shy racists who were excited about it, and it was already compromising my own social and family relationships. Suddenly, it seemed the vague ideas I had had for the show – how social and digital media affect our personal interactions and view of the world – were, like everything else, going to be skewed severely by Brexit.

Once the show was up and running, the new head of BBC2 came to see it and asked me if I'd meet him. He wanted me to do something for the channel, and had been disappointed to find that *Comedy Vehicle* had been cancelled when he took over. I couldn't do anything anyway, as I wanted to spend the next two years cashing in my chips live, not, on this occasion, giving material away at less than its live market value to the BBC. He suggested broadcasting *Content Provider*. I said it was too long and contained controversial political content and the c-word (cunt). He said leave it, it would be fine.

The stand-up character of Stewart Lee is different to the self-doubting newspaper columnist character of Stewart Lee. He has a much simpler vocabulary and genuinely believes in himself, thinking he is a great stand-up comedian, and that any of his apparent professional shortcomings are the result of the public's failure to recognise his genius.

Some of the things the newspaper columnist Lee writes can be spoken by the stand-up comedian Lee, and some of the things the stand-up comedian Lee says can be written by the columnist Lee, but on the whole they are distinct entities doing different jobs. The columnist Stewart Lee thinks he is not really clever enough to do the job he has been given. The stand-up comedian Stewart Lee thinks he is so clever his job is beneath him. The columnist wears glasses, but the comedian does not, and they would probably dislike each other were they to meet.

I, the third Stewart Lee, and the one who is writing this introduction (and the footnotes throughout this book), prefer the stand-up comedian Lee to the columnist Lee, whom I find more tragic. If I and the comedian Lee were to meet the columnist Lee, I think we would beat him up and leave him in a ditch with his glasses smashed.

During the closing previews of *Content Provider*, in October 2016, I (not the comedian or the columnist) wrote a diary piece for the *New Statesman*. Extracts from it follow here, some of which find later re-expression in the live show itself, but it sums up the state of mind I was in, trying to get my comedian self to assemble his new stand-up show in the gathering shadow of Brexit.

Brexit confusion is
scuppering my show

New Statesman, 6 October 2016

I am a stand-up comedian, and I am in the process of previewing a new live show, which I hope to tour until early 2018. It was supposed to be about how the digital, free-market society is reshaping the idea of the individual, but we are in the pre-Brexit events whirlpool, and there has never been a worse time to try to assemble a show that will still mean anything in eighteen months' time.

SATURDAY

A joke written six weeks ago about deporting eastern Europeans, intended to be an exaggeration for comic effect, suddenly just reads like an Amber Rudd speech – or, as James O'Brien pointed out on LBC, an extract from *Mein Kampf.*

A rude riff on Sarah Vine and *2 Girls, 1 Cup* runs aground because there are fewer people now who remember Vine than recall the briefly notorious Brazilian video clip. I realise that something that gets a cheer on a Tuesday in Harrogate, or Glasgow, or Oxford, could get me lynched the next night in Lincoln. Perhaps I'll go into the fruit-picking business. I hear there's about to be some vacancies.

SUNDAY

I sit and stare at blocks of text, wondering how to knit them into a homogeneous whole. But it's Sunday afternoon, a time for supervising homework and finding sports kit. My eleven-year-old daughter has a school project on the Victorians, and she has decided to do it on dead nineteenth-century comedians, as we had recently been on a Music Hall Guild tour of their graves at the local cemetery. I wonder if, secretly, she wished I would join them.

I have found living with the background noise of this project depressing. The headstones that she photographed show that most of the performers – even the well-known Champagne Charlie – barely made it past forty, while the owners of the halls outlived them. The comedian Herbert Campbell's obelisk is vast and has the word 'comedian' written on it in gold leaf, but it's in the bushes and he is no longer remembered. Neither are many of the alternative comedy acts I loved in the 1980s – Johnny Immaterial, Paul Ramone, the Iceman.

WEDNESDAY

I have the second of the final three preview shows at the intimate Leicester Square Theatre in London before the new show, *Content Provider*, does a week in big rooms around the country. Today, I was supposed to do a BBC Radio 3 show about improvised music, but both of the kids were off school with a bug and I had to stay home mopping up. In between the vomiting, in the psychic shadow of the improvisers, I had something of a breakthrough. The guitarist Derek Bailey, for example, would embrace his problems and make them part of the performance.

THURSDAY

I drank half a bottle of wine before going on stage, to give me the guts to take some risks. It's not a long-term strategy for creative problem-solving, and that way lies wandering around Southend with a pet chicken.* But by binning the words that I'd written

---

* This is how the music-hall comedian Fred Barnes, aka the Duke of

and trying to repoint them, in the moment, to be about how the Brexit confusion is blocking my route to the show I wanted to write, I can suddenly see a way forward. The designer is in, with samples of a nice coat that she is making for me, intended to replicate the clothing of the figure in Caspar David Friedrich's 1818 German masterpiece *Wanderer Above the Sea of Fog*.

FRIDAY

Richard Branson is on the Internet and, just as I'd problem-solved my way around writing about it, he's suggesting that Brexit might not happen. I drop the kids off and sit in a café reading Alan Moore's new novel, *Jerusalem*. I am interviewing him about it for the *Guardian* in two weeks' time. It's 1,174 pages long, but what with the show falling apart I have read only 293 pages. Next week is half-term. I'll nail it. It's great, by the way, and seems to be about the small lives of undocumented individuals, buffeted by the random events of their times.

Solihull, ended his days, having previously paraded along the Strand with a marmoset on a lead.

Content Provider: Stewart Lee Live

12–13 April 2018, Palace Theatre, Southend-on-Sea

AS THE AUDIENCE ENTER THE BEAUTIFUL VICTORIAN THEATRE, THE STAGE IS STREWN WITH THOUSANDS OF OTHER COMEDIANS' LIVE STAND-UP COMEDY DVDS, ARRANGED IN PILES AND AT RANDOM AROUND A SMALL CENTRAL STAIRCASE MADE OF JUNK, FLANKED BY BROKEN TELEVISIONS AND LEADING UP TO A MONOLITHIC WHITE CANVAS, WHICH HAS THE WORDS 'CONTENT PROVIDER' PROJECTED ONTO IT.[*]

---

[*] I met the designer Louie Whitemore to talk about the set in the spring of 2016, in a pub on Camden Parkway called the Earl of Camden. I wanted there to be some way of projecting an image onto a back wall, but the wall shouldn't look like it was just sitting there waiting to be projected onto. I wanted a staircase and a surrounding flange to the set, perhaps made of electrical junk, which would look like jagged clifftop rocks when seen in silhouette, as in the painting *Wanderer Above the Sea of Fog*. I wanted the stage to be covered with thousands of genuine second-hand stand-up DVDs. And all this had to be collapsible into a smallish white panel van, so that the usual one-man touring machine of James Hingley could handle it all, as I remained sceptical of touring overspends since the decade of loss-making live work I enjoyed in the '90s. In the end, Louie sourced a whole new type of screen, one where the image was sort of pre-sewn into the cloth but didn't show up until light hit it, so a canvas tower was constructed with lights concealed inside it. When the crowd came in, the screen merely showed a gobo of the name of the show, projected from the balcony, leading the punters to suspect it would never be used for anything (most theatre-touring stand-ups' set design stretches only as far as having their name, or the name of their meaningless show, written in big letters behind them, the

THE LIGHTS FADE. MUSIC – 'STEW'S BLUES' BY BLUESWATER*
– PLAYS.

[*Stew, from off stage*] People of Southend-on-Sea.† It's time to

---

lazy twats). Initial scouting of the comedy DVDs was done by the stage
manager, Ali Day, and her son, Ed, himself a new comedian, who saw
the death of physical-media comedy before his young eyes as he scoured
the second-hand shops of south London for my smashable stash, under
instruction not to spend more than 50p per item.

* Blueswater are a superb Edinburgh-based blues band whose
edutaining Fringe shows mix erudite commentary on blues history with
visceral interpretations of the songs referenced. I have seen them about a
dozen times, as well as their superb torch-song spin-off group, Smitten.
I knew exactly what I wanted for my intro music, and commissioned
Blueswater to write and record it, with the pauses and surges just where
I needed them to be for me to speak over. The resulting track, 'Stew's
Blues', is available to download free on my website in its fully realised
ten-minute form. Like King Alfred's Jewel, I commanded this to be
made, and I love it.

† I wanted to record the show in a town that (a) had voted Leave,
and (b) had a nice Victorian theatre, with good sightlines and nice
architecture. Southend fitted the bill, and the *Comedy Vehicle* TV team,
headed by producer Richard Webb and director Tim Kirkby, were
assembled, with financial assistance from my live promoters, Password,
my agent, Debi Allen, and Colin Dench, who flogs my DVDs out of the
back of a van to Netflix. Even though I had done Brexit material in the
leaviest of Leave places, like Lincoln, and hadn't had mass walkouts,
despite the fake news spread by right-wing newspapers and websites, I
knew that if I recorded *Content Provider* in a Remain area, critics would
say I had taken a soft option to avoid being booed off. Even in leavy
Southend, which was 58 per cent Leave, the awkward truth is that Leave
voters aren't heavily represented in the Theatre-Going Class, a statistical
fact that probably tells us some sad truths about cultural identity and
disposable income and voting intentions. My rooms would always be

endure the comedy of the comedian Stewart Lee.

STEW ENTERS. HE KICKS OVER A PILE OF STAND-UP DVDS
BY ACCIDENT* AS HE APPROACHES CENTRE STAGE. MUSIC
FADES. HE DISMISSES THE APPLAUSE AND IMMEDIATELY
STARTS TALKING OVER IT.

Right, er, just wanna crack on and tell you what's happening.
So there's a number of problems with this show. The main one,
right, is that I – I started writing this about eighteen months ago,
and the idea was it was gonna be two hours on the notion of the
individual in a digitised free-market economy. OK. And I was
gonna base it all around this painting . . .

STEW REVEALS A LARGE PRINT OF THE GERMAN ROMANTIC
MASTERPIECE *WANDERER ABOVE THE SEA OF FOG*, BY CASPAR
DAVID FRIEDRICH,† WHICH DEPICTS A MAN LOOKING OUT

---

skewed to Remain anyway, whatever I did, because they were in theatres,
but it was fun and appropriate for the angry Remain-voting character of
the comedian Stewart Lee to excoriate Southend-on-Sea for its perceived
crimes. Interviews with the mighty and accommodating comics wizard
and novelist Alan Moore, destroying my confidence in the way Armando
Iannucci and Chris Morris had done for *Comedy Vehicle*, were cut in
with the show about half a dozen times, but you'll have to buy the DVD
to see them, as I didn't want to break the flow of this stage transcript with
what was a device for the broadcast version. This text is assembled from a
broadcast edit of two performances.

* It was on purpose. I did it every night, so the audience, subconsciously,
would appreciate the stage was made of thousands of actual loose DVDs,
not just blocks stuck together. I wanted them to know it was difficult to
assemble, and real, and also to create the impression, by staging a minor
accident, that anything could happen and that this was live!

† In the spring of 2001, I was asked at the last minute by the producer
Richard Webb, who later became my *Comedy Vehicle* confidant, to

direct the comedy genius Simon Munnery's cheapo BBC Choice series *Attention Scum*, as I had been privileged enough to play supporting roles in various live incarnations of the project. Simon wanted to achieve an epic comedy travelogue on a tiny budget, though he was not necessarily forthcoming in communicating this, and the experience was one of the best periods of my life, giving me a purpose during a particularly meaningless and depressing period. I remember with great fondness the blue-sky summer days when we dragged Simon's un-roadworthy mobile-van stage around remote parts of the English landscape on a low loader. I am not sure I was ever happier. I learned TV directing on the job from the patient and supportive cameramen, Peter Loring and John Walker, and formed lifelong friendships.

In the end, I think we let Simon's vision down, though the series looked beautiful and the live sequences had a dream-like weirdness to them. To be fair, though, the original shooting script comprised a shoebox of crumpled notes. Nonetheless, *Attention Scum* was nominated for a Golden Rose of Montreux, embarrassingly, after the BBC, having deliberately scheduled it in a graveyard slot to bury it, had already declined to recommission it. Initially, we were forbidden from attending the Swiss awards ceremony by the top brass, but after Johnny Vegas threatened to do a benefit to raise funds for some of our travel, we were allowed to witness our loss, if we paid for the travel. As part of the series, in Tintagel, I chose to shoot Simon's League Against Tedium character, in his top hat and tails and holding a walking stick, with his back to the camera, ranting from a Cornish clifftop out into the blue horizon. I knew I had a half-remembered image in my head. That night, we stayed at the Rosemullion Hotel, near Falmouth, where my mother had spent some of her final holidays, and in the bar there was a framed print of Caspar David Friedrich's 1818 painting, *Wanderer Above a Sea of Fog*, the very half-remembered image I had been trying to recreate. I had looked at Friedrich's work when a teenager, after one of his paintings was used as the front cover of a 1985 compilation of new British psychedelia I really liked called *The Waking Dream*. (The album featured three tracks by Palace of Light, and I ended up writing sleeve notes for the 2017 reissue of their sole album, the 1987 classic *Beginning Here and Travelling Outward*.) I can't remember when I had the idea that the *Wanderer* image

... which is Caspar David Friedrich's 1818 German Romantic masterpiece *Wanderer Above the Sea of Fog*. Now, hopefully you've all had the emails, and you've done the reading you'll need to have done. Then I did about a month's work on that, and then the Brexit vote happened, right, and there seemed to be an assumption everywhere that I should've written some jokes about Brexit.

Now I haven't written any jokes about Brexit, 'cos I was trying to write a show that I could keep on the road for eighteen months, and as I didn't know how Brexit was going to pan out, I didn't write any jokes about it in case I couldn't use them in the show and monetise the work I've done. Right. So I haven't written any jokes about Brexit, 'cos I didn't see the point of committing to a course of action for which there's no logical or financial justification. [*Whoops and applause follow.*]

That's right, clap the things you agree with. Clap, clap, clap. Agree, agree, agree. 'Did you see Stewart Lee in Southend?' 'Yeah.' 'Was it funny?' 'No, but I agreed the fuck out of it. It was almost as if it was targeted at my exact social demographic. In a cynical attempt to maintain a future-proof audience for long-term mortgage-repayment purposes.'*

---

could form a central plank of the next live show, but photos were shot in the spring of 2016 for publicity purposes, in which I tried to dress like the character in the painting, and was indeed thin enough at the time to do so. Once you are aware of the painting, you see its echoes everywhere – in advertising, album sleeves and film and theatre design. I believe young people call this idea a 'meme'. It is a pre-Brexit referendum painting. The man is looking out into the world.

* This section has subsequently been shorn of context by alt-right types

Can it be, Southend, that the future of Britain, Europe, Southend, the world has been altered for ever, as a result, it would appear, of the ongoing competitive rivalry of a small group of competitive posh men? Right? It looks like that's, that's what's happened.

When he was a student, David Cameron put his penis into a dead pig's face, didn't he?* And then to outdo him, to do something even more bizarre and obscene, Michael Gove put his penis into a *Daily Mail* journalist.† Imagine doing that. Urgh. Urgh. Uh! That's 'caustic wit' that, like Toby Young. Do you like it?‡

And then to outdo him, to do something even more sick-making and wrong, Boris Johnson put himself into the role of foreign secretary. And if you think it's funny that Boris Johnson is foreign secretary – and it is, arguably – I guarantee you he's gonna be prime minister at some point. Theresa May has been

---

and put on the Internet to prove that even I realise people on the Left merely clap the things they agree with. I don't recognise this as being especially true of my audience, and the bit is meant as (a) a parody of this assumption, and (b) playful mockery of my own audience for their perceived folly, in the way one might make fun of a friend and expect that friend to understand that it was meant in a spirit of fun. I hate the Internet. Here's an example of the misappropriation of the bit, from Twitter: 'Stewart Lee's criticism of his own audience – "I didn't laugh, but agreed the f*ck out of him" They don't turn to this "comedy" to laugh, fir humour, they go to clap! To sneer. But never to laugh. They don't humour in them. Only sneering derision.' Thunderchunky

* He probably didn't do this, but it said he did in the 2015 biography of Cameron, *Call Me Dave*, by the toilet-tax fugitive Lord Ashcroft and the journalist Isabel Oakeshott.

† I am married to a woman who once worked at the *Daily Mail*, but only as a temp who ended up staying and operating beyond her portfolio.

‡ Boris Johnson had described the newly disgraced columnist and educationalist Toby Young's approach to humour as 'caustic wit'.

put in place, it's now clear, by the steering committee as a sort of a palate cleanser, kind of a nasty-tasting mouthwash that you swill around your gums before being forced to eat actual human shit.*†

A lot of casualties, weren't there, in the Brexit shake-up? A lot of people, you know. Michael Gove and Sarah Vine, they sort of disappeared initially, but they're back now aren't they, Michael Gove and Sarah Vine, and they're currently trying to reinvent themselves as the amusing celebrity political couple for young millennials so jaded they no longer find Neil and Christine Hamilton quite sickening enough. Michael Gove and Sarah Vine are the Neil and Christine Hamilton for the *2 Girls, 1 Cup* generation.‡ [*This joke does not go as well as he appeared to expect it would and Stew is momentarily thrown.*]§

* While this may have been arguably true when this joke was written, I think that now, in early 2019, perhaps even the Tories don't quite know what to do with Boris Johnson, who has rather outlived his usefulness. His future depends on how totally fucked the party is, but if calling for Brexit in order to end up leading the party pays off, it will be one of the worst things ever to happen in politics.

† I somehow mistakenly cut a section of the show here for the TV broadcast. It was this: 'It's a very difficult time to do stand-up. Because we live in a post-factual era, where any comment based on facts is dismissed as being the sort of thing one of these experts might say, you can't really do fact-based comedy, so you have to resort to petty scatological insults. For example, the observation that Nigel Farage looks like the sort of person who, before masturbating, would put on a pair of driving gloves. Ideally made of calfskin. So it felt like a calf was doing it.'

‡ This is a rare example of a line that worked equally well in print as on stage. Usually, I think the two media are mutually exclusive.

§ Don't worry, folks. I make these jokes fail on purpose, at the same points, night after night, using vocal inflections, anti-comic timing and neurolinguistic programming. It's like when Les Dawson couldn't play

Don't – yeah. Well, that's a shame. So, OK, here's what's happened, right. This is – this is two nights in Southend, and I am
aware that Southend's not really my target sort of town, but this
had a nice Victorian theatre, the theatre was available and the –
well, it's just that's normally the first big laugh of the night, that
joke there with a – but we've got a lot of people in. We've got the
sort of – you've got the target audience here, sort of comedy fans
and people that know about, about politics and stuff, and then
it's – I've put on too many dates on in Southend 'cos it's very –
this – look at these people, this isn't my crowd, is it? Look at that.
Essex – Essex filth, people that have – market traders on the run
from London, aren't they? Lost their nerve and come to live in
the white supremacist theme park.*

Should've been a bigger laugh, honestly, for that Michael Gove
joke. It's a good – it's a good joke. There's a – have people brought
friends with them? 'Cos that often makes it go worse, if people
. . . I know what's happened: people that used to come and see
me in the little cellar at the – at the Pavilion† like thirty years ago,

---

the piano and Tommy Cooper messed up his magic tricks. And when
Lux Interior, from The Cramps, fell off the speaker stacks in just his pants
and twisted his legs up, night after night. It's showbiz!

* This 'white supremacist theme park' bit is one of a number of
standardised local references that can be used in various parts of the
country, especially those characterised by the phenomenon of 'white
flight'.

† Oddly, Colin Dench, who has ended up releasing my work on DVD,
ran an alternative comedy gig in the cellar of the Southend Cliffs Pavilion
in the late '80s and early '90s. This was a bold move. In February 1990,
on a bill with Frank Skinner, the much-missed Donna McPhail, The
Calypso Twins and Bob Mills, I was booed off for being gay. Even though
I wasn't gay, I must have looked gay to the people of Southend. Earlier
in the evening, future TV chef Ainsley Harriot, in his Calypso Twins

you've gone, 'Oh he'll never fill the Palace Theatre, Southend, for two nights. Let's help him out and we'll buy four tickets and we'll bring Alan and Claire.' And they're, they're sitting next to you, your mates, nudging you and going, 'Is this him? Is he the main one? Is it just this all night, just a man complaining about things?' 'Yes, it is, until at least ten o'clock.'*

Don't bring your friends, 'cos it's filled it up with the wrong

---

double act, had been booed off for being black. And yet I read that the early circuit was a politically correct utopia. Luckily, compère Bob Mills handled all this professionally, gently rebuking the crowd, before bringing on the final two acts: a pottery-making lesbian and a recovering alcoholic. I think I wanted to record my snowflakey show *Content Provider* in Southend because it was the only town where I ever saw an act get properly racially abused, and that makes it a special town.

* I am aware that the Internet is awash with justifiably aggrieved hardcore comedy fans complaining that they have no wish to see me doing this 'pretends to complain about sections of the audience not getting it' shtick again. Well, (1) from where I am standing, every night, there are people who have been brought along and aren't getting it, for whom the show bears no relation to what they expected from stand-up, and who then go online explaining how much they hated it, and whom this stuff helps to put at ease or, at worst, neutralise. (2) Though there are hardcore comedy fans who know these moves, every time I tour there's at least 30 per cent more people hitting it for the first time, and the TV screening of this set won over people who have never seen that kind of shtick before in their millions. (3) If people tell me to stop doing something, I just do it more, which annoys my wife a lot more than it annoys comedy fans. (4) The fact that these audience-hating bits aren't totally set in stone and are fluid and tonally different every night keeps the show alive for 250 performances and makes for genuine surprises most nights. (5) It's necessary, I think, for the comedian to be a low-status figure, which is a hard persona to maintain where you are clearly playing a sold-out room, so I try to self-sabotage like this to bring myself down a peg or two. (6) I might stop doing it now, though (I definitely won't).

people, hasn't it, so perfectly serviceable stuff is floundering. It's not the . . . I don't need your help to fill up – this is all sold out. If you're going, 'No, it isn't, Stew, there's two seats there for starters,' like they're . . . All these seats are sold, right. Everything's sold. What's happened to me in the last few years, and I don't really understand why, right, but I've become popular enough that the ticket touts buy these seats, StubHub and that, and they try and resell them online, but I'm not popular enough for anyone in Southend to pay six times over the odds to . . .*

Don't imagine that disheartens me, those empty seats. That's – someone's bought them, right, so I've got the money, it's fine. And it's actually better 'cos it means I've got the money, but there isn't one of your stupid friends sitting in them going, 'What are

---

* As long as I don't go through major ticket agencies and avoid theatres run by Ambassador Theatre Group, which tend to be a bit porous to touts, I can usually avoid my sell-out shows ending up being overpriced on the kind of quasi-legal secondary ticketing sites that when he was culture secretary, the would-be Conservative Party leader Sajid Javid described as outlets for 'legitimate entrepreneurs'. I always try and put on enough dates to ensure the touts have no market, and when StubHub started pimping my tickets at five times their value, I just went into their Upper Regent Street office and hung around being weird and eating all their sweets, until they finally stopped ripping my punters off. I think most fans of mainstream shit have got to the point now where they never expect to be able to get a ticket for Springsteen or some boy band or TV comedian at face value, and regard getting one at all as some kind of lottery win. What should be a normal, easy process is obstructed at every turn by criminals and bots and bent industry collaborators who should be legislated out of existence. My son, who loves the band Twenty One Pilots and wanted to see them as his first stadium-rock experience, was taught a horrible lesson in criminal reality as we watched their tour tickets vanish offline and into the hands of organised criminals the moment they went on sale.

these nouns? How do words work?' You know. That's my dream, an entirely sold-out empty room. Which would eliminate the main problem with all my work, which is the public's ongoing inability to recognise its genius.

It's a – this is a very difficult time in history to do stand-up, and I would appreciate your blanket support, to be honest. It's very – it's very – Look, look, I went back on the road in September. I did a week in Oxford, right, and that's Remain. Then I did Doncaster, and that's Leave. And I did Glasgow – Remain. Dartford – Leave. This is about sixty–forty in favour of – of Leave, wasn't it? And the Remain-voting cities now, they loom out of the map, don't they, like fantasy citadels in a Tolkienesque landscape; wondrous walled cities full of wizards and poets, and people who can understand data, in the middle of a vast swampy fen with 'Here there be trolls' written over it.*

Yeah, down here, laughter. People there, people going, 'Hang on. Trolls, Stew? That's not a very fair way to, you know . . . We are in Leave-voting Southend-on-Sea.† Trolls. That's not a very

---

* This section is clearly having fun with the Remainer bubble's perception of the land beyond the Remain constituencies as a horrible wasteland, a self-mocking bit appreciated by the crowd, the self-awareness of which buys me the right to make frustrated attacks on Leave voters in the next section. Ideally, it shouldn't be sectioned off from it, but I don't control, or profit from, anything anyone chooses to post up on YouTube.

† This bit has a structural relationship with a line from the brilliant late-'80s/early-'90s double act Chris and George, whom I saw dozens of times in the early days, though I can't remember any of the nouns in the original bit: 'But, Chris, don't you think you should be careful. We are in . . .' George (Jeffrie) went on to write *The Windsors* and your favourite bits of lots of TV sketch shows, and Chris (Murray) writes loads of ace TV things, like *Lewis* and *Midsomer Murders*, and is currently in Amsterdam working on a reboot of the Dutch cop show *Van der Valk*.

fair way to describe the English and Welsh majority that exer-cised their democratic right to vote to leave the EU.'

And it isn't, to be fair, you know, and I think – look, we're gonna leave the EU, that is happening, and I think people have gotta put their differences behind them now and try and make it work. And I – and I don't know if you can make massive general-isations about people that voted to leave Europe anyway, because people voted to leave Europe for all sorts of different reasons, you know, and it wasn't just racists that voted to leave Europe. Cunts did as well, didn't they? Stupid fucking cunts. Racists, and cunts, and people with legitimate anxieties about ever-closer political ties to Europe.*

---

* How does this joke, which drew tears and cheers, even though I say it myself, night after night for the best part of two years, work? (1) Firstly, shock. I rarely swear on stage, and compared to most edgelord stand-ups, my swears count is probably only one level up from the sort of acts who market themselves as 'clean' to get gigs at hospices run by born-again Christians. So it is a funny shock to hear me abandon my usual vocabulary and say the c-word (cunt). The c-word (cunt) is probably a way-too-heavy word weapon to use here, and the deployment of such a disproportionately heavy weapon is part of what makes choosing to do so funny. (2) The structure of the bit has a relationship with the much-touted idea that liberal Remainers should look outside their bubble and seek to understand the fears and concerns that drove 17.4 million people to vote Leave ('People voted to leave Europe for all sorts of different reasons, and it wasn't just racists that voted to leave Europe . . .'), but then subverts that progression of thought by just calling them the c-word (cunts). To quote an old Lee and Herring routine, or possibly *Viz*'s Mr Logic, 'Our expectations were subverted, from whence the humour arose.' (3) This second idea is then given what we in the trade call a 'topper' by doubling back on the initial premise and conceding that some Leave voters may also have 'legitimate anxieties about ever-closer political ties to Europe'. There is then a second topper, in the form of a letter from a punter, which is a real letter (with the

name changed) received during an early stage of the show at the 2016 Edinburgh Fringe try-outs, which just replays the joke again but in a funny voice and with more swearing, and with the town the complainer comes from changed to some local place every night – in this case, Burnham-on-Crouch.

The Tory Brexiteer and *Sun* columnist Tony Parson, in the February 2019 edition of *GQ*, the sort of style and status bible Patrick Bateman in *American Psycho* would read in-between dismembering prostitutes in a penthouse apartment, wrote, on the subject of the c-word (cunt):

> In the little corner of Essex where I grew up, 'c***' was practically a punctuation mark among men and boys. It was in the foul air we breathed. But it grates now. It feels like the rancid tip of a cesspit that is the modern male attitude to women. And what I find bewildering is that it is not just thick ignorant oafs who use the c-word with such abandon. It is the woke. It is the enlightened. It is the professionally sensitive. It is the *Guardian* columnist, the BBC-approved comedian who can be guaranteed to dress to the left. 'It wasn't just racists that voted to leave Europe,' Stewart Lee recently quipped. 'C***s did as well. Stupid fucking c***s.' Does Lee's relish of the c-word sound rational or healthy? Does it provoke tears of mirth? Do you think it might persuade the 17.4m who voted to leave the European Union – the largest vote for anything in the history of this country – they were wrong? Some of my best friends are Remainers, but such spittle-flecked fury when using the word 'c***' makes Brexit sound like the very least of Lee's problems.

Obviously, like Julia Hartley-Brewer and other Conservative Twitter types who alighted on the Brexit bit, Parson removed the qualifying section that followed it, where I acknowledge the out-of-touch nature of the so-called liberal elite in north London, which in turn buys me some leeway, and also makes the subsequent attack on the so-called non-liberal non-elite more of a surprise; and Parson, presumably knowing little of my work, doesn't appreciate that the use of the c-word (cunt) reads to my audience here in a comical way precisely because using it is so out of character. It is not the swear word in and of itself that brought the house down nightly. It has to have context.

And, of course, the word isn't delivered with 'relish', and it isn't 'spittle-flecked' either. The c-word (cunt) is delivered here with a kind of despairing calm, as if the cuntishness of the Brexit c-words (cunts) was just a sad matter of fact. When I was directing Richard Thomas's *Jerry Springer: The Opera* at the National Theatre in 2003 (as I am sure I have written before), we were given the benefit of the theatre's voice coach for one session, who took the singers aside to teach them to enunciate all the libretto's swear words and curses, to spit them out with relish. I waited for the session to subside, respectfully, and then had to unravel the work that had been done. The swear words weren't necessarily to be sung in that spirit at all. For the most part, they represented the disenfranchised American protagonists working, in heightened emotional states, at the edges of the limited vocabulary that was available to them, and had to be used to convey not simply hate and venom, but also love, hope, despair and longing, the feelings expressed in Richard's music. If I'd really wanted this particular c-word (cunt) to read with spittle-flecked relish, you'd have known about it. There'd have been spittle on the lens. I'm not averse to spitting on stage (on an imaginary Graham Norton, for example), so a lens would hold no terrors for me. To me, the c-word (cunt) here was mainly about how utter despair drove the beaten and frustrated Remainer character on stage (me) to the outer limits of his inarticulacy, painstakingly logical arguments against Brexit having broken down into mere swears.

And I didn't 'quip' the line either. One thing you will never see me doing is quipping. My work is too laborious and self-aware to ever include a comic device as light-hearted as a 'quip', and if I see one, I usually have it surgically removed from my script, or at least quarantined behind ironic inverted commas ('Oh yeah, I can do jokes'). And obviously, the bit was not in any way intended to 'persuade the 17.4m who voted to leave the European Union – the largest vote for anything in the history of this country – they were wrong', so it is stupid to criticise it for failing to achieve something it never set out to do. That's like saying that *Fawlty Towers*, for example, was written to encourage hoteliers to control their tempers; or that the really funny playground joke that ends with the line 'Lemon entry, my dear Watson' was written to encourage Sherlock Holmes to keep suitable anal-sex lubricants close to hand for his congress with Watson, rather than relying on whatever out-of-date fruit preserves he could find in his larder.

Maybe I came onto Parson's radar of late because I talked about Brexit, which he and his employer the *Sun* support, or because I am now one of those 'cultural figures' that informed commentators like him are supposed to know about ('God! Haven't you heard of Stewart Lee, Tony? I can't believe it!'), who get praised in the *London Review of Books* and called the greatest living stand-ups in the world in *The Times*, irrespective of their perceived market penetration or popularity. For Parson, I am a 'woke . . . enlightened . . . professionally sensitive . . . BBC-approved comedian who can be guaranteed to dress to the left', which is hardly news, as it's essentially what I describe myself as on stage, having done lazy Parson's work for him.

Nonetheless, it's odd to be called out as evidence of 'the rancid tip of a cesspit that is the modern male attitude to women' in a magazine whose website has a 'Hottest Woman of the Week' feature. It's such an odd phrase, 'the rancid tip of a cesspit', that I had to go online and google pictures of cesspits to make sure I had understood what one was.

In my newspaper columns, I deliberately try to mangle my metaphors, writing in character as a man with imposter syndrome who is out of his depth in a posh newspaper and is trying to overcompensate with complex language that is beyond him. But Parson's incoherence, as brilliantly parodied each month in *Viz*, is effortless. A cesspit is, literally, a pit full of cess. It can't have a tip as it is not a conical solid. The only way a cesspit could have a tip is if it were somehow upended and its contents swiftly hardened in some kind of large-scale commercial drying unit, and the remaining cylinder or cuboid (depending on the shape of the pit that had moulded the cess within it) then sharpened at one end, perhaps using an enormous pencil sharpener rotated by shire horses on some kind of mill harness, or by Parson himself, until it formed the rancid tip Parson described. The only way a cesspit could have a natural tip would be if the body of the cesspit itself were conical, which perhaps they were 'in the little corner of Essex' where Parson grew up.

In fact, there is an Essex folk song, collected by the archivist Shirley Collins in the '50s from the old traveller singer Gonad Bushell, that goes:

'Dear Palace Theatre, Southend, please inform the "comedian", and I use that word advisedly,* Stewart Lee, who I had the misfortune of being taken along to see by friends last night, that I actually voted to leave Europe and I am neither a racist nor a cunt. Merely someone with genuine anxieties about ever-closer political ties to Europe. Yours, A. Cunt, Burnham-on-Crouch.'

It's where they live, isn't it? Yeah, Burnham-on-Crouch. D'you know what? I don't know anything about Burnham-on-Crouch. I just drove through it, I thought, 'That'll do for that joke.' It's the first time it's got a laugh. So yes, welcome to the music hall,† so,

---

> I'm a Billericay gypsy, Billericay is my home,
> My house it is a caravan, my cesspit is a cone.
> And if I want to see the cess become a rancid tip
> I tip the cesspit upside down, then dry and sharpen it!
> And the curlew is a-calling in the morning.

Parson may have a point about the c-word (cunt), though I don't really think my Brexit bit is hugely relevant to his discussion, and seems to be rather cranked in as part of some kind of twisted vengeance. Out of academic curiosity, I wondered what the dictionary definition of the c-word (cunt) was, and to my surprise, when I turned to it, there was just a massive picture of Tony Parson's face. And it had all arrows pointing towards it as well.

Imagine writing the sort of space-filling shit Tony Parson does, day after day. At least my columns are supposed to be stupid.

* I love it when they do this. It never gets old. Logically, though, by making my way around the country and earning a living as a 'comedian' for thirty years, I am a comedian, whether you personally find me funny or not.

† 'Welcome to the music hall.' I found myself saying this to amuse myself at this point on this night. I had performed the 'It's the first time it's got a laugh' line in a very self-conscious, Max Miller-y kind of way, and I looked behind me and realised I was on the Victorian stage of Southend's Palace Theatre, where Miller himself had probably spoken of not

er, no, it's difficult – you know, it's e— . . . I don't . . . you can't make massive ge— . . . to be fair you can't make massive generalisations about – about people who voted to leave Europe.

People did vote to leave Europe for all sorts of different – they did, don't snigger away down there – they voted for all, you know, not everyone that voted to leave Europe wanted to see Britain immediately descend into being an unaccountable single-party state exploiting people's worst prejudices to maintain power indefinitely.* Some people just wanted bendy bananas, didn't they? 'Oh no, I only wanted bendy bananas, and now there's this chaotic inferno of hate.' 'Oh well, never mind, at least the bananas are all bendy again, aren't they?' Like they always fucking were.†

---

knowing whether to toss himself off or block her passage, and keeping your bloody plough, and I was just momentarily overwhelmed by being part of this comedy tradition, in however small and professionally sensitive a way. Funny what goes through your head.

* At the time this act was assembled, there seemed to be no real opposition to the Tories' hard Brexit, so this line was broadly true. Then, after Theresa May's snap-election near defeat, it didn't seem to be quite correct, as she held only a slim and contrived parliamentary majority, but I glossed over it and got away with it live. At the time of writing these notes, in February 2019, as Jacob Rees-Mogg's European Research Group looks poised to enact a soft coup on the Tory party, and by association the country as a whole, it seems more true than when it was written.

† This bit crossed over with lots of column material, but as the *Observer* reader The Ducks pointed out earlier in this book, in March 2018, 'the EU did have regulations about bendy bananas, as Annex 1 Subsection II point 10 highlights, about there being no abnormal curvature allowed. They did of course later amend this due to all the ridicule they got – but why pretend that a regulation on bendy bananas never existed when it clearly did?' Point taken, and I never knew the banana issue had any basis in fact and couldn't be arsed to check, but I suppose the key thing

A lot of people voted to leave Europe as a protest vote, which I – I understand that. I sympathise with it. If you – if you spend your life driving around the country like me, you can see the disparity that would* – that would drive that. My – my best friend of thirty-five years, Ian, actually voted to leave Europe as a protest vote.† But I believe it was I who wrote –‡ [*There is a lone group of people laughing.*] Still these people doing the work, isn't it, down here. There's a big laugh there that was missed, right, and I'm filming this and I would appreciate . . .

OK, where – what – where the – d'you know what, I'm gonna try and – well, I'm gonna try and sort this out now, for the filming. So where the laugh should've been there, right, is when I

---

here is that bendy bananas were one of the main thrusts for leaving the banana-regulating EU, for both Boris Johnson and the kind of people in the *Question Time* audience who speak out without any apparent point. And yet the regulation no longer applied at the time of the EU referendum.

* I think gigging stand-ups, at any level, have a better working knowledge of the state of the UK as a whole than most politicians, having performed up and down it, and stayed in its Travelodges, and eaten in its service stations, even though they may still draw a variety of different political conclusions from the shared experience, from the soft Tory views of Geoff Norcott to the hard-left Remainer radicalism of Marcus Brigstocke.

† What follows is, on some level, an exaggerated replay of the relationship-compromising disagreements I have had with friends who voted Leave, twisted to make me, in the telling, seem funnier, cleverer and better informed that I am in everyday life.

‡ Again, I am sure this part of this sentence – 'I believe it was I who wrote' – has some sort of debt to a line by either Roger Mann or Ian Macpherson, both great stand-ups from the late '80s and early '90s who quit and were massive influences on me when I started, but I can't quite place it. I can just hear their voices saying something like it. Sorry, fellers!

went – I know you know, when I . . . [*There are more isolated laughs.*] I know, sir. That's the kind of people that like me, isn't it? Yeah, you. Cackling sycophants. The people that are with him hate him 'cos he – he goes to them, 'Have you not heard of Stewart Lee? He's amazing. I can't believe you . . . Probably the best comedian . . . no, he's not been on *Live at the Apollo*, obviously. You know, I think when you've seen him, you can't really watch other comedians. More like art really . . .' Yeah, that's the kinda people that like me, isn't it? Wankers.*

But you know, without them, that was a bit – OK, that was a – the laugh there should've been when I said, 'I believe it was I who wrote . . .' all right? What they're laughing at down there, they're going, 'Oh yeah, I . . .' It's parodying the idea of the perception of myself as a sort of patronising elitist who would quote his own work as a – but you know, you're just going, 'What an arrogant man,' aren't you?

But anyway, try and listen and close the gaps up, 'cos we need

---

* There is a trend among other comedians to dislike my audience, who seem to be perceived as some kind of judgemental, informed, snowflake Millwall. In a newspaper article, the Australian funnyman Brendan Burns wrote, 'Stewart Lee's audience are a bunch of satchel-carrying c***s so painfully unfunny they'll laugh at anything he says in the hope there's a chance of spotting the subtext and he'll throw them a fish'; the professional podcaster Richard Herring has tweeted that they are 'absolute pricks', while his audience, in contrast, are 'the nicest people'. Theatres round the country tend to like my crowd, as they are among the most well-behaved and polite of the hooligan comedy audiences, and yet consume record-breaking amounts of alcohol in the venue's bars, mainly, I imagine, because my shows are too long and they need refreshment to endure them. I like the people that come and see me on the whole. They can laugh at themselves. (For what it's worth, all theatre crews' favourite performer was Lemmy from Motörhead, whom they regarded without exception as a gentleman, while Jim Davidson is almost universally disliked.)

to – So I believe it was I who wrote – [*The whole room laughs now.*] I don't accept the second laugh, I only take the first one, so . . . It was me. It was in the *Observer*. It was a very clever piece. David Mitchell's away a lot, isn't he?* So I wrote, 'Voting to leave Europe as a protest vote is a bit like shitting your hotel bed as a protest against bad service, and then realising you now have to sleep in a shitted bed.'†

And my friend Ian, my best friend Leave voter, he said to me, 'Your metaphor doesn't make sense, Stew,' he said. 'By your own admission, the EU is institutionally flawed and freedom of movement can lead to exploitation of the labour market, so in a way,' he said, 'there was already some shit in the bed.' And I said, 'Yes, Ian, but if there's already some shit in the bed, you don't fix that by doing even more shit into the already shatted bed.' And my friend Ian said, 'No, you move into a different bed.' And I said, 'Yes, Ian, but what if that different bed, instead of some shit, has got Boris Johnson in it?' And my friend Ian reluctantly conceded that he would remain in the original shatted bed.‡

Now that joke initially appeared in the *Observer*, as I said, leading to a lively below-the-line online debate among readers

---

* David Mitchell is the actual *Observer* comedy columnist. I am just the sub.

† Eagle-eared comedy fans will notice that this is actually a twelve-inch extended remix of a much shorter joke from *Comedy Vehicle* that was initially about something else, but even I can't remember what it was.

‡ My best friend 'Ian' did not, in fact, concede that he would remain in the original shatted bed, and finds the idea that Brexit voters were duped by Boris Johnson's lies as patronising to working-class people. He voted Leave in order to cause total social anarchy, an admirably extremist position in some ways. And one that has, at least, worked to an extent, I suppose.

as to whether the past participle of 'shit' was 'shatted' or 'shitted'. Very much a key market for me, those people. The left-leaning scatological pedants community.*

But the out-of-touch metropolitan liberal elite, they didn't see that Brexit vote coming, did they, the out-of-touch metropolitan liberal elite? Who are the metropolitan liberal elite? Well, according to Garry Bushell in the *Daily Star*, if you're in my audience, it's you.† Never has that been less true than it is

---

* This online grammatical dispute actually happened, giving me some more material essentially written by the witty British public, but now I can't find the comment anywhere.

† 'Lee caters for the smug, right-on, middle-class *Guardian*-reading crowd who share his elitist prejudices' – Garry Bushell, *Daily Star*, March 2016. Bushell has made the predictable journey from being a teenage socialist in the '70s, via compiling the foolishly titled *Strength Thru Oi* album (with an actual gay neo-Nazi on the front cover) to being a UKIP supporter by 2011, when he said he would join the party, but didn't. Now, I expect he is, like lots of people, politically homeless and looking for someone to blame. I suspect the old punk and Python fan really likes aspects of my act, and he must recognise the creative oppositional relationship it has with the old-school comics he champions. Bushell probably can't square his obvious and counter-intuitive love of me with his increasingly conservative politics. Gal Gonad did his research, though, and noticed in a 2018 *Daily Star* review ('The Unfunny Face of TV Comedy') that in the broadcast of *Content Provider*, I was wearing a Les Rallizes Dénudés T-shirt, commenting, 'The '60s band were renowned for their tediously repetitive instrumental passages and painful use of guitar feedback. Pretentious? Naturally.' The irony is, nine months previously I had agreed with the producer Richard Webb that I would wear a fairly neutral, and much more flatteringly fitting, T-shirt of the Cornish record label Easy Action, and had been rotating three increasingly smelly ones all through the tour, which doubtless would have offended the sensitive nose of The Kane Gang's Pat Kane. But on the day of filming, at the last minute, the conscientious Webb decided that

here tonight in – in Southend-on-Sea, in a hive of racists.*

So who are – who are the metropolitan liberal elite? The metropolitan liberal elite, I think, are – they're the sort of people
who preferred the Labour Party in the '90s, when they looked
like a load of coke dealers at an advertising agency. As opposed
to now, when they look like Catweazle† and his army of furious

---

wearing the record-label shirt could fall foul of obtuse BBC regulations
concerning the promotion of commercial entities, so I had to wear the
unwashed, obscure Japanese psychedelic band T-shirt I had turned up
at the theatre in. I probably wouldn't have worn that T-shirt on stage
as, even though I have all the Les Rallizes Dénudés recordings that are
available, I think it does look pretentious to wear such a cultish thing on
TV. It's the sort of thing Russell Howard would try to do, and somehow
get slightly wrong in a way you couldn't quite put your finger on, like
when Prince Harry was photographed in his teenage bedroom next to an
upside-down XFM poster. That said, the on-stage version of me probably
would wear a Les Rallizes Dénudés T-shirt, so Webb's last-minute mind-
change really only focused the character as the pseud he is, which may
have been what the wily Webb wanted to achieve all along. Certainly,
Gary Bushell thought me rocking the Les Rallizes Dénudés look chimed
perfectly with his perception of me, right down to the fact that he found
a review of the band that described them as 'tediously repetitive' and
'painful'. If you are interested, the best Les Rallizes Dénudés track is the
particular version of 'Enter the Mirror' that is on the *Yodo-Go-A-Go-Go
(Flightless Bird)* compilation album, and is right in the zone where
tedious, repetitive and painful become sublime.

* My mainly liberal audience love being called racists because they know
they aren't. But I have been in audiences for the kind of acts who flirt
with an ironic populism that probably doesn't wash any more, for whom
such a line would get an unintended, and unironic, cheer.

† Weirdly, about three hours before writing this note, I walked
past Jeremy Corbyn on the Seven Sisters Road, as I came back
from trampolining at the Barry Sobell Sports Centre with my kids.
Corbyn did look like Catweazle (an eleventh-century wizard who

tramps.* Fighting each other to the death over the last bottle of Diamond White in a burning skip in a Lidl car park.

But I live in London, in N16, north London, which is classic out-of-touch metropolitan liberal elite territory, N16, north London.† This is how out of touch the metropolitan liberal elite

---

was transplanted to glam-rock England in a '70s ITV children's show, and who gave his name to a novelty wrestler) and was wearing some plastic-laminated grey jogging trousers. Oddly, I told my wife he was accompanied by an eight-year-old girl, but my son said I was wrong, and that Corbyn was in fact walking along with 'a little old woman'. How the mind plays tricks on us.

* This idea of 'an army of tramps' is, I think, indebted to an early-'90s Frank Skinner anecdote, in which he recalled a homeless fan's offer of, should Frank ever need it, an 'army of tramps'. I doubt even Frank himself can remember this incident now.

† I have lived in N16 since 1999, having moved there when it was still off the grid and cheap. Ten years later, I was blamed by the *Evening Standard* for being one of the 'media incomers' who had driven up the price of a cup of coffee in the café in the park. For two decades I have understood the world through wandering around multicultural Stoke Newington, formerly squat central, and so many of the routines in my material from 2004 onwards were inspired by it, from interacting with veiled Muslim women at the Weight Watchers to being accused of racism by black people for objecting when the jazz club was turned in a Nando's chicken outlet. But the Victorian pleasure park that once hummed with Turkish barbecue parties and Rastafarian frisbee tournaments is now mainly the preserve of the white middle classes and a few orthodox Jews. We have hung on here, where we are at home, because getting two series of *Comedy Vehicle* commissioned back to back meant we were financially able to, but maybe the place escapes me now, and most of the people I knew have been priced out. Perhaps the increasing self-loathing of the Stewart Lee character reflects his being marooned on this odd social archipelago, imposter syndrome eating away again. Maybe it's time to go and live in a wood and write stand-up about squirrels and wild boar. The

are where I live in north London. The weekend before the vote, the Brexit vote, bloke I vaguely know, er, he sent out a tweet and he said, 'Don't worry about the Brexit vote,' he said. 'I've just been out for brunch in a gastro pub in Islington and absolutely no one there's voted to leave.'* So in a way they had it coming, didn't they? With their spiralisers. Yeah, the courgettes taste the same, don't they, whatever shape ... [*There is some isolated laughter.*] That tells you a lot about the room, doesn't it? Look, down here, among the elite, the spiraliser jokes, 'Ah-ha! Spiralisers!' And as we spread up there, friends of the theatre, 'What is a spiraliser?' And then right at the top, some lone usher, 'What's a courgette?' The joke, the joke failing on three levels. Three levels simultaneously. Only I can give you this, triple simultaneous joke failure there.†

So, but, whatever your line of work, whatever your politics, you're gonna be affected by the Brexit. I am a content provider, that is my job, and I've spent the best part of, er, three decades now travelling around the country, providing stand-up comedy content from a sort of centre-left liberal position. I've done very well out of it, I'm not gonna lie, but the problem I've got now is, how do you write a one-size-fits-all stand-up show to tour around divided Brexit Britain? It is very difficult, you know. You

---

world that shaped me has shifted. Perhaps I am the archaic relic Brendan McCarthy, the *Mad Max* writer, says I am.

* This tweet is a verbatim quote, except it was 'Stoke Newington' and not 'Islington'. In London, or areas of the country to which priced-out Londoners had decamped, I would say 'Stoke Newington', which requires a more nuanced understanding of the capital for it to be funny. Elsewhere, I would say 'Islington', which still stands for the idea of the metropolitan liberal elite nationwide.

† There was usually some way of bouncing off the spiraliser line and getting this semi-improvised bit to work, though it didn't always pan out as neatly as it does here.

315

might have a joke, Tuesday night, you're in Harrogate, Oxford, Cambridge, Glasgow, round of applause. Next night, Lincoln, glassed in the face. By the mayor.*

So I don't know what this show's gonna be when I finally abandon it at the end of the tour. All I know is, whatever it ends up being, it will always open with the following sentence:

THE LIGHTING CHANGES TO A SHOW STATE, THE WORDS 'CONTENT PROVIDER' DISAPPEAR FROM THE SCREEN, AND STEW ASSUMES A BUSINESS-LIKE STAND-UP TONE. THE SHOW PROPER HAS BEGUN.†

So my multiple British Comedy and BAFTA award-winning BBC2 series got cancelled, presumably because it was unprecedentedly critically acclaimed while also being incredibly cheap to make.‡ Although I notice there is money at the BBC for a proposed remake of *Are You Being Served?* Educate, innovate, entertain.§

Now, the weird thing I think about trying to remake *Are You Being Served?* at the moment is that the British retail industry doesn't really exist any more, does it? The new – the new *Are You Being Served?* should be set in an Amazon delivery warehouse. Mrs Slocombe stands in a massive shed off the M6, making incomprehensible cat-based double entendres about her own vagina to loads of poorly paid and soon-to-be-deported east European workers.¶ [*waits for a laugh that isn't there*] No, again, nothing from you on that.

---

* Another proper pull-back-and-reveal gag. It was the mayor all along!

† Half an hour late.

‡ This blunt statement of fact was always well received.

§ This is a misremembering of the BBC's statement of core values, 'Inform, educate, entertain.'

¶ This is a fun example of a routine that survived the news changing

316

It's a big – a big news story, that, the, er . . . Actually, you know what? That used to be a big – all last year that was a big laugh, that joke, but it's sort of gone off the boil since Christmas.* It's not – it's not really your – your fault. It stopped working, that joke, and I was, erm, I was trying to think why it was. It was good. It was all last year it worked, and it – what it is, I think, is, OK, you think about how stand-up works, right, you basically – you either overstate a perceived truth for comic effect, or you overstate a contrary position for comic effect. And all stand-up is basically those two, er, binary positions recombined. Er, yeah, that's ruined it for everyone, hasn't it? That's bankrupted Netflix.

But – so why that was working last year was 'cos the perception was, wasn't it, that the – the Europeans weren't being told they could stay after Brexit, and that was a sort of a negotiating tool for Theresa May in Brussels. So I'd go, 'Soon-to-be-deported European workers,' and the audience would go, 'Yeah, that's true,' like that. But then, last gig I did before Christmas was December the 9th,† and I did that joke in London and it sort of went off half cocked, like tonight. And I thought, 'Well, why is that?' There's normally some reason.

So I went home and I googled it, and what happened that day, or the day before, and I didn't know but the audience obviously did, was that in Brussels Theresa May had said that the Europeans

---

around it. As the exact post-Brexit status of EU citizens in the UK kept changing, so the routine was able to double endlessly back on itself and become a way of reflecting the fog of Brexit through the sheer impossibility of trying to write cast-iron comedy comment on something that was itself unstable.

* Frustratingly, the show has been immediately derailed again into diversions and cul-de-sacs.

† 2017.

could remain after – after Brexit. So I went, 'Soon-to-be-deported east European workers,' and some people went, 'Ah-ha, ha-ha!' And then other people with them went, 'No, she said they can stay now.' 'Is that right?' 'Yeah.' 'Well, it's not funny then.'

So that was the last gig before Christmas. Next one was January the 2nd,* and I thought maybe I should cut that line, but I didn't want to 'cos it gets me from the joke about Amazon into another joke about, er, charity shops, right, and it's just a smooth . . . So I thought I'll hold on to it, see what happens, you know, and then – So I did it again January the 2nd, ba-ba-ba, and – and it's a well-constructed joke as well. I know that 'cos it goes – it goes, 'Ne-ner-ner-ner-ner – ne-ner-ner-ner – ne-ner-ner-ner, soon-to-be-deported east European workers,' bang!† Like that, it's got hard – it ends – it ends on or near a hard consonant, which is important as well. 'Work! Workers!' Bang! Like that.

That's how – if you look at Frankie Boyle or Jimmy Carr, all their jokes end on hard consonants, bang! And that sort of triggers the laugh. With me it's a little bit different. I – I – I don't always end on a hard consonant. Sometimes I put an extra beat in after it, and that's why a lot of you are sitting there going, 'This guy's hilarious, but I don't know why.' And it's because I'm, I'm – the comics you go and see normally, they're sort of in four–four time, but I'm like – it's like a jazz thing really, it could go – I know where the beat is but I'm – it's probably too advanced.‡

So it's . . . I'm not saying it's better than them but it's – it is. Right, it's . . . but so – anyway I did it again on 2nd of January,

* 2018.

† Most mid-length jokes by mainstream stand-ups, in the space between one-liners and shaggy-dog stories, follow this rhythm.

‡ I sort of think all this stuff a bit, but I am exaggerating to appear like a comedy snob.

'soon-to-be-deported east European workers', bang! And there was even less laughs than three weeks previously. So I thought, 'What's going on here?' So I went and looked on all the news. What had happened, I didn't know, was a few days after Theresa May had said that Europeans could stay after Brexit, somebody – a reporter – said to David Davis, the negotiator, said to him, 'So the Europeans can stay?' And he went, 'Well, we said that in – in Brussels, but we can just change it, we don't have to abide by it.'

So I think what happened on the night was I went, 'soon-to-be-deported east European workers', and some of 'em went, 'Ah, yeah,' and then other people went, 'No, she – Theresa May said they can stay.' 'Oh.' And then someone else went, 'No, David Davis has said it's . . .' And in that moment the laugh . . . the laugh had gone really, 'cos if you think about it, laughter's a very instinctive thing, isn't it? You just laugh. You don't sort of canvas opinion about . . . from the people around you and then decide.

So it doesn't work, that joke, but what I'm saying is, it's not my – it's not my fault. It's because there's not – there's – we don't know what the government position is, so it's – you can't write a joke in relation to it when it's not clear – see what I'm s— . . . what I'm saying is, there's no – it's not my – there's not enough – the problem is at the moment there's not enough clarity in the negotiating position for that joke to work. Do you know, I dread to think how this is affecting people in other lines of work.*

Because, you know, I mean I – I'm trying to – I'm just trying to get a joke that will get me from Amazon to charity shops, and

---

* The punchline, but it relies on the audience having followed the argument and filling in the unspoken section themselves. When people say I 'have no jokes', they are right to some extent. A lot of the jokes have been removed, and the audience are invited to find them for themselves in the joke-shaped spaces that have been left behind.

the lack of clarity in the Brussels negotiations means it's – you know, what if you're trying to order staff or supplies, it's just . . . I'm not trying to make this all about me, I'm saying it's a – it's a bigger – you know, whatever your politics, you've gotta admit it's a difficult – I mean, I don't know if there's enough trained negotiators in this country for vast swathes of this show to ever be funny again, to be honest.*

But anyway, what I'm saying is, it's – there used to be a big, big laugh there, but the – the – the circumstances haven't so much changed as they've just become unclear, so it's very difficult to know whether to cut it or rewrite it, because you could change it, couldn't you, and then the next thing you know . . .

Who even goes shopping now?† Yeah? See? That feels weird now, doesn't it, 'cos that's – that's supposed to come off the back of 'blah-blah-blah, Amazon, who even goes shopping now?' Who even goes shopping now? Even the – oh, come on. Even – yeah, but I can hear one person clapping on their own. You know, and that's the terrible thing, I've got hear— . . . I've got hearing aids now the last couple of years, so in the – in the silence I could hear one man clapping in a sort of encouraging, patronising, 'Go on' way. People up there, the friends of the theatre, I can hear them going, 'He doesn't seem to be able to do stand-up.'

I can, I – I'm very good at it. I can do what you think stand-up is. This is what you like, isn't it? 'Who even goes shopping now?'

* The topper makes the relationship between being unable to plan post-Brexit comedy and being unable to plan post-Brexit industry clearer, and gives the slower punters a second chance to get on board.

† I performed this with a diametric shift from unfocused pleading and mumbling into *Live at the Apollo* stand-up salesman mode, and the audience recognised the different performance registers and laughed at that, as the comedian tried to reset his act and begin again.

[*runs round and round the stage like a TV comedian for ages*]*
'Who goes shopping now? Oh, I don't, do you?' 'No.' 'Oh.' That's what you like, isn't it? 'Who even goes shopping now? You know – even the charity shops are doing home deliveries, aren't they?' No. They fuck— . . . they fucking are! If I say . . . 'Who even goes shopping? Even the charity shops are doing home' – they're not, they are, so, they are, so if you ever fancy getting a hundred copies of the last Rufus Hound live stand-up DVD for a pound, 1p each, yeah, you don't even have to leave the house. 'Why?' ''Cos the charity shops are doing home deliveries.' 'They're not, mate, it's not cost effective.' 'They are. They've got kids on bikes. Got drones doing it. If you – if you – if – the charity shops are doing home deliveries.' 'They're not.' 'They are, so if you ever fancy getting a hundred copies of the same Alan Carr live DVD for a pound . . .' '1p each?' '. . . Yeah, you don't even have to leave the house.' 'Why?' 'The charity shops are doing home . . .' You know what? Forget it, forget the fuck— . . . I don't wanna do this routine.

I'm on high-blood-pressure medication.† It's not – it's not safe for me to perform this routine with the level of commitment the upper circle of Southend appear to require. I'm gonna die doing this here. I wouldn't mind dying on stage if it was like Tommy Cooper. D'you remember that, older people? Tommy Cooper when he – he died on stage at the London Palladium.‡

---

* I also did this running around in the 2011/12 live show *Carpet Remnant World*.

† I would aim to visibly exhaust myself during the *Live at the Apollo* running-around stand-up section, so that the audience, and I, were genuinely concerned about my health. On this recording for BBC2, I look positively unwell.

‡ This was actually at His Majesty's Theatre, Westminster, 15 April 1984, and was broadcast live on the LWT show, *Live at His Majesty's*. Jimmy

And I'm not trying to take the piss, it was an amazing thing, a brilliant way to go out for a comedian. 7,000 people in the room, all laughing, and he's died and he thought – they thought it was a joke. It was an amazing way to go out for a comedian.

But I wouldn't wanna die here in this gig. [*A man claps alone.*] With him, clapping, a sycophant, on Twitter afterwards. 'Uh, I've just seen Stewart Lee's last gig.' 'What was it like?' 'Well, it was a struggle for him, in many ways. It's a shame, a lot of people weren't that into it, but yeah, it was a – it w— . . . it was not his best. He looked ill, actually, he looked ill. He looked like he was struggling, you know?'

We'll drop the charity-shop routine, we'll move on to the next bit. [*There is audible disappointment in the room.*] There is no charity-shop routine. There is no charity-shop routine, mate, every night I'm gonna pretend. It's the best bit as well. What a shame, what a shame.*

All I'm saying is this, right. All those '90s and '00s TV panel show, *Live at the Apollo*, Netflix comedians, right, you can get all their live DVDs second-hand on the Internet, on Amazon, on eBay for 1p each, all of them 1p! But the cheapest that you can get – [*A woman laughs.*] Well, we'll see how funny it is, won't we, madam, when we hear – when we hear how much it is. The cheapest that you can get my 2004 live DVD for, second-hand on the Internet, how much d'you think it is, madam?

[*The woman he has chosen mumbles incoherently.*]

This is a quick little exchange usually.

[*The woman says, '£5.'*]

Tarbuck's manager pulled Cooper back through the curtain, and the rest of the show was performed in the limited space in front of it.

* Here I addressed this to an individual near the front, but this section would pan out differently on different nights.

£5? Have you seen this show before? Have you tried to fuck this up on purpose?* For God's sake, tonight of all the – it's not £5, no. You panicked, didn't you? You were asleep? £5. It's £3.67. Now, right, what's happened the other 208 nights of this tour, it's – it's £3.67, my DVD, I go to the person there and say 'How much d'you think it is?' And they go, '50p' or 'A pound' or '10p' or something, which is less than £3.67. And then I say, 'No, it's £3.67!' and there's a kind of mock-heroic triumph in the room. 'Yeah, ha! More than they said, yeah!'

But what's happened tonight . . . you weren't to know, were you? It's very kind of you to think that it would be five. What's your name, madam? What is it? No, you ha— . . . Don't shake your head, you have a name. Listen, what is it? Annette. Yeah, Annette very kindly has massively overestimated the – she's gone £5, I've gone £3.67, and where there's normally joy, the people of Southend are already struggling. Look at them, they've gone, they've gone, 'Oh, that's awkward, isn't it, 'cos it's less. It's much less than he said.' So that's ruined. But that's normally another bit where there's a bit of a lift where all those bits tonight are being sabotaged. So that's good. But, erm, so, er, I'll – I'll be really amazed if this makes the edit, but if it does, then that's the camera to get it on, there.†

So, it's – it's £3.67, right, which is still – yes, that's right, cry

* After a few weeks of touring I had developed various routes that could get me to wherever I needed to go whether the chosen punter said a price higher or lower than the actual price of £3.67. Needless to say, people assumed I used plants, but I didn't need to. I would go online once a week and try to buy the right amount of copies of *Stand-Up Comedian* to keep its online second-hand price at or near £3.67.

† In the filmed version I started talking to this camera behind me, which looked quite funny in the edit, but I don't really know what I was doing or what I was trying to achieve.

and blow your nose – it's, it's still 367 times more than anybody else's second-hand live DVD, right? But that would've been . . . you could've cheered a little bit there, couldn't you, and recovered from the damage that your representative has done to the evening, but instead, Brexit-voting Southend just sat there and thought, 'Let's make this bloke suffer and then . . .'

It's 367 times more than anybody else's, right, which is – Oh, you know what? [*The audience cheer.*] Don't patronise me, it's too late. No! Forget it. The moment . . . [*The audience cheer and clap.*] Right, you can clap! You can clap and cheer as sarcastically as you like, Southend! But it doesn't change the fact that I am the £3.67 king of the obsolete-physical-media market.* Right. But there's a reason for that, and it's this, OK. I always sell DVDs and books after the gig. I probably won't bother tonight, to be honest, but I normally do, and the cheapest that I can get the 2004 live DVD at source, new, from the warehouse in Colchester, is £3.50. OK. So I have to put it on for ten quid, right, 'cos I have to give 10 to 25 per cent commission to the venue, that's £2.50 off the ten. 15 per cent to the promoters, that's another £1.50 off the ten, that's four gone. Another 15 percent to the, er, agent. That's £1.50, that's £5.50 gone off the ten. £3.50 for the DVD in the first place, that's £9 gone, er, off the ten. [*There are a few isolated laughs.*]†

---

* There was usually some way, most nights, of intuitively driving the audience to clap and cheer at the points I wanted them to, without apparent prompts, making them think they had chosen their responses themselves, but I honestly couldn't tell you how exactly I was doing it. As I write these notes, I am also starting to think about my forthcoming show, *Snowflake/Tornado*, which will open in the autumn of 2019, and suddenly I feel like I can't remember how I ever used to make anything work. It's terrifying. Every time I feel like I am starting from scratch with nothing. I can feel the vomit in my mouth.

† Usually, but not always, there would be odd laughs from a minority of

Er, this doesn't normally get laughs, but I'm happy to take whatever comes . . . from the Southend accountants' theatre trip up there at the back. 'This is the bit I told you about, it's hilarious. 'Cos presumably he's self-employed schedule D, but he doesn't seem to have realised that he could put the initial DVD purchase through as a tax-deductible business expense.' I do, right. [*There is much laughter.*] Why is this going better than proper jokes? Just – right, I do know that, but I put the – I put it through at the end of each quarter, not with the balance of each – it doesn't make any difference as long as – who are you? Who's come to this? 'Politics, words, we're not interested in that. What we like is numbers being added up.' You've got a pound – when I did this tonight, I thought, 'I hope it's a really unique night that we're filming,' and it fucking is.*

Right. So you've got a pound left, right, that's taxed, isn't it, at business rates, 22 per cent, so you've got 78p left from the ten, er, then there's other costs, transport, storage. So basically a £3.50 DVD sold for ten quid, I'm normally looking about sixty or seventy pence profit, right? So what I do, OK . . . I can never sleep after gigs, right, because of the crazed adrenaline rush that is surging . . . Come on, look at what you've seen me dealing with! I've got a woman here, right, normally, who says, '10p.' That works, but she said '£5', and that is the highest anyone's ever said in eighteen months, but it didn't floor me, did it? No, I've rolled with it. I came – I went, 'No, it's not . . .' I did. You couldn't do

---

the room here, which would usually, but not always, get me into some kind of improvisation about who was in the room – for example, the accountants' theatre trip.

* The ill-considered and unnecessary use of the word 'fucking' here tells me that I was genuinely improvising, and so using the swear to buy time and make the rhythm work, rather than for any especially valid reason.

this – if you had to do this, you'd cry. You couldn't do this, and that's why I'm up here like a god, right, and you're down there in the dark, like pigs in an Essex ditch.

So I wait, so what I do, I can't sleep. I go on the Internet and go on Amazon. I go on eBay, drunk, right, and first of all I buy loads of 1970s Turkish funk albums, right. Yeah, Moğollar, Selda, Erkin Koray – the usual names. 'Bunalım, Stew?' 'No, too metal.' So, what do you want? So, 'I love him adding up and the Turkish funk stuff. Other than that . . .' It's getting applause for the Turkish funk stuff. Yeah, I'm bang on the meme. So does that exist, that phrase? Bang on the meme? Have I invented it? What's going on?*

So then, when I've – when I've bought all the Turkish funk, right, I start looking around for that 2004 live DVD, and if I see it anywhere, second-hand, for less than £3.50, £3.40, £3.35, I buy it, slip it in with the new ones, I'm looking at an extra ten or fifteen pence profit. I tell you what, tonight – for that bit it's good to

---

* I do like '70s Turkish psychedelic funk, having got into it via the 2003 *Love, Peace and Poetry* compilation, on QDK Media, and I thought it was a funny, obscure thing to choose as the genre I am searching for. Each night I would try and improvise a different bit about it, using different real band names, to amuse myself. Oddly, during the course of the tour, Daniel Spicer published his ground-breaking study of the genre, *The Turkish Psychedelic Music Explosion: Andalou Psych (1965–1980)*, and the rise of a more authoritarian state in Erdoğan's Turkey led to a reassessment of the kind of cultural freedoms that had allowed the music to flourish in the first place. Meanwhile, Umut Adan is among the contemporary artists reviving the genre. It's not really an album music, but my favourite Turkish psych album would be Erkin Koray's *Elektronik Türküler* (1974). I used to do a world-psych show on Resonance 104.4 FM called *Global Globules*, in the guise of my Canadian comedy alter ego Baconface, and the Turkish episode can be accessed here: http://www.baconfacecanada.com/global-globules/episode-34-turkey/.

be out of London and to be in Essex, 'cos in London, the sort of people that live there now, I do that bit and they go, 'Huh, fifteen pence? What a waste of time!' But all you lot, ex- . . . ex-patriot cockney market traders, aren't you? 'Fifteen pence, that's a good return on that.' 'We've left London now.' I know why.*

Sometimes you get lucky. There's a company on the Internet called Music Magpie. They had twenty copies of it for £3.40 each, right, and I bought them all, OK.† And the bloke at Music Magpie – Rick he's called – he sent me a sarcastic note with the order, he put, 'How sad,' he put, 'How sad, buying your own DVD second-hand on the Internet.'‡ But it isn't sad, is it, 'cos I made two quid on that, clear profit.§

So my DVDs are £3.67. That is 367 times, Annette, more than any other stand-up's second-hand DVD live, but to be fair, er, there's a reason for that. I'm like a corrupt banker, aren't I? I've kind of manipulated the market to drive up the perception of my commodity in the marketplace. You know, to be fair to Jimmy

* The inference here is that the people of Southend have left London because they are racist. This is drawn from the kind of coded speak that elderly people used to use with me when they talked about leaving Birmingham.

† At some point during the tour, Music Magpie stopped taking my orders for my own DVDs.

‡ Something like this happened, but I forget exactly what, and there was a bloke called Rick involved. Good luck to him!

§ This is funny because the amount of profit is very small given the effort involved. And, of course, it is more absurd because I was actually doing this sort of thing, going online to buy the DVDs cheaply to make small profits. In the end I forgot whether I was doing it 'in character' as the mad, obsessive, on-stage Stewart Lee, as some kind of ongoing off-stage method act, or whether I was just doing it as the real me in my own time, but it was getting done, all the same, by one of us.

Carr, for example, whose DVDs are all 1p second-hand on the Internet, he's not awake, is he, at two o'clock in the morning, buying his own DVDs second-hand on Amazon to resell off a trestle table in Southend-on-Sea. He's not doing that.

Imagine if he was, imagine if Jimmy Carr was on Amazon buying something that he never paid the tax on what he got paid for doing it in the first place, from a company that don't pay any of their tax either. Is it possible to imagine a more tax-avoiding transaction than Jimmy Carr buying a Jimmy Carr DVD on Amazon? Only if he found it using Google on a Vodafone phone, while paying Gary Barlow to spit cold Starbucks coffee into his splayed anus, while the cast of *Mrs Brown's Boys* stand around, singing 'I Still Haven't Found What I'm Looking For'. There's not a single taxable juncture in the entire transaction.

Now if you've been looking carefully, you'll notice the whole of this set tonight is actually made entirely out of other stand-up comedians' second-hand live DVDs.* I wasn't trying to make fun

---

* Though the initial scattering of second-hand stand-up DVDs for the set was sourced by the production manager, Ali Day, as the tour went on it became necessary for tour manager James Hingley and I to replenish them, so that there were about a thousand ready to be crunched underfoot each night. It was funnier if there were enough fresh DVDs for them to make a good shattering noise when I stood on them, as people are still rightly horrified by the wanton destruction of cultural artefacts, however lowbrow they are. It seems like fascism. I wore special steel-heeled cowboy boots to aid the crushing and shattering, and it would be obvious to anyone who watched the show that I had worn them for this purpose. Nevertheless, the fact that I was wearing steel-heeled cowboy boots was used as evidence by online posters that I was pretentious or old or whatever. You try shattering hundreds of Jason Manford DVDs, night after night, in trainers. It can't be done. For the year or so of the tour proper, if we had time between shows, whenever we saw a CeX DVD-exchange shop, we would clean all the 50p stand-up DVDs off the shelves

and load them into the van. It would take the staff ages to find them all behind the counter, and though some were good-humoured, many were understandably resentful of being asked to spend hours carrying out the odd task of packing the DVDs. Even though we told them we wanted only the packaging, an odd internal rule meant they were obliged to give us the actual DVDs in plastic wallets. This meant that throughout the tour, customers at the merch stand were incentivised with the offer of free sleeveless stand-up DVDs, from a box of thousands, by the likes of Frankie Boyle, Rufus Hound and Jethro. In Liverpool's CeX, they wouldn't sell us any stand-up DVDs as they suspected us of working some scam, whereby we emptied all the CeXs in the land of Michael McIntyre DVDs in order to drive up their value, due to scarcity, and then drip-fed our own stash back to CeX at inflated prices. Inevitably, there were more McIntyre DVDs for 50p than anyone else's, and this is the reason we chose to pile them up uniformly for me to kick over, but pretty much every stand-up who'd ever had a DVD out could be found in CeX for 50p, with two exceptions. There were never any of my DVDs in CeX, because I didn't do them with the kind of companies that have to saturate the retail market to try and make back the act's advance; and because, I suspect modestly, people think they might watch them twice. There were no 50p Dylan Moran DVDs either, as they seemed to hold their value at around £3.50–£4, probably for similar reasons.

In February 2019, an article in *The Times* proclaimed the death of the stand-up DVD as comics began to aim directly for streaming services like Netflix, who will not release actual viewing figures to any stand-ups who upload their content to the Netflix app. I countered this trend by saying that I would continue to make DVDs, as I see them as finished pieces of work, and also planned to put out vinyl, both of which I can always sell personally at shows. Dara Ó Briain helpfully tweeted the journalist Dominic Maxwell to correct some information about me, by pointing out that he had also had stand-up specials on terrestrial TV this decade, and to express his delight at the death of DVD and its impact on the globalisation of the industry and the international expansion of his own customer base. 'Glad to see someone notice this; the whole industry has gone international in the last five years. DVDs are dead, but tours are now international; both due to digital media.

of anyone, what I wanted to do was get all the DVDs and pile them up and then hang hessian sacking over them, so they look like the rocks in cliffs, er, in that painting, but I didn't do that idea in the end. But I don't want anyone to think I'm trying to make fun of the other comedians by making the set out of their DVDs. I'm not, it's just that other comedians' live DVDs are currently the cheapest building material available.*

Honestly,' concluded Ó Briain, 'I'd happily trade the DVDs for the shows in Norway, say. Just tons of fun.' I am offered shows in Norway, but as I treat each tour as a finished piece of work, often with a set that relates to it, it is not ideal for me to have to break the material from these shows down into isolated sections, or to take the sets to, for example, Norway. This is not to say these types of shows are better than the more utilitarian shows Ó Briain, for example, might delight Norwegians with; they're just different. The logistics of taking a heavy set made mainly out of worthless stand-up DVDs – a large percentage of them Dara Ó Briain's – over the sea to Norway don't really add up. It barely makes sense to go to Ireland even. Honestly, I'd happily trade the shows in Norway for writing, performing and touring fully realised stand-up shows with sets and cues, rather than just generating interchangeable slabs of monetisable content. Just tons of fun! Why does Dara Ó Briain need to do stand-up in Norway anyway? If he wants to go there, can't he just make another one of those programmes where the BBC film him and Ed Byrne going on holiday? And if I felt doing stand-up was 'just tons of fun', I'd think I was doing it wrong. Stand-up is a job of hard work, and it should feel like it for both performer and audience, Norwegian or not. 'Just tons of fun' is something you have at Center Parcs, unless you are too fat to go on the waterslides.

* On reading this line back, it appears to be indebted to an old Simon Munnery joke that went something like: 'We do not burn the American flag because we are anti-American. We burn the American flag only because it is the cheapest available in this region.' Except that, in this instance, all the information is factually true, so the line probably evolved out of that realisation.

Of course, what I haven't factored in is it's actually quite depressing to – to look at this every night for – well, you know it is, 'cos I am a comedian, right, and you know, I got all of these DVDs for 1p online, or 50p in that, er, CeX exchange place, and of course what is sad is there are actually lots of really good ones here and it's very depressing to think of them just becoming a sort of pile of worthless landfill. [*He tramples on the DVDs with glee and enthusiasm, until he is weak, finally kicking a pile of discount Michael McIntyres sky high, some of which, ideally, rain down on the audience's heads and upturned laughing faces.*]

No. It is sad because – because, well, this was a big deal, wasn't it? The Christmas comedy DVD market, and that's over, and everything's in collapse, you know? The government are trying to close down the BBC. I don't know how that'll affect comedy. Actually, after the second series I did for the BBC I got offered more money by Sky to go and do two series for them,* but I didn't. I didn't go to Sky and I stayed at the BBC for less money, and I've not talked about this on stage before . . .† All right, I'll tell you why, it's because I think if you make an ethical choice about something, it's a private matter, and you shouldn't go around crying it, crying it from the rooftops to try and engineer the perception of yourself as some kind of national cake-baking treasure.‡ Know what I mean?

---

* I was offered more money by Sky to do two series for them after series two of *Comedy Vehicle*, after the BBC initially declined to recommission it, but in the end the possibility of reaching a larger audience for less money at the BBC made more sense in the long term, with regard to building the live crowds.

† Here the audience delighted me every night by laughing, unprompted, at the deliberate display of what the alt-right call 'virtue signalling'.

‡ This is a joke about Mel and Sue's now forgotten decision not to follow the *Bake Off* money from the BBC to Channel 4, for which they were praised.

But I started talking about it on stage last year, and in the summer Sky's lawyers sent me a very threatening cease-and-desist letter, saying I wasn't to say Sky had offered me more money than the BBC, 'cos they hadn't.* And I went through the paperwork, and I went, 'There's the offer, there's the minutes of the meeting,' so they – they backed off, but that gives you an indication of the extent to which I'm a pariah in the comedy business. A broadcaster would take legal action to deny ever having wanted to work with me.

But there's all sorts of reasons not to appear on Rupert Murdoch's evil Sky, and one of them, of course, is that I know it's not really me they want. They don't want me. They want you. They want you to watch Sky 'cos I'm on it.† They want you, the ABC1, going-to-the-theatre, reading sort of people, to start watching Sky so they can advertise the sorts of things that you buy. Like cappuccinos and spiralisers and courgettes.‡ If you watch Sky at the moment, all the advertising is for knives, masking tape and bin bags.§

You know, I wish – I wish I had gone to Sky for the money, right, but I can't. 'Cos if you're a sort of broadly liberal comedian and you appear on Rupert Murdoch's evil Sky, my concern is you're gonna lose your core audience, which tonight is about

* Sky's lawyers did do this, but the fact that the story was demonstrably true, and that we had the paperwork to prove it, headed them off.

† This strategy of Sky's, weirdly, doesn't seem to be working. Some great comedians go and do shows for the channel, but no one anyone knows ever sees them.

‡ Call-back. Nice!

§ This joke exploits the unfair stereotype of long-distance lorry drivers being murderers.

seven people down there, in Southend.* Alan Partridge, the fictional character, he can appear on Rupert Murdoch's evil Sky because that is exactly the kind of channel Alan Partridge would appear on if he was real, isn't it? In fact, if you were watching Sky News and Eamonn Holmes came on and then Kay Burley and then Alan Partridge, you'd go, 'Oh, Sky have raised the quality of their journalism.'

And I wish I could appear on Sky for the money, I wish I could, right. But I can't. Because the character of Stewart Lee that I've created would have smug liberal moral objections to appearing on Sky.† And I'm coming to hate the character of Stewart Lee. I'm coming to despise the character of Stewart Lee in the same way as Rod Hull came to hate Emu. I even hate this, what I'm saying now. Pretentious metatextual self-aware shit. What's wrong with proper jokes? That's what I say to me. You know, Russell Howard's not involved in an ongoing interrogation of the divided self, is he? No, he's going . . . [*performs an interminably long sequence of wordless pelvic thrusts, of the type used by young male stand-up comedians to punctuate their acts*] 'We've all done it. You run out of toilet roll, you use a sock.'‡ His own clothing.

---

* For over a decade, writing two £60 record reviews a week for the *Sunday Times* was my most dependable source of income. But my editor left, and the childcare for my newborn cost more than I'd earn writing reviews, so the decision to step away from the paper was made for me before writing for Murdoch would have become untenable for a self-professed snowflake in the Brexit era.

† Here the on-stage character of Stewart Lee is talking about how he dislikes the on-stage character of Stewart Lee. Lee will eat itself.

‡ This was a line that appeared over and over again, coming out of Russell Howard's face, in the trailers for his 2016 Comedy Central series, *Stand Up Central*. To be fair, it is possible it was snipped off the end of a very good routine, as often happens in these cases. I suspect it also

For excrement. What is that? Observational comedy from a Victorian mental hospital? 'We've all done it, you wake up probably about six in the morning, get up, then about eleven o'clock, then gentry come around, don't they, in their top hats, smashing you in the face with canes. Then in the afternoon you're chained to a bed and spat at. You're trying to escape, we've all done it.' I'd go and see that.

All the young twenty-something comedians in their twenties, they all complain to me about me doing a joke about Russell Howard, all the twenty-somethings. They go, 'Oh, mate, mate, oh, mate, oh, mate, oh. Oh, mate. Oh. Oh, mate. Mate, no. Oh. Oh, mate, no. No. No, mate. Oh. Mate, no. Oh, mate. Oh, mate. Mate. Mate, mate. Mate. Mate. Mate. Mate, what – why, er . . . Mate, why are you having a go at Russell Howard for? Mate. Mate, why – why [*unclear*], uh. 'Mate, what you, mate, what, what, mate, what you, what you, mate, what. Mate, mate. Mate, what – urr . . .! Ur! Mate. Mate. Mate. Maaaaaaate. Maaaate. Whatyouhavingagoatrussellhowardformate? Whatyouhavinga goatrussellhowardformate? Mate. Mate. Mate. Whatyouhaving-agoatrussellhowardformate?'* They all stick up for him. It's not

---

related to masturbating, rather than defecating, as I have pretended to assume, but the edit the show's producers (Avalon) have chosen to use to promote the product leaves both interpretations possible, presumably to work the twin defecating and masturbating markets.

* I had one or two mithering young comics in mind here, many of whom are involved in unacknowledged Oedipal struggles with me, but the main inspiration for this bit came from where we used to live, in Stoke Newington, in the 'oos, two doors down from a shared student house. The students used to have parties and would send all the neighbours invites to 'come and boogie the night away', like we were going to do that at our ages. And I don't think the disabled ninety-year-old lady who lived underneath them was especially keen on continuing

even fair. I did one joke about Russell Howard, about ten years ago, and that's all, one joke. Admittedly, it was fifty-eight minutes long.*

It wasn't even about him, it was about a press release about him which was stupid, right. I liked him, to be honest. I hate him now, though. It's not even his fault, it's my fault entirely, right, and why I hate Russell Howard is this, OK, now this is – right

---

to rave until six or seven the next morning. I went out one time to try and calm things down, as our babies were weeping and could not sleep, and saw a man through the window DJing while wearing a motorcycle crash helmet with the visor on. I had come straight from my bed and was naked except for a dressing gown and walking boots. A young man was in the street, shouting the name of another young man up at the window over and over again. 'Da-a-a-a-a-ve. Da-a-a-a-a-ve. Da-a-a-a-a-a-ve.' I lost my temper and found myself asking him how old he was, the implication being that standing in the street bellowing was immature. 'How old are you?' I said to him. 'I'm twenty-six, mate,' he kept saying, over and over again. 'I'm twenty-six, mate.' It was the 'mate' that really made me lose my rag. I wasn't his mate. It's the kind of thing Rod Liddle would call you on a panel show to needle you. The next week, at my kid's Saturday-morning football, one of the other dads, a university professor, said his students had said the comedian Stewart Lee had abused their friend in the street the previous weekend. The annoying student was who I had in mind for the speech patterns here, and the incident also became the basis of my contribution to an improvised piece, 'Crash-Helmet DJ', on the 2018 industrial-jazz album *Bristol Fashion*, by capri-batterie and me (Dirter Records). It was a fun bit to do live, and panned out differently, and at different lengths, and with different levels of intensity, every night, despite being based around only a few words, repeated ad nauseam.

* An old routine inspired by Howard's admittedly impressive charity work, and the way it was used to market his products by his PR people, grew so long live that it was eventually split over two episodes of the second series of *Comedy Vehicle*.

this – OK, this is the last sort of seven-, eight-minute bit of the first half, this, er, this ends on a sentence that normally gets such a big laugh that I don't even have to wrap up the show, I just walk off while people are still going, 'Ha-ha-ha.'*

That won't happen tonight, and I think we know why, it's because . . . God bless 'em, loads of people have come along tonight, they thought, 'Oh, something's come to Southend, let's go and see it.' And this joke relies on people having seen me before or knowing something about me. I'd like to drop this bit, to be honest, but I can't, but it's . . . erm, it looks very relaxed but actually it's a very tightly structured show and I can't drop this bit 'cos there's stuff in it that sets up things in the second half, so I have to do it, so we'll just get through it and then . . .

Right, OK, the reason I hate Russell Howard is this, OK. It's because my family, right, they're very nice, OK, but they don't – I love them, but they don't read the sort of papers where I get good reviews.† They don't know the sort of people that would – that would like me.‡ They're like a lot of people that have

* Here I am setting up the end of the show to fail on purpose. It can't possibly match the hype.

† This is increasingly not true, though it was once. My step-father is a digital subscriber to *The Times*, and so sees some positive press, and even though my mum wasn't a *Guardian* reader type, after her death I found a scrapbook where she had stored local, and some national, clippings about me. It is awkward for family members, though, to have to deal with the fact that someone they genuinely don't find funny at all is getting press saying he is literally the world's greatest living stand-up (I am not saying I am, by the way; I'm just quoting *The Times*). Family can be relied upon to humble us all.

‡ My mum, who always worried that I had wasted my life, started to get what I was doing a bit more towards the end of the 'oos, when younger workmates or the children of friends told her they were excited about

336

come tonight. And, er, and if they ever see a bit of film of me on YouTube or something like that, they – they think it's so bad, right, what I do that they can't believe I can actually make a living out of this, and in fact they don't believe it.*

And so when they talk to me about stand-up, they talk to me about it in a sort of sympathetic tone of voice, as if they think I'm a delusional madman who imagines that he's a stand-up comedian. And if I was to find out that I wasn't, I would have a mental breakdown. So they sort of ring me up and they go, 'Hello, and how is your stand-up comedy going? 'Cos that's your job, isn't it, and you . . . and you do that, don't you, for your work in your actual life?' I'm going, 'Yeah, it's fine, I'm just coming to the end of an eighteen-month tour actually.' 'I'm sure you are, son, you've been going all round, haven't you, and people are all laughing and no one's walking out . . .'†

---

going to see me. She came to the *If You Prefer a Milder Comedian* . . . tour twice: the first time with her partner, where she read the inbuilt struggles and micro-managed deliberate failure as real and clearly pitied me; the second with a younger friend, where she saw all the same apparent failings play out again and realised it was an act, and that the people who were laughing understood that. It can't be fun, I suppose, to watch the child you have nurtured fabricate an apparent breakdown. She used to love Les Dawson's deliberately bad piano-playing, though, which is the same. I wish she had lived to see me succeed in terms that would have been easier to understand. I feel like I let her down and betrayed her trust, and the choice she made to scoop me up out of the Lichfield orphanage cot in December 1968.

* In the mid-'90s, I remember my gran, astonished, saying she literally could not believe people paid me to do what I did.

† This sort of patronising conversation is usually followed, all stand-ups will tell you, by the relative asking if you have played Jongleurs, as they went to a works do there, or if you will be appearing on *Have I Got News*

The worst one is – is my brother-in-law,* right, he's a really nice bloke, he's fifty-seven, I really like him, I'm very lucky to – to have him, but we're different sort of people, he – he's the kind of bloke who – he'll ring me up and he'll go, 'Yeah, I saw you on TV last night having a go at Farage, quite badly misjudged, I thought.'† But he's really great, and . . . no, he is, I really – no, I do, I really like him, but he came to see me once about three years ago in London and it was a proper normal – Right, this is a five-star show, right, I'm just letting you know. This has had across-the-board five-star reviews, right, so I'm just letting you know that if there's a problem in this room tonight, it's not on this side of the stage, that's all I'm saying, all right? OK. A five-star show, all right. Doesn't feel like it tonight, does it? It feels like a four, with occasional lurches down towards a three, but it is a five.‡

Anyway, my brother-in-law came to see me in London, a proper normal five-star night, not like tonight, full of wilful obstruction, indifference and people wandering out. It was a normal five-star – but he just didn't like it, you know, and he – you know, afterwards, he looked so ashamed and embarrassed he couldn't meet my eye, I thought he was gonna be sick in the – in the foyer. But to be fair to him, my brother-in-law, he has no frame of reference whatsoever for this, right, 'cos he's only ever

---

for You. When you tell them how little *HIGNFY* pays and how all the acts on it use writers, they kind of glaze over and can't process it.

* This brother-in-law is a composite of various relatives. I don't have a brother-in-law who fits this description.

† This was actually said to me at an eightieth birthday party, not on the phone.

‡ I usually worked this 'five-star show' bit in somewhere near the top of the show, and then did a crowd-pleasing call-back to it at this point, but somehow, on the night of the recording, I forgot to do it and had to cram it all in here in one splurged bit. Amateur.

seen one other thing live in his whole life, and that was in 1986 at Lancaster Polytechnic, he saw Deacon Blue.* I can see him with his mate in the room, he's going, 'What is this? It's nothing like Deacon Blue, what is it? What's going on?'

Anyway, he rings me up. 'Hello, how's your comedy, that's your work, isn't it?' I'm going, 'Yeah, it's fine.' I said to him, 'You sound in a good mood'. He said, 'I am in a good mood.' I said, 'Why?' And he said, 'Well,' he said, 'we've been very lucky,' he said, 'we've managed to secure two tickets, eighteen months in advance, to the sold-out Royal Albert Hall run of our favourite TV stand-up comedian of all time, Russell Howard.'† And I went, 'Oh.' And

---

* My ex-brother-in-law had only ever seen one band live, and it was '80s Scottish soft-rockers Deacon Blue. He couldn't remember their name, but I managed to work it out by a process of elimination. Had I set out to find the perfect joke band to be the only band an imaginary ex-brother-in-law had ever seen live, I couldn't have chosen a more perfect one than Deacon Blue, the one my ex-brother-in-law actually saw. The great thing about Deacon Blue for comedy purposes here is they are actually a pretty good version of the thing that they are, and they wrote some great songs, so it isn't fake-sounding, like if I had chosen a more route-one comedy option – Bucks Fizz or Nickelback or Kajagoogoo or something. Deacon Blue frontman Ricky Ross's 1996 solo album *What You Are* is a solid power-pop set and features the guitar-playing of Jeff 'Skunk' Baxter, of '60s Boston psychedelic group The Ultimate Spinach. Skunk's computer skills, oddly, led to him becoming a defence consultant and chairing a US Congressional Advisory Board on missile defence in the '80s. Bizarrely, a re-formed Deacon Blue were leap-frogging us around the country, so punters in the theatres had usually passed posters for their reunion tour on the way in.

† I do have a relative who clearly can't stand what I do but loves Russell Howard. I understand why this is and, at worst, find it mildly amusing, but have decided to pretend to be angry here for comic effect. But in terms of our respective critical acclaim, it is a bit like running a Michelin-starred restaurant and your relative saying they prefer Burger

he said, 'You sound surprised.' And I went, 'Well, it's just I never met an adult, you know, that was going . . ."*

And, but, er, and he said to me, 'Don't you think he's any good?' I went, 'Yeah, he's great,' you know, and then he said to me in a sarcastic voice, my own brother-in-law, he said to me, 'Yes,' he said. 'Not like you then,' he said, 'the most critically acclaimed stand-up in Britain.'† [*a small laugh*] Well, that's where the big laugh is normally at. [*a big laugh*] Nothing was there. [*a big laugh*] Yeah, well, I said that . . . [*applause*] OK, right, why that normally gets a laugh, right, honestly that's normally such a big laugh, I just – people are going, 'Ah, genius,' and I just walk off, OK.‡

OK, they – it's doesn't matter, it's nice actually that so many people have come that didn't really know me and have . . . OK, what – what it is, why that's – OK, you don't know, right, but why it's funny, right, he said to me, 'Of course you're the most critically acclaimed stand-up in Britain.' Like I'm not, but I am. Right? So that's why – and they know that, that's why they're laughing, while the rest of you are going, 'Well, he can't be, can he?' Well, I am, I am. I'm not – no, that's why it normally – don't fucking shake your head at me, right, this – it's not up for debate, right. I am, I'm the most critically acclaimed stand-up in Britain

---

King (which is not to say I am better than Russell Howard; merely that broadsheet newspaper critics think I am. He has obvious skills that I don't).

* A joke among comedians is that Russell Howard's large ticket sales are down to the parents of his fans having to accompany them, as they are too young to go out on their own.

† This was actually said to me, in a branch of Wagamama.

‡ Every night there were enough people unaware of my critical standing to make this work.

this century, so it's funny that your own family member wouldn't – would not – I'm not – I'm not saying I'm the best, right, I'm the most critically acc— . . . I'm not saying I'm the best, there's loads of stand-ups better than me, I mean, there's – there's Daniel Kitson.* There's loads.†

But there's – no, I am, I know, so people are going – I can see them going, 'He can't be, can he?' What? People are walking out.‡ You've made this seem arrogant, but it's actually a very humble joke 'cos it's about how – fuck . . . I – look, I have got – I have got – I've got a – two – I've got three British Comedy Awards, I think. I might have two, I can't remember, I've got so many, I've got . . . I've got a BAFTA, I've got an Olivier Award, I've got – none of these people have got that, have they, an Olivier Award?

* This joke, which follows the structure of the 'all the different types of cheese – Red Leicester' joke from *Comedy Vehicle*, is for comedians and comedy fans, for whom the consensus, certainly for the most part of this century, was that Daniel Kitson was unassailably the best stand-up in the world, but that he had chosen to remain invisible to mainstream media. When members of the public, like cab drivers, who don't believe I am a comedian anyway because they haven't heard of me, ask me who my favourite stand-up is, and I say, 'Daniel Kitson,' they become angry and defensive because they haven't heard of him, especially if you then tell them he can crash the National Theatre ticketing website the second he announces a run of shows there. People seem to take their comedy very personally, as if you are insulting them by liking something they don't know about.

† The deliberately arrogant suggestion here, of course, is that there aren't loads, because I can't think of any.

‡ People always walked out. They probably needed wees as much as anything, as I said the half would be an hour long but always ran it for seventy to seventy-five minutes to create stress. I always pointed out the people leaving, rather than ignoring them, as it created the feeling that the evening was collapsing around me.

I've got six Chortle Awards, which is the industry . . . so, yes, I've got six consecutive ones for best touring show. What d'you want me to do?

I can . . . I – you know, listen, this isn't an end to a half, is it, a man pleading the case for his own genius while people file out? For Christ's sake, let's sort this out, right, let's – right, OK, I appreciate so many people coming, taking a punt on this, not knowing what it is, I know it's hard to get babysitters, all that sort of thing, let's sort this out, let's kick the second half up – up to a five. Right? We can fix this.*

What I'm gonna do . . . Don't go! Stop hanging around the doorway, give me two minutes, right, I'm gonna fix this. What I'm gonna do just quickly, right, I'm gonna go over some of the jokes that are coming up in the second half, no, because then they can ask people about the – the when – I can't afford to lose any more of you. Right, in the second half, right, there's gonna be – this'll take a minute, right – there's gonna be two more jokes about Deacon Blue, the '80s Scottish – right, they're not hilari-ous jokes, right, but what they are, they're what we call call-backs and they tie back to the earlier mention of Deacon Blue and they give the show the illusion of – of structure. Right? Which is what raised us above the apes, I think. Or visiting American stand-ups, as I call them.†

* Here the audience are invited to become stakeholders in the success of the show, rather than passive observers.

† After Hannah Gadsby's show *Nanette* hit Netflix in 2018, American stand-ups realised that in the rest of the world comedians were taking the time and trouble to structure their long-form shows and make them about something, as if the comedians gave a fuck, which explained why acclaimed Americans that came to the Edinburgh Fringe just got three-star reviews and went home crying and complaining about 'the tyranny of the British hour'. Once American stand-ups started to try and write

Oh, come on, you've seen them, haven't you? You're at the – you're at the O2, seeing the American stand-up, it's ninety-five quid for their forty-two-minute club set, and you're sitting there watching the American stand-up, and you're going . . . 'We don't have those cakes here, mate. Sorry. Don't have those cakes.' OK, all I'm saying, right, is I don't go to New York and do two hours on Mr Kipling, do I? You know? I'm not in Madison Square Garden going, 'And there's like a shortbread bit. Then there's jam on there, then there's like a Bakewell – is this on?'*

So to get everyone in the mood I thought I'd play the first Deacon Blue album, *Raintown*, at half-time, right, and I found it second-hand on the Internet, 69p. That's not very good, is it, Annette? 69p! No! I can teach Deacon Blue a thing or two about online reputation management. What I don't understand is, there's six of them, they should be on the Internet in shifts

---

proper shows too, nearly thirty years too late, think-pieces began to appear in American magazines and on culture websites about this new kind of stand-up, in which I was at best a footnote and the real '90s Edinburgh Fringe grandaddies of the form, Ireland's Sean Hughes and Australia's Greg Fleet, were never mentioned at all.

* Here I am thinking, unfairly, of Jim Gaffigan's acclaimed routine about an American cake called a Hot Pocket, which I have never seen, and which he performed for weeks at the Leicester Square Theatre, in a country where Hot Pockets are not available. In 2000, in Melbourne, I was on with a famous American comedienne, whose name I genuinely can't remember, who told me she was dying every night. I went to see the show. Much of it was about the brand names of confectionery that was not for sale outside the US. This kind of American comedy parochialism was parodied brilliantly in the '90s by Paul Putner's American stand-up character Earl Stevens, who was often accepted by cocaine-blasted Britpop-era trendies as a genuine out-of-touch American, and booed accordingly.

driving that price up. D'you know, if there was six of me, my DVD would be about £5.*

That's right. You were right to clap. So what we do there, we get a problem, it's not a problem, you store it away, bring it back later on. I know you're laughing, the people up there, they're going, 'No one could be that good, she is a plant, that woman. He takes her round the whole country, and she shouts out "£5".' You're not a plant, are you, Annette? No. Only four more shows left anyway. You don't know what's going on now, do you?†

So I ordered it off, er, Music Magpie, Deacon Blue's first album, and the bloke, Rick at Music Magpie, he sent me an email, he said, 'We're sorry to inform you that *Raintown* by Deacon Blue,

* By complaining to Annette about her suggestion of £5 earlier in the show, I set up bringing it back as an unexpected positive. It worked better, for this call-back, if the person earlier in the show suggested a number that was higher than £3.67.

† As usual, online commentators assumed the person was a plant. When I took my dad to see Al Murray the Pub Landlord being brilliant in a massive theatre in the late '90s, he assumed the three dozen or so audience members Al bantered with were plants, and was impressed by Al's ability to learn all their names before the show and remember where they were sitting. My dad ran his own packaging consultancy, yet would not accept that the logistics of touring thirty-six people around the country, night after night, merely to make some standard top-of-the-show banter work, would render his assumption impossible. The chat-show host James Corden, it must be said, did all of us who genuinely improvise a disservice by having a plant that he 'improvised' with every night when he starred in the 2011 National Theatre production *One Man, Two Guvnors*, thus destroying public trust in genuine comedy improvisation. Corden would say he was hungry, and an 'audience member' would throw a hummus sandwich at him, allowing Corden to say, '*Guardian* reader.' Ah well, it's a living!

order 2032917358, has failed its final quality inspection.'* So I said, 'Well, don't worry if the case is damaged, I just need to play the – the music at half-time in my show.' And he said, 'No, not its physical-quality inspection. Deacon Blue's mix of soulful singer-songwriter sensibilities and plastic mid-'80s production values has not aged well. But we notice from our files that all your fans who buy your live DVDs from us then go on to buy 1970s Turkish funk albums.† So as a goodwill gesture, here's some to play in your interval.' And that's the interval now.

STEW WANDERS OFF, CONCLUSIVELY. ERKIN KORAY'S 'CEMALIM' STARTS PLAYING IN THE INTERVAL,‡ FOLLOWED BY A MEDLEY OF OTHER '70S TURKISH PSYCHEDELIC FUNK.

* This is a genuine note I received from Music Magpie the first time I tried to order *Raintown* from them. Obviously, I changed the next part of the exchange for comic effect, but really it was too perfect.

† Multiple call-backs! The bodies of every call-back in the show pile up on stage – *Hamlet (Pow Pow Pow)*.

‡ In the end, it would have been too expensive to clear this track just to hear a tiny snatch of it in the TV broadcast of *Content Provider*, to crown the multiple call-back pile-up. Instead, my ten-year-old son showed me how to use his GarageBand software, and he 'produced' a fake '70s Turkish psych-funk track for me, 'Yarasa Adam', by Toz Hasat. *Toz Hasat* is Turkish for Dust Harvest, which was the name of my '80s Dream Syndicate-copying student band, which played only four gigs and had three line-ups. On 'Yarasa Adam' I played bendy guitar, we swathed the drums in massive echo, and dropped in obscure Turkish dialogue. You can download the track for free here: http://www.stewartlee.co.uk/ what-is-stewart-lee/what-is-stewart-lee-2018/. I make no claims as to its quality, but it did the job.

SECOND HALF

Right, in the first half I said, didn't I, I was trying to do two hours on the idea of the individual in a digitised free-market economy. I said I was gonna base it around this painting, Caspar David Friedrich's 1818 German Romantic masterpiece *Wanderer Above the Sea of Fog* [*crosses the stage with the painting and leans it against a pillar stage left*], and I said I couldn't do that 'cos I had to talk about Brexit, then I did talk about Brexit for about twenty-five minutes, then I got back on to talking about digital media, physical media, so that was all right, that was the first half, that was done.

Then about sixteen months ago I started writing the second half, and that was coming together all right, and then America voted for Trump and there seems . . .* there just seems to be an expectation everywhere that I should've written something about Americans voting for Trump. And I haven't written anything about, er, Trump because I'm trying to write a show that I keep on the road for eighteen months, and as I didn't know how America voting for Trump was gonna pan out, I didn't write anything about it in case I couldn't keep it in the show for the full length of the tour and monetise the work I've done. So I haven't written anything about America voting for Trump 'cos I don't see the point of committing to a course of action for which there's no logical or financial justification.

---

* There was a laugh here as the quicker punters realised the opening of the second half was deliberately mirroring the opening of the first, with Trump replacing Brexit.

Well, typically, it's going better down here, isn't it, down here, the elite of Southend. They're going, 'How amusing, Lee, how amusing, Lee has used exactly the same syntax at the start of both the first and second half, with only two nouns changed in order to drive home the notion that both the Trump and Brexit victories are driven by the same populous rhetoric. How clever.' People up there are going, 'How embarrassing, he's done the same bit twice.' 'He must be drunk.' 'He's an alcoholic, I saw it on Twitter.'*

* I keep reading on Twitter and in below-the-line comments that I am drunk on stage. If you are good at acting mad, people assume you must be. I have been drunk on stage about four times, and one of them was in New Zealand, which doesn't count. The best fabricated story of my drunkenness is this one, from a YouTube user called Funday's Child, who seems to be trying to mess with my head: 'I was Stage Manager for Stewart Lee. It wasn't performance art, stand-up comedy or satire. It was a fucking train-wreck. That man could not read an audience 3 feet away. And yes, I got to know his act well during the rehearsals and Tech rehearsal. I also got to know the fact that the man is a functioning alcoholic, finishing nearly 12 cans to himself before going onstage, and that he is banned from the entire chain of Theatres I used to work at for being rude, dismissive of staff and responding terribly to bad audience feedback. I don't hate this man in the slightest, I pity him. Where he tries to wear the "never hitting mainstream" as a cloak (Even naming a tour after it) the cracks appear when you're one on one with him. He is angry, and I don't think he know who he's angry at.' Needless to say, I don't really have a 'stage manager' and don't really understand what this job title refers to here. I don't rehearse my act, ever, and certainly not on-stage in theatres. I could not drink 'nearly twelve cans' under any circumstances, and I am too tight to ask for any kind of rider, having seen the break-even points disappear in a fog of apparently complimentary sandwiches and Carling Black Label on Lee and Herring tours during the Avalon years. I do like the idea that I finished 'nearly' twelve cans, though, as it suggests someone was checking and tipping

347

So, you know, 'cos I've got a Trump bit, I have to check at half-time every night that he's not been assassinated or fallen into a barrel of porn actresses* or something, and, er,† but it does mean that I see the same crass anti-American generalisations online every night, social media, and it – it annoys me, to be honest, because I don't know if you can make massive generalisations about Americans who voted for Trump.

Because Americans voted for Trump for all sorts of different reasons. And it wasn't just racists who voted for Donald Trump

---

them out individually to see what was left in them. How many cans was it? Eleven? Ten? What is 'nearly twelve'? I am not, quite categorically, banned from any chain of theatres either, though I have chosen not to play some of them. In fact, James Hingley, the tour manager, and I are welcomed back by delighted staff and crew members all around the land every year, as we are an efficient, low-impact unit who clear up our own mess. I am not offered 'audience feedback' by any venue, and it is not standard practice to offer it to comedians, so I am not invited to respond to it by anyone, though it is true that even if that were the case, I wouldn't see it as my duty to adapt to it anyway. I wonder what or who this all relates to? Perhaps Funday's Child has got me confused with Adam Hills, from *The Last Leg*. Or Alex Brooker. Or Toksvig. This all sounds like the sort of stuff one of them would do.

* How quaint that in April 2018 I was still worrying that Trump might not outlast the tour. I write this in March 2019, and he's still there, clogging up the pipe.

† As a purist, this 'er' here irks me, as in this instance it is an example of the stand-up trick known as Ó Briain's Truncated Appendage. Here the comedian appends a stray 'er' to the end of a sentence to give the audience time to catch up with the joke, while appearing to be merely pausing for thought, not waiting for them to laugh. It is so named as it is a key element of the work of *Mock the Week*'s Norway-conquering, DVD-hating host Dara Ó Briain, who has had a number of his specials screened on terrestrial TV.

348

[*delays moving on and milks the laughter of anticipation, like a milkmaid of swearing*]. Cunts did as well, didn't they?*

Yeah. Stupid fat American cunts. The worst kind of cunts, aren't they? Much worse than our British cunts, ain't they? Salt of the earth, British cunts. [*sings*] 'British cunts. British cunts. British Brexit-voting cunts from Southend.'†

But it's you, isn't it? But I don't know – well, I don't know if you can make massive generalisations about Americans who voted for Trump. Seriously. I mean, not all Americans who voted for Trump wanted to see America immediately descend into an unaccountable single-party state, exploiting people's worst prejudices to maintain power indefinitely. Some Americans just wanted to be allowed to wear their Ku Klux Klan outfits to church, didn't they?

Perked up, haven't you, at half-time! Had a little chat, have you, with the people that brought you? 'Oh, d'you think he's funny, John?' 'Yes.' 'Oh, I do as well then.' You make me sick.‡

It's very difficult, though, nowadays to write a joke that everyone either understands or finds funny, you know, er, or relates to. And it's partly because we live in such fragmented times in terms of how we consume news information, there's no dominant trusted news narrative, no news source, everyone's going down their own little digital wormholes, and you'll be on some

---

* Although Tony Parson would doubtless disagree, it is not the c-word (cunt) in and of itself that is getting the laugh here. The laugh comes from the telegraphed inevitability of the fact that the word is going to be said, as the act is mirroring the same section in the first half.

† The c-word (cunt) is out of the bag now and can be bandied about with gay abandon, willy-nilly.

‡ This is standard start-of-the-second-hour shtick from me, and has probably appeared verbatim elsewhere.

website and it says, 'D'you agree with this? Then click on this 'cos it's the same as what you already think.'

And no one – no one's got any overview, have they, and that's partly how a Trump and a Brexit can – can happen. It didn't use to be like that, did it, Southend, we used to be part of a collective consciousness, didn't we? In 1978, for example, 28 million British people watched the same Christmas *Morecambe and Wise*, as it was broadcast in real time. Half the population. And this is held up as a sort of apogee of our collective experience. But it doesn't really hold water 'cos there was no competition then, was there? There was no DVDs, there was no Internet, and there was only two other TV channels. And on one of them was a documentary about Burnham-on-Crouch. And on the other was a drawing of a clown sitting near a blackboard. And that got 27 million viewers. 'Did it?' No.*

But young people today are very proud of the fact that they don't interact with conventional terrestrial media at all, aren't they? They go, 'Mate,† I don't even know what that is, mate.

---

* The image I am talking about here, as older viewers will remember, is called Test Card F, and was usually accompanied by music from reliable Brit-jazz sessioneers like Alan Hawkshaw. It was shown on screen whenever there were no programmes on the BBC, like in the afternoon or the middle of the night. Yes, kids, in the old days, sometimes, there was *no TV*! I had it in my head that the image had been designed by the father of the hilarious Irish actress and stand-up Tara Flynn, who appeared in, among other things, *Comedy Vehicle*, but having checked on the Internet, I see this is absolutely not the case. In fact, she tells me, her father worked for a soft-drinks company in West Cork. I wonder why I thought he designed Test Card F. Am I mad? Is the act of writing these footnotes actually documenting early-onset Alzheimer's disease? Can I trust any of my memories? My brain seems to be just linking random things together. If only there were some way to monetise this.

† All this stuff was done in the voice of the Russell Howard fans from earlier.

Terrestrial media? I just watch the Internet, Netflix, cable, download computer television. I haven't even got the thing that you need to – I haven't even got any eyes. Mate, I haven't even got any, you know, senses to perceive any physical stimuli. I just have memes Bluetoothed into my cortex, you know?

'Have you not got the Internet, Netflix, cable, Sky computer-download television, Stew, have you not got that, mate? It's amazing. Some amazing things on, er, Internet, Netflix, cable, Sky. I mean, there's er, there are, there's some really good stuff. I mean, there's *Game of Thrones*, for example, which is – oh, have you not seen *Game of Thrones*, mate?* Have you not seen *Game* – uh. Not seen *Game of Thrones*, mate? Uh, it's not just about a gnome, Stew. He's a dwarf anyway. You're racist against gnomes. You're a gnome racist. It's a completely different thing.

'Have you not seen *Game of Thrones*? It's – it's not for kids, Stew, no, I mean, yeah, there's – there's magic in it, but it's not like, you know, *Harry Potter* or the *Faraway Tree*† or something like – you know. I mean, what is magic anyway? That's what I say to you. I mean, magic could be, like, kind of energy force that we just don't understand yet. Could be? Think about it, I mean, once upon a time, you know, people would've run away from Doritos, wouldn't they?‡ But there are people eating them now

* I have still not seen *Game of Thrones*.

† As mentioned earlier, I was reading the *Faraway Tree* series of books to my daughter at the time. My mother had read them to me while I drank my milk in my pyjamas and cuddled my bear. I was six years old, and not twenty-eight, as you imagined.

‡ On reflection, this bit has an obvious relationship with a line in a '90s Lee and Herring routine, where Richard said, 'They laughed at the idea of toast, Stew, once upon a time.' Perhaps I included Doritos here as a subconscious acknowledgement of this, as Richard's father, famously and enjoyably, used to mispronounce Doritos as 'Doritoss', making the

and dipping . . . I don't, but it's what – you know, some people, I've seen people eat them.

'Have you not got – have you not seen *Game of Thrones*? It's – I don't know when it's set, Stew, no, you know, could be in the past, yeah. Could be in the future after Brexit. There's a big wall coming off the north of the country, everyone's in rags, no one's got any Toblerone, so it could be.

'Have you really not seen *Game of Thrones*, mate? It's – I mean, it's not just about a dragon flying around with a hat on, it's really – So actually, Stew, *Game of Thrones* is a really amazing programme because actually it's very clever, *Game of Thrones*, 'cos what it's actually about, it's about history and, you know, philosophy and politics and things like that.'

'Is it? *Game of Thrones*? Peter Stringfellow's *Lord of the Rings*. Bilbo Baggins at the Spearmint Rhino. I'm not going to watch *Game of Thrones*, I can get the same experience from sitting around with a Terry Pratchett novel in one hand and a copy of Hustler's *Barely Legal* in the other.'

'It's not like that, mate, have you actually watched *Game* . . .?'

'I haven't watched *Game of Thrones*. If I want to understand the ongoing weft of history, while simultaneously being mildly sexually aroused, I'll forcibly dress David Starkey in Agent Provocateur underwear* and pay him to give a lap dance† to Simon Schama.'‡

Mexican snack sound like some kind of cleaning fluid or Hispanic semen discharge. We went to visit him in about 1987, in Cheddar, and he said, 'Have you tried these new Doritoss?' I still call Doritos 'Doritoss' to this day, because of him.

* Punchline.

† Topper.

‡ Double topper.

'It's not like that, mate, have you actually watched *Game of . .*'
'No. I haven't watched *Game of Thrones*. And I shall never watch *Game of Thrones*. "I shall take no wife, hold no lands, father no children.* I shall wear no crown and win no glory, and I shall not watch *Game of Thrones*."' [*There is limited applause from* Game of Thrones *fans who recognise the quote from the series.*]

D'you like that, do you, *Game of Thrones* fans? D'you know what? I don't even fucking know what that is. I copied that off the back of a cup in HMV.† Right? OK? No, I did. And everything I need to know to do an hour of stand-up on *Game of Thrones* I can get off a cup. So grow up, you stupid Warhammer twats. You're about forty-five years old.

'Have you – it's not like that, have you actually w—' 'No, I haven't watched *Game of Thrones*. If I want to understand the ongoing collapse of ancient dynasties while simultaneously being barely semi-tumescent,‡ as usual,§ I'll read Tolstoy's *War and Peace* while sitting over the wheel arch of a diesel-powered double-decker bus'¶ – first laughs from the friends up there.

---

* Here I would scan the audience to single out people who looked like *Game of Thrones* viewers and pitch this quotation at them, so that they would applaud as a minority and I could then berate them for liking *Game of Thrones* and recognising the quotes.

† A version of the *Game of Thrones* routine was already in place when I gave some free tickets for the show to a musician friend of tour manager James Hingley. The man thanked me for the tickets and gave me a *Game of Thrones* mug from HMV, which had this original version of the quote on it. I used the quote and detailed its source in subsequent versions of the joke, as seen here.

‡ Punchline.

§ Topper.

¶ This got laughs from only a small minority of the audience, as it was calibrated to, who were aware that the chugging of a diesel engine can,

353

Some of the older supporters of the theatre going, 'Yeah, remember the old days? You could get on, couldn't you, could get on the bus in Billericay,* and by the time . . .'†

'Hey, I've got a joke for you now, Southend, it's a *Game of Thrones* joke. Hey, I tell you what, you may laugh, madam, if you were my daughter, I'd still be bathing you.‡ It's a joke . . . Come on. It's the 1970s, it was a different time. It was a time of innocence and fun, laughter. So, got a joke for you, it's a *Game of Thrones* joke, hey, so, you may laugh, sir, if you were my son I'd still be bathing you.

---

apparently, cause involuntary erections in some men.

* Coincidentally, this is Tony Parson's home town, where as a young man he 'breathed the foul air' that was thick with the c-word (cunt). Obviously, I only said 'Billericay' when I was performing in Essex. In other places I'd say a different town. These are the secret tools of the touring comedian, which an ordinary person like you, reader, could never master.

† The suggestion here is that the diesel engine has caused the male passenger to ejaculate semen from his penis. A few people laughed at this, and I didn't clarify what I meant. In the ensuing confusion I segued quickly into a kind of Roy 'Chubby' Brown/club-comic voice, making my getaway from the previous bit, and began doing '70s-type working-men's-club material. I don't know why. I don't remember ever writing this bit down, so it grew out of an improvisation, until it became a fluid bit that I performed every night. I don't quite know what connections were firing here, but it seemed to work, and it allowed me to do *Game of Thrones* material as if it were being performed by a '70s club comic, in a time before *Game of Thrones* was ever broadcast.

‡ This is an old Bernard Manning bit. You can see footage of him using it at all the different stages of his career. When he does it to young women, when he is really old and unthreatening, it is almost charming.

Different times weren't it, '70s, it's – all the children were clean, weren't they? In the '70s. Weren't they? Get in the bath. Get out the bath. Dry yourself off. Get back in the bath, now! Get in the bath! So there's people up there going, 'Oh, now it's picked up. A proper comedian's come on.' So got a joke for you now, it's a *Ga*— You may laugh, sir, if you were dead I'd still be bathing you.* Different times, weren't it, the '70s? You could bathe the dead, couldn't you? 'Is he dead?' 'Yes, but he's clean.' 'Oh.' 'Nice and clean.' So I've got a joke for you now, it's a *Game of Thrones* joke. Hey, I tell you what, right, there's so many naked young women in that *Game of Thrones* programme . . . [*looks into the wings, as if to check that there is no one monitoring him*]†

Now I'm just checking back there for the old PC thought police. Gary Lineker's liberal Stasi.‡ No offence, the metropolitan liberal elite of Southend, but how fucked are you when the main champion of your liberal values is Gary Lineker? 'My name's Gary Lineker, I like to wake up in the morning and send out a succession of tweets in support of broadly progressive causes. Then, in the afternoon, I like to relax with a great big bag of crisps.'§ Are you there, Gary? He's not there tonight. Are you

---

* Our perception of '70s light entertainers has changed in recent years.

† This trick of checking if there is anyone listening to the act in the wings is copied from Max Miller, and it makes the audience feel like they are in on a secret that must not be shared.

‡ Crisp-advertising ex-footballer Gary Lineker has distinguished himself over the last few years as a prominent liberal voice in the Twittersphere, much to the disapproval of the largely right-leaning sports commentariat.

§ I could more or less get Lineker's Leicestershire accent right if I thought, each night, of how the actor, comedian and Silver Age DC Comics expert Colin Hoult actually speaks in real life, although he is from Nottinghamshire, so it doesn't really make sense.

there? Some nights he's there and we have a – we have a little chat, don't – hello. But no, Gary, I don't think – well, given how the first half ended I don't think tonight's the sort of night where the audience will go with a long improvised dialogue with an invisible off-stage Gary Lineker. So I know, Gary, it worked very well in Leicester, but that's your . . . that's your home town, and what began as a regionally specific ad lib has gradually depreciated in value as we've gone further south. I know. So he's not coming on tonight, he won't – he won't – he's not there anyway, he w— . . . he won't come this far south, Gary Lineker. He won't cross water. In case his crisps get damp.* Anyway, I need to get on with the joke now because, er, the longer I talk in this voice the more I realise I've not really given enough thought to who this is supposed to be.† Just started off as a throwaway thing. So – anyway, so I've got a joke for you now, it's a *Game of Thrones* joke. Hey, I tell you what, right, there's so many naked young women in that *Game of Thrones* programme they have now, it's hardly surprising what stunted Tyrion Lannister's growth.‡ It

* This invisible Gary Lineker bit began as an improvisation in Lineker's home town of Leicester, where his family have a fruit stall in the market, and then became one of those fun bits of the show that keep you sane over 250 performances, which could expand or contract nightly in different ways and go off on different tangents. There were much longer versions of it than the one here, which is the only documented version.

† Indeed. The voice is some kind of generic Roy 'Chubby' Brown/ Bernard Manning composite, which isn't really sustainable without further finessing, but I left it deliberately in this unresolved state.

‡ Tyrion Lannister is the 'imp' character in *Game of Thrones*, played by Peter Dinklage, who has a form of dwarfism. Dinklage addresses his condition head on in Tom DiCillo's brilliant 1995 film *Living in Oblivion*, in which he plays an actor of small stature sick of being cast only in dream sequences. Here, like Boris Johnson, I am aware that I am

were wanking, ladies and gentlemen. He's wanked hisself into being a dwarf.* He was six foot six in the pilot episode.

[*adopts an annoying, whining voice*] 'Oh. Hang on a minute, mate, wasn't that a sizeist joke?† About the dwarf community?'

[*as himself again*] Yes, it was. But I ridiculed the dwarf community in order to satirise the ongoing exploitation of women in mainstream media, so it cancels it out. It's the kind of split-second collateral-damage decision Frankie Boyle has to make every time he opens his mouth.‡

------

having my cake and eating it, making an un-PC joke with relish, while supposedly parodying old-school un-PC comedians. Look, I'm holding my hand up to that, OK? Am I now #cancelled?

* I have a strange pride in having got the phrase 'He's wanked hisself into being a dwarf' onto the BBC.

† The Russell Howard fan voice from earlier returns here.

‡ I wonder if Frankie Boyle and his joke-writing team do have these kinds of discussions. Is there a decision-making process whereby them accusing the glamour model Katie Price's blind autistic son Harvey, who was eight at the time of Boyle's and his writers' joke, of wanting to rape his mother is balanced out, as legitimate collateral damage, against the idea that his mother's lifestyle and choice of romantic partners make her fair game for such harsh mockery? When, in his 2011 book *Work! Consume! Die!*, Boyle described the blameless campaigning comedian Josie Long, who was probably not even on the radar of the average Frankie Boyle fan, being raped by a monkey crossed with Hitler, did he feel the obvious distress this would cause her was counterbalanced by striking a well-deserved blow at . . . well, who knows what? Similarly, was the decision to repurpose the '00s Frankie Boyle sick-comedian character as a liberal satirist made by the real Frankie Boyle and his writers for some reason they have never made clear, or had Boyle and his joke-writing team exhausted the possibilities of the Frankie Boyle/nihilist character and understandably wanted to see it evolve? Was this repointing an attempt to ease his, and his writers', return to the BBC,

[*as the whiner again*] 'Oh, hang on a minute, mate, who's the sole arbiter of taste in stand-up comedy? Who's the self-appointed moral judge of right and wrong in stand-up comedy?'

[*as himself again, but almost incoherently furious*] It's me, I am! It's been me for about seventeen years now! And there's nothing the passive-aggressive indifference of the people of Southend-on-Sea can do about that! Not now!

[*makes a sudden jarring shift into a friendly, chatty, observational-comedy stand-up persona*] But, hey, the world's gone mad, hasn't it? Yes. D'you know what, I blame – I blame the young people, by which I mean people under forty, and I hope there's none in.* 'I'm under forty. I'm disillusioned. I like Russell

---

which he had previously said was too cowardly to handle him and his writers, after the cancellation of the badly produced 2010 Channel 4 series that failed to facilitate their talents? And what makes me making fun of a dwarf actor any better than Boyle and his writers at their least accountable? Is it simply the fact that I have acknowledged what I am doing in a post-modern way? Is it in fact worse than Boyle and his writers because it is dishonest? Probably. I don't know.

People do change. They come to realise that jokes might have consequences and might exacerbate hatreds that they can't square with their consciences. We all have material we are happy to have left behind, and Boyle has tried to move on. The likes of Toby Young, Boris Johnson and Jeremy Clarkson have a professional interest in not doing so, and they continue to deny that a joke is ever anything more than just a joke.

* The initial thrust of this bit survived from the 2015–16 *Room with a Stew* tour and was too bulky to fit into its intended place in series four of *Comedy Vehicle*, becoming the first bankable building block of *Content Provider*. It didn't make quite as much sense now, as it suddenly seemed a long time since the days when Labour leader Ed Miliband was seeking the endorsement of the newly politicised Russell Brand, who was running around advising people not to vote as there was no point.

358

Brand, I didn't vote, yeah. Oh no, I've got no future now. Never mind, I've got this phone.'

STEW MIMES A YOUNG PERSON TAPPING THEIR PHONE FOR ABOUT SIX MINUTES, WORKING WAVES OF LAUGHTER THAT GROW, SUBSIDE, THEN RECONFIGURE, UNTIL THE ACTIONS HE IS PERFORMING NO LONGER BEAR ANY RELATIONSHIP TO PHONE USE AND HAVE BECOME A MEANINGLESS, REPETITIVE, RITUAL DANCE. FINALLY, HIS TROUSERS FALL DOWN, AND HE ADDRESSES THE AUDIENCE WITH A CONFIDENCE THAT IS NOT AFFECTED BY HIS HUMILIATING PARTIAL NUDITY.[*]

* This bit grew and grew, until I could dance around in a frenzy of pretended phone-screen tapping for minutes on end, surfing the waves of baffled hysteria. A clip of this section, shorn of the spoken-word material either side that explains it, has appeared on the Internet, courtesy of some alt-right nostalgist, as an example of how bad 'modern' comedy is, and how much better *Dad's Army*, Bernard Manning and Max Miller were. Those viewing it without context could be forgiven for feeling bewildered, but the idea that this furiously incoherent dance represents 'modern' comedy is demonstrably wrong. It is ancient comedy, and it is possible to imagine the earliest of shaman clowns, perhaps before language had even taken shape, performing a similar absurd dance around the fires of their Palaeolithic caves, three million years ago. I have written before how the music of Julian Cope's proto-metal/Detroit pre-punk revivalists Brain Donor has affected my comedy, suggesting that if you persist with something apparently simplistic to the point of stupidity for long enough it can eventually become transcendental. I'm not saying I achieved that here, or that I am the equal of genuinely transporting art and music, but it was a lot more fun doing this every night than saying sentences with words in them that, because of their position in relation to each other and the meanings they have, could make people laugh. As for the falling trousers . . . I gain and lose weight erratically on tour, due to a toxic mix of post-show drinking, motorway food, sedentary van

People under forty, what a shower of shit, aren't you? That's you! This is you.*

_____

journeys and suppressed stress. I wore the same 1980s skinny black jeans all through the run, and at a Bristol date about halfway through I must have been significantly slimmer than at the start, as my trousers suddenly started slipping down my hips during the mad phone dance. I could have pulled them back up, but I found myself wondering what would happen if I let them fall, and just ignored it, already calculating in my mind that it would be great to be performing high-status slag-offs of young people, while looking like a ridiculous old man who couldn't keep his trousers up. In fact, doing the routine with my trousers around my ankles should have actually made it funnier for proper clown-theory reasons. And it did. With a little practice I realised I could swivel my hips in such a way as to make my trousers fall down every night, like some kind of out-of-shape Chippendale, which was even funnier for the front few rows because both of my two legs are covered with scars from insect bite infections, including the bite of a rare and invasive species of spider, and blotches from patches of decayed flesh left over from a bout of cellulitis. They are the kind of legs that encourage GPs, who don't know that I am a successful comedian, to ask 'if there is someone at home looking after me' and to remind me that at fifty I now qualify for free local council sessions of 'chair-based activity'. One night someone helpfully heckled that my trousers had fallen down, and I answered that I was aware of this, and that it was a deliberate attempt to lower my status to enable me to mock people from the position of a lowly outsider, a theory I had learned from studying, and living with, the Native American shaman clowns in Arizona and New Mexico. About one in ten times people would tell me my trousers had fallen down, and I was able to answer with a similarly pretentious discourse, and I wish it had happened for the live recording, but it didn't. There! If I had plants, like James Corden, I could have fixed that.

* I am genuinely sick of these phones, especially in theatres and cinemas. They take everyone out of the moment and ruin the climaxes of long, and painstakingly structured, routines. On this tour I warned everyone at the start (edited out of this transcript) that if they used phones, I would

STEW BEGINS THE PHONE-TAPPING DANCE AGAIN, AND
CONTINUES IT WHILE MOCKING THE AUDIENCE.

'I'm under forty, I like the Pokeman Go.* I'm under forty, in
the morning I don't eat bread for breakfast like an adult, I suck
drinking yoghurt out of a pouch [*sucks*]. I'm under forty, this
is my food [*sucks*].† I'm under forty, this is me on the bus to
work in the morning [*pokes his phone, dances and sucks*]. People
under forty, you like stupid fads, don't you? A Japanese cat's
face drawn on a satchel, that's what you like, isn't it? 'We'll get

---

come down, get their phones and smash them to bits. In about one in
ten shows I would see someone on their phone, so I would run down
and snatch it, easily taking them by surprise as they were looking at their
screen, and take it back to the stage. The audience would expect me to
smash the phone as promised, but instead I would turn round, pull down
my pants and wedge the phone into the actual point where the lower
end of my buttocks crack meets the start of my perineum, and then pull
my pants back up and carry straight on from where I had left off with
no comment. The phone would remain wedged in my rectum until the
end of that half, sometimes causing me visible discomfort as I moved
around the stage. Then, after putting the phone in a jiffy bag, it would be
returned to the punter via front of house, ideally with pieces of suspect
physical matter visible on it. GET OFF YOUR PHONES!

* Throughout this section I am affecting ignorance of the modern world,
based on half-seen videos, adverts and memes, which I often genuinely
fail to understand in real life anyway.

† The idea that drinking yoghurt was amusing in and of itself dates
back to a mid-'90s Lee and Herring routine, which I have forgotten.
Richard has gone on to do pioneering work with yoghurt-based humour,
but in this bit I was specifically thinking of an annoying contemporary
advertising campaign for a new Australian breakfast drink, Up & Go,
which aimed to increase sales among men by visually suggesting there
was a link between sucking up some breakfast drink and receiving oral
sex from a hot surfer chick.

up early and get down the market.' 'Why?' 'The Japanese-cat-satchel-face man's coming.' 'You've got loads of satchels with a Japanese cat's face on, mate.' 'I know, but they might be a blah blah blah aaaaaaah . . .' [*dissolves into an incoherent frenzy of twenty-something babbling*].

Bondage sex and S&M and the fetish scene, that's the new thing, isn't it, for the under-forties? Which they think they've fucking invented. 'Cos they read about it in *Fifty Shades of Grey*. Or they saw it in a FKA Twigs video.* I know who he is actually, mate, so you can fuck off.† This is exactly my problem actually with the under-forties, if you're – if you're fifty like me and you make some joke about popular culture, people under forty go, 'Ah-hah, grandad, you don't know who FKA Twigs is.' Well, I do know who he is, FKA Twigs. They don't know, do they, the Southend theatre people. But I do know who FKA Twigs is. FKA Twigs, right, he's not a twig, like you think. 'Is he a twig? Is he from the woods?' FKA Twigs, he's a – he's a rap singer, he's one of these – he is, he's one of these rappers, he's – well, he is, I've – you know, he's done loads of tapes, I've got his tapes.‡ And he's – he's got a video, FKA Twigs, where all sort of Japanese bondage ropes go round him

---

* Usually, one person would laugh at the mention of FKA Twigs, who is a female dance-music artist from Cheltenham, Gloucestershire, and is on the fringes of the average person's consciousness. She was chosen for this joke because only a tiny minority of the audience would recognise her name, so the joke would semi-fail.

† I don't, because I have got Twigs's gender wrong. On a good night, people would call out to tell me that FKA Twigs was a woman, and then I would accuse them of gender fascism and say they were worse than Hitler. But it didn't always happen, and it didn't happen here. That is the beauty of live performance: great moments are lost for ever, as they should be.

‡ Bizarrely, audio tape is now the latest cool retro format.

and he flies up in the air and he has to try and – right, has anyone seen this?* 'Cos I'm looking for stuff to drop, to be honest.† No. I've seen it, I – I saw it on, er, oh, not *Top of the Pops*, what is it they have now? The Internet, it was on that. It's like *Top of the Pops*, isn't it, the Internet? Full of pop music and sexual predators. Yeah, see, see, I can write jokes, I could be on *Mock the Week* easily.‡ This is *Mock the Week*, isn't it? [*backs off from the mic, and then scampers back up to it,* Mock the Week-*style*] 'The Internet is a bit like . . .' – fuck off for God's sake. Pathetic, isn't it? 'Oh, I've written a joke.' Imagine writing jokes. What a waste of time. 'Oh, this thing is like this, only this is different.' For God's sake.

People under – 'I'm thirty-seven, I like bondage sex. I had a

---

* If anyone had seen this video (for the 2015 single 'Pendulum'), and it only needed to be one person, I would go on a lengthy digression about exactly how FKA Twigs had got tangled up in all the string. I would remember that it happened near a row of shops just by Gloucester Quays shopping centre, where there is a Burger King, a Toys 'R' Us and a Laser Quest centre. If anyone in the room knew the geography of Gloucester, which I know well, the bit could gain an extra five minutes. I remember that the routine ended with someone jumping out on FKA Twigs, who was listening to rap tapes on a Sony Walkman and so not paying attention, and luring Twigs into a disused shop, where he/she was tangled up in string. I remember it concluded thus: 'And FKA Twigs says, "There isn't loads of string in there, is there?" And the bloke said, "No." But there was.' But sadly, the lengthy FKA Twigs/Gloucester shopping centre extemporisation was never written down and was not recorded, so like many other classics from my oeuvre, such as the Latvian Radio Station routine, the Icelandic volcano slide show and the Boy Who Cried Wolf bit, which was very similar to a section of Ricky Gervais's subsequent debut stand-up show.

† And tonight I did drop this bit.

‡ When I do find myself writing a normal set-up/punchline one–two joke, I feel I then have to apologise for it, as it is so unexpected.

363

mask on and some jam went on me.' Did it? D'you remember proper bondage sex that we used to have? In the '80s, in the '70s, in the '50s, friends of the theatre, remember? Proper, you know, degrading, you know, if you weren't in hospital at the end of it, you'd done it wrong. And you had to do it again.*

Not like now. 'I'm thirty-four, I like bondage sex, a feather went on my bum.' Did it? Were you asphyxiated in a career-ending accident? No? Shut up then, get your fucking pouch of yoghurt, get your fucking cat-face bag and fuck off!† And that is my message to the under-forties.

* An elderly volunteer usher, at a small theatre in an out-of-season Yorkshire seaside town that I play out of pity, talked to me after the show. She said she had never seen comedy like it and enjoyed the bondage part, where, she explained to me, I was making fun of how people always said the past was better than the present, but using the maddest modern thing I could think of as an example of the good old days. I will never tire of touring. Television feels like throwing shit at a wall and hoping some of it will stick. But working live, even at this late stage in my career, I feel like you are making new fans one by one in the most unlikely places and sometimes giving people new experiences they would never have imagined they would enjoy.

† It was very enjoyable to shout this odd sentence every night. At some point during the routine I was able to contrive, apparently unintentionally, pulling the standing strut of the microphone out of its base, which was another accident which became a bit, and then use the remaining stalk to gesture at people or smash random bits of the stage to pieces in fabricated rage. We had our own, increasingly damaged, mic stand for the tour, which you can see is visibly on its last leg in the BBC film of the show. I never understand stand-ups choosing to use clip-on head mics, or even radio mics without cables, for shows. The mic stand identifies you as a stand-up comedian, and with that powerful visual signifier of identity literally in your hand, however far you deviate from the rules of what a stand-up is supposed to be, you are still anchored to that identity. Plus, the stand and the cable are multipurpose props that you are *allowed* to use in an utterly

But, joking apart – yeah, I was joking. I took an exaggerated position for comic effect. I've been doing it all night. A little peep for you there, Southend, behind the wizard's curtain.

> [*dances and sings in a high voice*]
> Behind the wizard's curtain, with Stewart Lee,
> He is gonna show you all the secrets of comedy.
> Well, what would you do if a woman said '£5',
> When you were hoping that she'd say '50p'?
> Would you squirrel it away at the back of your head
> And bring it back later on instead?
> Behind the wizard's curtain.

Behind the Wizard's Curtain.* It's a thing I'm working on for Dave.† Hey, get this, right, it was my idea and I wrote it, but

---

uncontrived way – they are supposed to be there anyway – and which ground you. The mic stand can be a sword, a stump to lean on, a baton, a wizard's staff and even, as I remember in a very old Julian Barratt routine, the tiller of a barge steered by a strange pipe-sucking captain (what a great stand-up Barratt was in the pre-*Boosh* days, but secretly he always wanted to be in Keith Tippett's Centipede, and so was never content with comedy). Meanwhile, the mic cable (always use cable mics, not radio mics with no cable, which make you look like someone doing a mattress marketing event in a regional shopping centre) can be a whip, the crest of a wave, a hangman's noose. Don't mess with this. This is a powerful archetype now, and it has everything we need. The mic and the cable are the tools of the trade, like the bladder on a stick the morris men's clown must wave, allowing himself licence.

* By thinking on my feet I could usually improvise lines in the 'Behind the Wizard's Curtain' song that would tie it in to the earlier part of the show, when I asked a punter to estimate the second-hand value of my DVD, whatever that estimate had been.

† The Dave channel always invested in the cost of BBC comedy productions, in exchange for repeating them on Dave, but unexpectedly

apparently it'd be better if Greg Davies presented it. Doesn't seem fair, does it?*

Anyway, I was talking about the S&M and the fetish thing there, right, it's an exaggerated example to choose, but let's stay with it 'cos it dovetails into something I wanted to talk about, which is this, right: I think any area of interest people have, any hobby, whether it's woodwork, sailing, you know, er, collecting stamps or something mad like the fetish thing, whatever it is, it's so much easier now to find out about these things and to meet like-minded people because of the Internet. So much more so than it was, say, even twenty-five years ago that I don't know if any of our passions, if any of our hobbies, our interests, will ever have the same depth of meaning that they had to us a quarter of a century ago, because you're not required to put yourself out, you're not required to – to commit to anything.

You know, let's take the, the fetish thing for a laugh, right. Now if you wanted to get into that twenty-five years ago, you know, you probably couldn't even have done it in Southend, right, you'd have had to, you'd have had to go to Burnham-on-Crouch,† right,

---

declined that option for the second series of *Comedy Vehicle*, leading to a deficit in the projected budget, which ultimately streamlined the show in a beneficial way.

* I have never seen *Taskmaster*, which this refers to, but I am told it is very good, and I am pleased that things have worked out for its creator, Alex Horne.

† Obviously, all these local references would be rejigged in different regions. But I don't like doing too much that feels bespoke to a particular town and its adorable quirks, as I think it looks like pandering to the audience – or entertaining them, as some people would call it. That said, Mark Steel's BBC radio show *In Town* is brilliant, and it does only that. I suppose the difference is the character of the comedian Stewart Lee wouldn't really know or care where he was, or whether there was

so – to the very worst part of Burnham-on-Crouch – and you'd be in – in some underpass and there'd be some horrible shop there with a bloke behind the counter drinking amyl nitrate out of an egg cup and he'd sell you some tickets to some fetish event in London in about two years' time, and you'd go there, to The Clink or something, and go, 'Hello, where d'you get that collar thing? Who are you? How d'you do this? When's the next meeting?' And it would take you ages, wouldn't it, to get into any kind of subculture, but when you finally did, it would mean something because you'd committed to it, right?

But it's all changed now. One of you could go home tonight from here, couldn't you, and think, 'Oh, I'd like to be in the fetish thing,' and you could go on Amazon, bop, bop, bop, next-day delivery, Taiwanese fist glove, and that's there tomorrow, midday. And your partner goes, 'What's this?' 'It's a Taiwanese fist glove.' 'I didn't know you were into all that.' 'I am.' 'Since when?' 'Last night, about half past ten, I just decided.'

But it wouldn't mean anything, would it, it wouldn't mean anything. Right. You know, I – OK, I used to collect records, right, and, er, I started about 1979 and I spent the next two decades wandering around with a little list in my pocket, looking for these things, and then I'd go – I started touring in '89 and I'd go to these different towns in Leeds, Birmingham, Glasgow, I'd go into the record shops, 'Have you got this?' 'No, we'll ring the dealer.' And he'd come, and it would take me ten years sometimes to find the thing you were looking for.* And when you finally

---

an annoying one-way system or a crisp factory. That said, I do enjoy surreptitiously using the phrase 'all round the Wrekin' whenever I am in Shrewsbury.

* It took me five years, five years of crate-digging, to find a copy of Country Joe and the Fish's 1967 classic *Electric Music for the Mind*

did, it was amazing. Then, in 1997, I got online, in an afternoon I found everything I'd been looking for for twenty years, right. But it didn't mean anything. It did not mean anything.*

---

and Body, after John Peel played 'Death Sound' to my childhood ears in 1981. I remember he wanted to show psychedelic revivalists what real psychedelia was. Today, you could download it in an instant. In November 2000, I ended up having breakfast in a Seattle hotel with two of the Fish and my acquaintance, Nick Saloman, of The Bevis Frond. I travelled light for a three-day trip to plug into the psychedelic mainline at the Terrastock Festival, back when I was young and free and had a disposable, if small, income. I seemed suspicious to Seattle airport's security staff because I had no luggage. They asked me why I was coming to Seattle, and when I said it was to see a version of Country Joe and the Fish, they detained for me two hours, searching me and questioning me. In a related record-collector's tale, it took me thirty-four years of googling misremembered titles to acquire a record I heard once on Peel in 1984, which had haunted me ever since. I finally found the twelve-inch version of 'Hep Cat Gloss' by Dundee's Beefheartian obscurists Boo Hooray at an online dealer (which is cheating), and it was like being reunited with a long-lost friend. But today's young music fans have had the real-world challenge of finding physical things taken away from them. We were big-game hunters, coming home with vinyl trophies. What are they? Squares with Spotify accounts. Nobodies. Nothing.

* I do remember getting online, when an Internet was set up for the first time for me and Richard Herring in our writers' office at Avalon's HQ in Leicester Place, in around 1997, and wondering what would happen if I put Green on Red's 1981 EP *Two Bibles* and Markley, A Group's 1970 album *Markley, A Group* – two records that had been on my wants list for a while – into the AltaVista search engine. And when I realised that all that stood between me and them was raising the rather large sums the dealers wanted for them, my heart sank a little. It was all over, the great record-collecting adventure, and now those record-collector heroes of the post-war era who invented the concept of Delta blues as a thing by going round shacks in the Deep South with handfuls of cash, would be at home, pallid and unhealthy, clicking online buttons in dimly lit rooms.

And it's changed so much in our life that if you talk to your grandparents or your great-grandparents* about trying to do bondage sex and fetish sex and S&M, you know, in the war, when it was Hitler, Adolf Hitler, or in the '30s, when a lot of the things they needed were very scarce, very hard to come by, it was harder for them to get into all this stuff, but I think it meant more to them – well, you snigger because you ca— . . . you're – you're of a generation where you cannot conceive, can you, they cannot conceive of not being able to instantly get what they want. And it is – it is a tragedy, I think.[†]

And, and I remember talking to my – to my gran about this, and I remember her saying that in the '30s, you know, if she wanted a deluxe latex sort of, er, like a sex harness for bondage, so she could be hung up from a beam or something, erm, you know, it wasn't like now. They – they couldn't just go into Ann Summers, you know, there was no Ann Summers. They lived in Kidderminster. People still live there now. Still live there now.[‡]

What – what they had to do in the '30s in rural Worcestershire if they wanted a sex harness, is – yeah, ha-ha – is . . . they would have to walk, they would, and they would walk and walk and walk and walk, miles and miles and miles, all round rural Worcestershire, all round Bromsgrove, Redditch, Alvechurch,

---

* The trick in performance here was to have talked about general nostalgia so much that when I suddenly doubled back into talking specifically about S&M, it was a shocking and funny surprise.

† I do think this, so it was easy to perform with conviction, but I am also aware it is ludicrous.

‡ I have set this routine in the rural Worcestershire landscapes that I remember my adoptive mother's parents describing to me as a child. All their tales would take place there. I have used this trick before because, along with lapsing into their Black Country accents, it helps to give these kinds of routines the patina of remembered truth.

Inkberrow,* Rowney Green,† er, Bellend, Fishponds, Upper Piddle, Wyre Piddle, all these sort of places,‡ just looking on the floor. For an old bit of string and twine, and sturdy weeds and vines, and then they would knit all these together, and they would make their own sex harness, just out of old rubbish from off the – And d'you know what? A sex harness made out of all stuff off the floor in Worcestershire in 1937, that would've meant more to them than probably any possession any of you have ever had, or any feeling that any of you have ever had, or any thought that any of you have ever had, because you live, don't you, in a time that is of no value, and consequently you are of no value. And you are like an empty husk billowing across a desolate landscape, bereft of all sense and meaning, and you know it.

And I remember talking, I remember talking to my grandad about this sort of thing. My grandad. And he said to me, he said it was different, he said to me in the '30s in rural Worcestershire, if he wanted a deluxe latex zip-up gimp mask for sex, a sex mask, it wasn't like now. He couldn't just go on Amazon and order a sex mask. What they had to do in the '30s in rural Worcestershire,

* I was fascinated by Inkberrow as a young teenager, as it was the home village of the mysterious rural goth band And Also the Trees, whom I was a fan of at around the age of fourteen. AATT were 'folk horror' decades before it was a thing. Their enveloping literary soundscapes, tragically compromised by the often wayward pitch of their singer, remain big in Europe, if not in Inkberrow. I finally drove through Inkberrow a decade or so ago. You can see the shape of what it was, with Barratt Homes newbuilds now blurring its boundaries.

† My adoptive father's sister lived here, and she would have us to biweekly Sunday lunch. On the way home I would listen to the Top 50 rundown on Radio 1 as we drove through the dark countryside.

‡ Pronounced as 'play-zes'.

if they wanted a sex mask, is they would have to walk, and they would walk and walk and walk, miles and miles and miles south from Kidderminster, down what is now the M5.* You've got the M5, haven't you, the M40, coming in here, then the 42, Banbury Way, the 50, Ross-on-Wye, South Wales, the M4, Reading, Twy—, Twy—, course back then it was a leafy lane.†

Then about – then about halfway down there, where Droitwich, junction 5, is now,‡ they'd go off east, not west round the back of Frog Ponds, Bromsgrove, east, Pershore, er, Evesham, Vale of Evesham, where all the vegetables comes from, and they would find a potato farm, and Gran would distract the potato farmer with rhetoric and dance. And Grandad would creep in the potato farm, and when he's found hisself a potato sack, he'd empty all the potatoes out of it and then cut two eyes holes in it. And that was his sex mask, an old potato sack. And he'd put it on, and the hessian would gouge horrible wounds into his crying face, but that was their sex mask, the potato sack.

---

* How utterly tedious it was, as a youngster, to listen to adults discussing routes around the country in their boring voices for ages and ages. This is a form of revenge.

† As a child, it seemed I overheard endless discussions about routeways around the Midlands, and how they had changed, which would end with the observation that 'back then it was a leafy lane'. How silly, it seemed to me. And yet now there are busy residential roads on the once-rural fringes of Solihull, like Hay Lane, a tree-canopy tunnel through fields flecked with newt-spawn and gorse, which I remember from the '70s, back when it was a 'leafy lane' where we would wait for flocks of geese and herds of cows to cross on the way to school. It is time for me to die.

‡ On a good night a lone person would laugh at this, and I would realise there was someone in with local knowledge, whom I could then engage with at even greater, and more tedious, length about the geographical specifics of Worcestershire roads and motorways.

And d'you know what? A potato-sack sex mask from off the floor in rural Worcestershire in 1937, that would've meant more to them than – OK, what's the most treasured possession you've got? 'Oh, Stew, it's a photo of our daughter the moment she was born.' Is it? 'Cos that's meaningless, isn't it? Compared to a potato-sack sex mask. But it is. 'Cos what did you do with that image the moment you took it? You sent it off, didn't you, to two hundred people, in your address book, a hundred of whom you don't really know, fifty of whom you actively despise, and every time that image lands, like a wet sock falling into a urinal, a layer of meaning is shaved off it, isn't it? Shave off the meaning, shave it all away! Until you're left with a Turin Shroud gossamer-thin tracing-paper imprint of this supposedly profound moment in your life that no longer has any value because you fucked all the meaning out of it again!*

And these are the old stories the grandparents used to tell. You're probably like me, Southend. Your grandparents used to tell these old stories and you used to think, 'I must write them down or tape-record them before they're all forgotten,' but we never do, do we? I actually did. In the 1970s, I tape-recorded all these old stories of my grandparents, but in the '80s, when my

---

* I don't think the end of this bit was ever well written or focused enough, but I used that sort of American stand-up comedy trick of just increasing in speed and velocity throughout the routine to nudge it over the line and trigger nightly applause on the button, like some kind of West End music-theatre slut. On some level, the puritan in me still thinks such performance tricks are a filthy con and the only honest way to perform stand-up is in a flat monotone, stripped of all cheap applause-provoking prompts. But I spent twenty-five years doing that, so I suppose I have earned the right to sell out and entertain people. I am a barrel-organ monkey prostitute.

brother-in-law moved in, he taped a Deacon Blue album over them.*

Right, that's the first one of them. Well done. The second and final Deacon Blue joke is – it's right up near the end of the show, but it isn't the actual end of the show. I do it, and then there's about thirty seconds more until the actual end of the show. So when you hear the second Deacon Blue joke, don't go, 'Oh, it's finished now', and start getting your coat on and wriggling around. Just – wait!

So I was talking about the S&M and the fetish scene, and it's a mad, exaggerated example to – to choose, but, er, it's a good way, I think, of looking at – at how our access to information, our access to different cultures has – has changed, and our grand-parents and our great-grandparents did see incredible changes, and my – my grandad was still around at the sort of start of the Internet age.

And he – I remember him talking about it, and I think, you know, he said he couldn't believe it, and he did, he did say to me once that – he said in the – in the '30s in rural Worcestershire, if he did want to do, er, S&M and fetish stuff,† er – seriously, I'm not doing a, a joke now – but he said it was, it was very different. I mean, he said to me they just couldn't get the – couldn't find things, you know. He said to me, for example, back then if they wanted to do that sort of thing, you know, there was no Ann Summers deluxe strawberry-flavoured sex lubricant gel, there was nothing like that. Well, there wasn't.

* Ka-pow! I told you I was gonna do dat, and I still dun it, and you still fell for it, sucka!

† The audacity of returning to this idea, which the audience had presumed abandoned, especially after the lengthy misdirection of the previous minute or so, is what gets the big laugh here.

And, and, er, all they had then in the '30s, in, in rural Worcestershire, if they wanted to do that sort of thing, was a big lump of dripping.* And this was kept, wasn't it, the dripping, on a – a marble slab out the back, in the pantry to keep it cool on the marble, and, er, yeah, on the marble slab, and, erm, I know, it's funny to you. 'Didn't they have a fridge?' No, mate, they didn't have a fridge.

And, you know, maybe it was Christmas, and Grandad was in a – in a good mood, he'd go, 'Come on, Gran, let's have bondage sex.' Not his own gran, obviously, he wasn't sick. That's not – he

---

* I never really understood what dripping was, but after my parents split up, I lived in my grandparents' house, where dripping was ubiquitous. Older adults would often have, as a treat, 'a bit of dripping' – or if they were feeling extravagant, 'a bit of bread and dripping' – in the evening after supper. Dripping was/is congealed animal fat, left over from the cooking of beef, pork and lamb. Its commercial equivalent is lard. But in the world of congealed animal fat, lard is a blended whisky, while dripping is moonshine, potcheen, distilled in a hillbilly fat still. Bread and dripping, a dish popular in the Midlands, where I grew up, and the north of England, is congealed fat spread on bread. Wikipedia tells us that if the brown sediment has settled to the bottom of the dripping, the same dish is known in Yorkshire as a 'mucky fat sandwich'. Towards the end of the last century, healthier options, such as vegetable, olive and sunflower oil, displaced dripping, but they were still lapping it up in '70s Birmingham. To be fair, these were people who entered the Second World War knock-kneed and malnourished, emerging from it into protracted rationing, in a world where a big lump of congealed animal fat was a potentially life-saving treat. In my grandparents' house, the dripping was kept, as I suspect it always had been, on a little plate on a marble slab in the pantry beneath the stairs. They had a fridge but remained suspicious of it, and my gran still used iron weights to measure out cake ingredients and a museum-piece mangle to hand-crank the water out of wet, washed clothes. Above all, in this bit, 'dripping' is a lovely word to say over and over again in a Black Country accent.

wasn't – that's what he called his wife, 'cos he loved her. And they would get undressed there in the freezing black darkness of the – of the hovel they lived in, shivering and crying in the black dark, the flea bites bleeding all over them. They would put their potato-sack sex masks on. And the hessian would gouge horrible wounds into their faces, horrible weeping sores, and they'd be shivering there and crying, in the black dark, and bleeding, and all the while trying to maintain a state of arousal, and doing it because unlike your cosseted generation, they believed in something, they had values.

Not like now. 'I'm thirty-three, I like bondage sex. Get under the duvet where it's warm and I'll harm you.' I've seen, I've seen where they lived: the wind howling through the cracks in the stonework; the floor just straw and mud and dung, animal dung; all the farm animals in there with them, sheep, goats, ducks. Some of the ducks were traumatised by the things they saw. They were laying square eggs for years afterwards.*

And then finally Gran would go, 'Now it's time to go down in the cellar and get the coal and light the fire to put the dripping in the skillet† to melt it down.' And Grandad would go down in the cellar, shivering and crying and naked and bleeding in the freezing black dark, digging up the coal. And the coal dust would billow up into his potato-sack sex mask and he'd be coughing up huge toxic black clogs of poisonous black phlegm and bleeding and crying in the frozen darkness. Until finally the fire was lit.

And then Gran would hold up the dripping, and at this point she'd always say the same thing to him, and when we were kids and she was telling us this story, we'd go, 'Come on, Gran, say the dripping thing!' And she'd go, 'No. That's in the past.' And we'd

* The rhythm of this sentence is pure music hall.

† Likewise, 'skillet' was another delicious word to say.

go, 'Come on, Gran, say the dripping thing.' 'No, I can't remember it.' And we'd go, 'Come on, Gran, say the dripping thing!' 'No, people don't wanna hear about that.'* Christmas Day, six kids round the table, 'Say it, Gran, say it, say the dripping thing, go on.' And finally she'd give in.

Well, she'd hold up the dripping, and she'd say to Grandad, she'd say, 'Now, here's the dripping, but remember, before we melt this dripping down, as well as being a lubricant for your selfish pleasure, this dripping is also your dinner.'†

---

* My grandmother was similarly reluctant to talk much about her life before the Second World War, as I suspect she thought she had 'bettered' herself and didn't want to be drawn back to the past. She wouldn't ever talk about working on the shop floor at Cadbury's, and thought the National Trust's decision to salvage the last of Birmingham's back-to-back Victorian slums, around the courtyards of Hurst Street, where I first saw Ted Chippington, was ridiculous. Why would anyone want to preserve them?

† Punchline. When I was putting this routine together, I specifically had in mind the *trad. arr.* Billy Connolly joke that ends with the line, 'I need somewhere to park my bike.' Connolly told this joke, probably the most obscene thing that had ever been heard on British television at that point, on the *Parkinson* chat show in 1975, and on a 2011 radio show Jack Dee recalled the broadcast as being a pivotal moment in his life. Though I didn't see the show, my mum would often describe it as the funniest thing she ever saw on television. Was this routine a belated attempt to win her approval, years after she had passed away? It is also influenced, it must be said, by the eloquent filth of the young Frank Skinner, though not by any specific joke. It's just that a long story in which some old people end up using dripping as an anal-sex lubricant feels like the sort of joke Frank should have written, even if he didn't. And above all, I also have in mind the Max Miller routine that ends with the line, 'You can keep your bloody plough,' which I have previously ripped off in a 2016 newspaper column about why I wouldn't accept an OBE. I suppose I was experimenting with trying to write a

And then they'd have to make a choice, a very stark choice; a choice unlike any choice your cosseted, spoiled, lazy, facile generation will ever have to make; a choice between the pursuit of selfish pleasure and basic human sustenance and survival.

But talking to my grandad years later, he said if they did choose the pleasure, if they were careful they could normally scrape together enough of the dripping . . .*

So it's an exaggerated story, that. They didn't live in Kidderminster. They lived in Malvern Link. Not as funny a name, is it? So I've changed it.

Weird that, isn't it? Why's one – why is one name funny and another one not funny? What – what – what makes things funny? Well, if we knew the answer to that question, there'd be no need for this whole charade, would there? If you knew what made things funny, you could stay at home, couldn't you? Making yourselves laugh. Instead of having to pay a professional to do it for you.

And the under-forties have my sympathy. They've grown, grown up thinking the values of the free market are normal, that everything's up for sale and that we're all customers in a set of transactions whose needs must be met, and everything is up for sale, isn't it? The forests, national parks, education, health.†

You know, further education, for example, wasn't supposed to be a transaction which increased the cash value of the customer

---

classic old-school comedy routine, and having a legitimate narrative reason to perform it in a regional accent, like an old-school comic, liberated me to do so.

* There was never any need to make this suggestion explicit. The laughter always overwhelmed it, thankfully.

† Does this segue make complete sense? Not really, but the end of the show is in sight and it's a sprint to the finish.

in the job marketplace. Further education was supposed to be an opportunity to participate, ideally for no charge, in a quest to enlarge the global storehouse of all human understanding, admittedly while drinking heavily subsidised alcohol. And losing your virginity in a tower block named after Winnie Mandela.

But we're all customers now whose needs must be met, and the best example of this customer mentality, I think, I saw on the guest book of the TripAdvisor holiday review website.

Now I've got a ten-year-old boy, and he's a massive *Doctor Who* fan,* and his favourite *Doctor Who* thing is not the multi-billion-pound Doctor Who World place in Cardiff Bay, it's a little museum in the cramped two-room cellar of a little cottage in the square of the Herefordshire market town of Bromyard, and this cellar is full of the eccentric owner's mad collection of *Doctor Who* props and costumes and sets, all crammed in there. It's called the Time Machine *Doctor Who* Museum,† and all around Bromyard there's posters of the Tardis. It says, 'The Time Machine *Doctor Who* Museum', and it is made abundantly clear that the Time Machine *Doctor Who* Museum is an entirely *Doctor Who*-based museum.

But there is a one-star review of this *Doctor Who* museum on TripAdvisor. And it says, 'The Time Machine *Doctor Who* Museum has very limited appeal, except for *Doctor Who* fans. We were in and out in 25 minutes and that was after going around twice.'‡ They

---

* Thank God for *Doctor Who*, which gives the lives of certain boys meaning.

† It is not called the Time Machine *Doctor Who* Museum. It is called the Time Machine Museum of Science Fiction, but all the marketing, and the window displays, are *Doctor Who*-themed. I tweaked the name to make the joke work. I lied.

‡ The real review was a three-star one from GWRTSY, in April 2014,

went round twice. They went round once and they couldn't believe how little non-*Doctor Who* content there was in the *Doctor Who* museum. They thought if they went round again, they might see a diorama of the life of Isambard Kingdom Brunel or an interactive display of the mating cycle of the Asian short-clawed otter. It's a *Doctor Who* museum. You can't complain that there was too much *Doctor Who* stuff in the *Doctor Who* museum. It's not aimed at you. Not everything's aimed at you. Reminds me of an elderly relative who, on having gone to see Andrew Lloyd Webber's musical *Cats*, complained to me afterwards that she hadn't been expecting it all to be just about cats.*

---

which said, 'Stopped out of our way to pay a visit. Nothing in Bromyard was open, except the museum. Very limited appeal except for *Dr Who* fans – not that much relating to Anderson series. We were in and out in 25 minutes, and that was after going around again!' So as you can see, I have tweaked it a bit, but not much.

* This quote was a genuine comment made by an ex-girlfriend's auntie, whom I liked very much. I have a feeling I once gave her an Incredible String Band album and a print of a photo of Captain Beefheart because she told me she had enjoyed both as a teenager. In fact, the same woman's son-in-law was the man whose online comments about me I read out in the *Carpet Remnant World* show in 2011: 'I know this guy . . . not well . . . but I can in fact confirm that he is a cock! I've spoken to him several times in the past at various get-together's (although not recently) and he is a bit of a pillock! He used to go out with my wifes' cousin. He came up a few times for Xmas and one or two other things. I found him condescending and arrogant . . . Anyway they've split up now and my wifes cousin seems a lot happier.' I was a bit shocked by this, as I remember going out with the bloke and his wife and thinking we all got on well, and I had a night out with him in Newcastle after a gig there in the year 2000. I had no idea he hated me so much. It's like finding out years later that the bloke from The Kane Gang said you stank. Ah well, that's two bits of material out of one family.

And a person under forty came up to me after a gig, and he said to me, 'I didn't really enjoy that, to be honest, mate.' And I said, 'I don't know what you expect me to do about it. You just paid to see me, and I am me.'*

But we've turned away, it would seem to me, from the wider world.† Everyone's looking inwards, back through their own boundaries, back through their own borders, and you have to pay for everything now, and nothing comes for free. Except the last U2 album. Whether you wanted it or not. Like a Trojan virus. And I – I don't really know what I'm supposed to say to any of you now, 'cos you all live in a reflecting hall of digital mirrors made of Facebooks and Twitters and Snapchats and Instagrams and Deliveroos and selfies and WhatsApps. You're the kind of people who were run over by a bus because you were crossing the road while looking at a bus-timetable app.

And they say you shouldn't keep dolphins in concrete tanks, because the endless sound of their own sonar bouncing back at them eventually drives them mad, like someone locked in an aluminium-lined cell listening to an endless loop of every ill-considered 2 a.m. tweet they ever sent out. And that is you, you are the mental dolphins of now. Inward-looking, self-obsessed people with no attention span, hurling yourselves fatally out of your tanks in the self-inflicted wounds of your

* I had forgotten about this exchange, which happened outside the Underbelly's cow-shaped tent in Bristo Square, Edinburgh, in the summer of 2007, until a punter who overheard it reminded me of it.

† At this point, 'Für Seelenbinder' would play, by Kosmischer Läufer, a contemporary Glaswegian group writing in character as a '70s East German radiophonics composer, press-ganged by the communist state into writing inspirational music for the East German Olympic team. It provided the perfect uplift for the end of the show. The lights would gradually darken here.

imagined democratic choices. And it's no surprise to me that you've all gone mad. 'Cos you've all got phones on you all the time, haven't you, with cameras, and they all take photos all the time, don't you, with your face over and over again, your face, your face, your face, your face.*

Why? Surely you all know what your own faces look like now. And your entire online digital history is just an endless succession of images of your face, obscuring an endless succession of things that are all more interesting than your face. 'Here's me at Stonehenge. Here's me at the Taj Mahal. Here's me at the Deacon Blue reunion concert.'† And I don't know what I'm supposed to say to you, or what anyone is supposed to say to anyone, because nothing that anyone could ever have to say could possibly be as interesting as the ongoing moment-by-moment documentation of your entire lives.

And so when I look at this painting,‡ Caspar David Friedrich's 1818 German Romantic masterpiece *Wanderer Above the Sea of Fog*, I see a man like me, two hundred years ago now, looking out into the world and trying to make sense of it, and his place in it, instead of just using it as a backdrop for his own narcissism.

But this is you.

Now.§

---

* At this point I would ascend the staircase through the DVD rubble.

† Now I would put on a concealed black frock coat, with tails, and wield a stick.

‡ At this point, the image of the painting, stitched into the backdrop, would be revealed, usually to applause.

§ Here I would pose, with my back to the painting, for a smartphone camera on a selfie stick, which mirrors the cane in Friedrich's painting, the frock coat echoing the subject's clothes – the Wanderer in twenty-first-century reverse.

PART III:
WHAT NOW?

Epilogue

The comedian, actor and broadcaster David Mitchell, for whom I am the supply-teacher fill-in at the *Observer*, kindly allowed me to write the column due the weekend after Brexit was supposed to happen. I explained that my forthcoming book was working to a schematic that would benefit from the appearance of my printed comments, on the week Parliament finally enacted the people's will.

Of course, we all know how that ended, but my initial plan was that the immediate post-Brexit column, the one that now concludes this book, would bring things to a neat, if not climax, then at least resolution.

I could have delayed delivery of this book until Brexit was concluded, one way or another, I suppose, but how long would that take? Weeks? Months? Years? And how many more words would be added to the work's already unwieldy weight?

Besides which, I need this book out by the autumn of 2019 so that I can flog it on the next tour and make back the advance for Faber & Faber. Welcome to the world of the modern writer. And I am luckier than most, as I have this farmers'-market system in operation, whereby I can take the product to the consumer at theatres around the land. 'Books! Get yer books! Fresh from the Faber & Fucking Faber factory!'

As I write this final section, on 1 April, of all days, it is just past 10 p.m. and I am in a holiday cabin in the Forest of Dean, watching a second set of possible Brexit options rejected. I am on a final-edit retreat with my eight-year-old daughter. She was driven to bed early by Brexit, as the live-action *Cinderella* movie was overruled by me in favour of live coverage of the indicative votes. Both are grim tales.

We are in the last available cabin, a 'dog-friendly' one, even though we don't have a dog, and my eyes are watering a little. It could be a dog allergy, I suppose, or maybe it is watching Ken Clarke, Nick Boles and Caroline Lucas crumble live on TV in front of me as the true desperation of the situation becomes all too apparent.

For the final column before I delivered this book I decided to cover Nigel Farage's March to Leave. I knew this meant I had to go and see it for real somewhere along its route, so that I wouldn't subsequently be accused online of being some kind of lying pawn of George Soros and his MSM. Maybe I saw the march as the physical realisation of the imaginary March of the Lemmings I had already chosen to name the book after. It seemed like a ritual to me, almost folkloric, a theatrical enactment of an idea, a clown crusade; it reminded me of the films of the visionary artist Andrew Kötting, who, in *Gallivant*, *Swandown* and *By Our Selves*, set his cast off on journeys across our island, pilgrimages which he seems to feel will, if persisted with, reveal some sort of truth; and it felt like something that happened in the ideological chaos of post-Civil War England, bands of bewildered peasants briefly falling into line behind the hopeful absolutist certainties of ranters like Abiezer Coppe or Gerrard Winstanley.

My wife accompanied me on my trip north, and when she read the finished column, I could tell she disapproved of it. She was sympathetic to the soon-to-be-disappointed patriot pensioners trudging along the lanes, whereas I saw them as people only six degrees of separation, or less, from the fascists, racists and self-interested opportunists piggybacking off their parochial concerns.

At the end of the day, she is working class, despite her many appearances on Radio 4, and she recognises the protesters as people, irrespective of her ideological opposition to them;

whereas the education and privilege I unexpectedly benefited from means that for me they are 'other', and represent attitudes and values from which I have spent my life in retreat and curtains that twitched as black people moved in over the road.

Am I why Brexit happened? And maybe Brexit, to date, has been, for all of us, a struggle to define our own idealised selves in opposition to the values and/or prejudices of others, even if at the expense of the country as a whole. Now, something needs to change, as the final reader comment in this book, from the mysterious Disabled Scapegoat, goes some way to suggesting, even though they erroneously ascribe me with enough money to rescue Hartlepool single-handedly.

This social division was crystallised, quite comically, two days later. On Friday 29 March, the day that Brexit failed to be implemented, we went with our son to see Morgan Lloyd Malcolm's new play, *Emilia*, about the unsung black female Elizabethan poet Emilia Lanier, at the Vaudeville Theatre on the Strand. I had arranged to meet my wife and son opposite Charing Cross station, at the statue of Oscar Wilde, to whom I have been compared sarcastically in the *Daily Star* by Garry Bushell, but their progress had been slowed by police officers ushering them away from the surrounding area.

Farage's March to Leave had swollen in its closing hours, from a hundred or so diehards to nearly two hundred thousand people, including a hardcore far-right contingent attending a breakaway rally hosted by the Islamophobic tax fraudster Tommy Robinson, and the police thought it was going to turn nasty.

So picture this. It is half-time in *Emilia*, a wonderful, vibrant piece that attaches contemporary concerns about representation, race, gender, exclusion and identity to a vividly realised historical drama. I and the other metropolitan elitists are in the theatre bar on the first floor, drinking wine and looking out of the windows at the Strand, where police riot vans are storming towards Trafalgar Square. The pro-Brexit demonstration is turning nasty, the skinhead contingent making it look like a Sealed Knot re-enactment of the far-right '80s rallies we grew up fearing as teenagers.

There was something brilliantly absurd about the situation. It seemed like a reimagining of a pre-revolutionary scene from the early reels of *Dr Zhivago*, the citizens rioting outside in the Moscow streets as Lara and Victor Komarovsky look on from some bourgeois balcony, but this time the peasants were revolting in favour of their oppressors.

Nonetheless, with the parties fragmenting along Brexit lines and the riot vans rolling down the Strand, it was clear there was no future in writing more polarising polemics about the Brexit impasse. And the Leave loyalists knew it too. Not a single one of the 1,098 below-the-line comments on my final column of the first Brexit era was pro-Brexit. The Brexit Internet warriors, too, had given up on their sustained kamikaze flights into the rock-walled fortress of my certainties.

And yet the fucking thing was still dragging on. And the divisions Brexit has exposed will drag on for ever now, even if the superficial, and comparatively trivial, question of our membership or non-membership of the EU is finally resolved.

So what next? I don't know. What do I say, and what voice do I say it in? I've a new live show due in September 2019, and I return to temporarily fill Mitchell's *Observer* slippers once more in May. I'll figure something out, I suppose. This isn't really about me, is it?

All I can offer, as an unsatisfying conclusion to this book, is my final column of the first Brexit era.

With the end in sight, Brexit pulls into a layby

31 March 2019

The March to Leave is a sparsely attended, fortnight-long, 200-mile protest ramble, aimed at securing Brexit, a trembling Parliament its final destination. I wanted to see it in the flesh so I could tell my grandchildren 'I was there', before taunting them with descriptions of toilet paper.

Nearly three years ago, during the week of 13 June 2016, I watched members of the public on live TV debates, people bamboozled not only by funny Boris and those Leave lies, but also by how percentages work and what words mean. And I realised Remain would lose the referendum.

And so, as a metropolitan elitist snowflake and cultural Marxist, I was disappointed by the referendum result, but when the departure date of 29 March 2019 was confirmed, I knew how to weaponise my inconvenience. I would treat all my subsequent newspaper columns henceforth, until we left the EU, as interrelated episodes of a complete work that would only make total sense when read as a whole, like my inferior literary forebear Charles Dickens would have done had he experienced a Brexit, instead of just Christmas and some misery.

I would make recurring novelistic characters of the likes of Michael Gove (the Vengeful Orphan), Sarah Vine (the *Daily Mail* hate funnel) and Boris Piccaninny Watermelon Letterbox Cake Disaster Weight Loss Haircut Bullshit Wall-Spaffer Johnson; and I would gradually unravel the resolve and tolerance of the work's defeated and unreliable narrator (me) as Brexit dragged on.

And, finally, I'd use neurolinguistic programming to provoke the regular below-the-line comment providers and automated Kremlin bots on the paper's website into performing as a predictable dramatic chorus. I would play you all like a pipe!

In a stroke of genius, I arranged to deliver the completed manuscript of *March of the Lemmings* (as the work was to be called) on the weekend we finally left the EU, creating the definitive, and most balanced, overview of the Brexit era, from the street-level point of view of a middle-class, middle-aged man, working in media and living in a 78.5 per cent Remain-voting constituency.

But the departure date is suddenly postponed, and among Brexit's many unforeseen consequences is the fact that tonight I have to complete the last chapter, a story that, like that other great European cliff-edge caper, *The Italian Job*, has no convenient dramatic conclusion. Those cheeky chancers thought they'd get out of Europe with a fortune! But did they?

On Wednesday morning, I woke early to drive to Towcester, in Northamptonshire, to intercept the March to Leave, in the hope that the pro-Brexit trek might provide me with the ending my story suddenly lacked. Perhaps I would die in a head-on collision with the Led by Donkeys van that shadows the ramblers showing film of Leave politicians' lies, my death creating a final scene rich in dramatic irony.

I drove north-west, listening to the radio. Ranking Roger, from Birmingham's 2-tone pioneers The Beat, had died of cancer. I was sad. The days when popular culture closed ranks against racism and the far right seemed long distant. Meanwhile, news reports made it clear the last wheel on the fiction-festooned Brexit bus was finally falling off, with desperate diehard Brexiteers expressing support for a deal they had already acknowledged was worse than being in the EU. No-deal reality bit.

Driving through rural Buckinghamshire, past village-green

memorials and Second World War airfields, it was easy to understand the nostalgic national fantasy that psychic vampires like Rees-Mogg and Farage fed off. I stopped to see the great eighteenth-century garden at Stowe, its vast follies suddenly remnants of a soon-to-be-fallen civilisation, Mayan pyramids in waiting, crumbling and caked in guano.

In a layby on the A413, just south of Towcester, the hundred or so attendees of today's leg of the March to Leave were assembling, the coach that carried their cases stowed nearby on the A43.* I passed between them as they filled their mobile toilets with their micturations, tied their laces and raised their flags. I wasn't the droid they were looking for.

It's Day Twelve and, Farage long since vanished, today's celebrity is Tim Wetherspoon, who moves among the faithful, raising morale with his scoutmaster charm, his chiselled calves like the carved legs of a decorative pew-end woodwose, his burly body an Albert Uderzo cartoon of a pirate.

I waited on a bench to watch the protesters walk through Wood Burcote. No one had turned out to see them, apart from me and a bloke in a Human League T-shirt, and though there were occasional supportive car-horn toots, a pointedly positioned EU banner at the marchers' next mobile-toilet layby provided more editorial balance than any edition of the *Today* programme since Sarah Sands took over.

Farage's friendly flag Wombles looked like any random group of affable English eccentrics, a flock of Fairport Convention

---

* My friend, the performance artist and writer Ben Moor, emailed me after reading this piece to say he had lived in the area described many years ago, so I sent him a photograph I had taken of the layby where the march assembled. 'Yes, that's it,' he replied, 'we'd ride our bikes and find porn mags in that exact layby.' Ben and his friends were all twenty-eight years old. I am now retiring this joke.

fans or a gaggle of real-ale enthusiasts. It was just that these hale fellows had voted to leave after the unveiling of that 'Breaking Point' poster, had assembled here in Buckinghamshire at the behest of a man busy building alliances with far-right leaders all across Europe, and were marching to a drum that inspired neo-Nazis worldwide, irrespective of Tim Wetherspoon's land-lordly bonhomie.

Events hadn't offered me the definitive final paragraph I needed, so I fired up the humane punky reggae of The Beat's 1980 debut, *I Just Can't Stop It*, and drove south. The song 'Two Swords' puts forward the notion that opposing political forces only sharpen their respective blades by slashing at each other, and that you must remember your opponent is your brother, 'even though that cunt's a Nazi'.

This evening, as I write this, eight indicative votes, designed to give some direction to the country's next Brexit move, have all been rejected by Parliament. Michael Caine's coach cantilevers on the cliff edge. The gold he coveted slides towards the doors. You shoulda killed me last year!! Save. Press 'send'.

Stewart Lee. When all this Brexit shite is over people like you better be prepared to bung some money up North to places like Teesside or Hartlepool. Disabled Scapegoat